Postmodern Auteurs

Also by Kenneth Von Gunden

Twenty All-Time Great Science Fiction Films
(with Stuart H. Stock, 1982)

Alec Guinness: The Films
(McFarland, 1987)

Flights of Fantasy: The Great Fantasy Films
(McFarland, 1989)

POSTMODERN AUTEURS

Coppola, Lucas, De Palma, Spielberg and Scorsese

by
Kenneth Von Gunden

McFarland & Company, Inc., Publishers
Jefferson, North Carolina, and London

All photos are from the author's collection unless noted otherwise.

British Library Cataloguing-in-Publication data are available

Library of Congress Cataloguing-in-Publication Data

Von Gunden, Kenneth.
    Postmodern auteurs : Coppola, Lucas, De Palma, Spielberg and
Scorsese / by Kenneth Von Gunden.
      p. cm.
    Includes bibliographical references and index.
    ISBN 0-89950-618-6 (lib. bdg. : 50# alk. paper) ∞
    1. Motion picture producers and directors—United States—
Biography. I. Title.
PN1998.2.V66   1991
791.43'0233'092273—dc20   *791.43092*
[B]   *V946*   91-52594
                                            CIP

Manufactured in the United States of America

McFarland & Company, Inc., Publishers
  Box 611, Jefferson, North Carolina 28640

For Donna

Acknowledgments

I wish to gratefully express my deepest appreciation for the generous criticism, advice, and assistance I received from five outstanding scholar/teachers during the writing of this book: Thomas W. Benson, Dorn Hetzel, Robert Secor, Kenneth A. Thigpen, and Daniel Walden, my thesis advisor.

Professor Walden's support and commitment to my research is a debt which cannot be repaid; I can only acknowledge it thankfully and offer *Postmodern Auteurs* as a testament to his caring, dedication, and hard work.

Contents

Chapter 1
Introduction

Much has been written about the generation of young filmmakers who began to take over Hollywood in the seventies and eighties, the brash young men who came to be known collectively as "the movie brats" — a group which included Martin Scorsese, George Lucas, Steven Spielberg, Francis Ford Coppola, and Brian De Palma, the five directors examined in this book. Many of the articles and studies about this generation of directors, screenwriters, and producers have focused on several key similarities: technical expertise, almost encyclopedic knowledge of the classic Hollywood canon, and strong commercial sense, at least in the way they have been able to tap into some vast collective (and often juvenile) desire for straightforward and unchallenging narrative films. Less, however, has been written about how these (almost exclusively) young males are embodiments of their postmodern times and their film-school educations.

Quoting literary critic Lucien Goldman, another scholar has written:

> All great works of literature express the "vision of the world" of a specific social class — a class to which the writer himself belongs and which constitutes, therefore, both the source and the destination of his works.[1]

Their personal histories and childhood interests demonstrate, I believe, that the five young lions of this study are undeniably children of the postmodern age. At the same time, a clear link can be demonstrated between their shared film school background and their familiarity with the films of Hollywood's classic period, the works of certain directors, and their mastery of a wide range of film styles, genres, and techniques.

Before the training and backgrounds of these five young lions are examined, the postmodern world they were born into should be revealed.

Postmodernism

To begin with, just what *is* postmodernism?
Clearly, we should begin our attempt at definition with the idea of

1

"modernism," for if our subject is "postmodernism," we must know what preceded it.

Modernism, according to Todd Gitlin, was itself a response to nineteenth-century realism in which "the work of art was supposed to express unity and continuity." One of realism's goals was to mirror reality, to comment upon it, and to present it clearly and unambiguously. In modernism, however, "voices, perspectives and materials were multiple." The work now was assembled from many pieces, its unity deriving from fragments audaciously juxtaposed to reflect life in a calculatedly modern way. High culture now quoted from popular culture.[2]

Gitlin sees postmodernism, unlike modernism, as

> indifferent to consistency and continuity altogether. It self-consciously splices genres, attitudes, styles. It relishes the blurring or juxtaposition of forms, stances, moods, cultural levels. It disdains originality and fancies copies, repetition, the recombination of hand-me-down scraps.... It takes pleasure in the play of surfaces and derides the search for depth as mere nostalgia.[3]

Gitlin notes that postmodernist "currents" are especially strong in audience members "born in the 1950s and 1960s," adding that to have come of age in the 1960s and 1970s is to have the experience of "aftermath, privatization, weightlessness; everything has apparently been done. Therefore culture is a process of recycling; everything is juxtaposable to everything else because nothing matters."[4]

Frederic Jameson notes that one of postmodernism's key features is "the erosion of the older distinction between high culture and so-called mass or popular culture." Jameson's view of postmodernism's blurring of the lines separating high and popular culture is not far removed from Gitlin's.[5]

"One of the most significant features or practices in postmodernism today is pastiche," argues Jameson. "Both pastiche and parody involve the imitation, or, better still, the mimicry of other styles and particularly of the mannerisms and stylistic twitches of other styles." Jameson suggests that art has become fragmented, speaking to different audiences, each with its own language, each as separated from other audiences as islands. Since no one group knows the language or the private codes of any other group, this is "the moment at which pastiche appears and parody has become impossible. Pastiche is blank parody, parody that has lost its sense of humor."[6] Thus, Jameson seems to be saying, artists who follow earlier styles do so earnestly, rather than tongue in cheek, since many of the other audiences won't get the joke, won't understand what is being referenced.

If one accepts this idea of pastiche, a key notion which I believe is vitally important to understanding the directors of the 1970s and 1980s and their audiences, then one can agree with Jameson's argument that in an artistic landscape in which it is all but impossible to be stylistically innovative, "all that is left is to imitate dead styles . . . and . . . contemporary or postmodernist art is going to be about art itself."[7]

Jameson introduces the idea of a particular type of pastiche film, the "nostalgia film," and suggests that one of the earliest films in this special category is George Lucas' *American Graffiti*. Jameson posits *American Graffiti* as a nostalgia film because it sets itself the goal of recapturing a past era, the United States of the twilight years of the Eisenhower era. Jameson places Lucas' *Star Wars* in this new genre as well. Jameson argues that *Star Wars* is not remembering the galactic future but the Saturday-afternoon matinees of the 1930s, 1940s, and 1950s. As he puts it, "*Star Wars* reinvents this experience in the form of a pastiche; that is, there is no longer any point to a parody of such serials since they are long extinct."[8]

I agree with Jameson that Lucas' *Star Wars* represents the pastiche nostalgia film. Indeed, I hope to show that Lucas is the young lion most prone to pastiche and self-parody. On a scale of highest pastiche level to lowest, I would rank the five young lions in this order: George Lucas, Brian De Palma, Steven Spielberg, Francis Ford Coppola, and Martin Scorsese.

Let us now consider the children born during and after World War II, the baby boomers and their brothers and sisters who followed them in the sixties and seventies – the postmodern generation. Born in the thirties, forties, and fifties, the young lions were *consumers* of popular culture long before they were *producers* of it. They grew up with television's recycling of Hollywood's films of the thirties and forties and the vast outpouring of multimedia entertainment directed primarily at youthful audiences. Hence, the lions and *their* audiences share an easy familiarity with the same inter-multitextual elements. Postmodernist filmmakers like John Landis, Spielberg, Lucas, and the others are not only the creators-authors of their films; they comprise those texts' ideal readers as well.

And television – not movies, not radio, not comic books – is arguably the single largest factor in the cultural lives of the postmodern generation. Some postmodern theorists insist that "TV is in a very literal sense, the real world, not of modern but of *postmodern* culture." As they see it, TV is not a "mirror of society, but just the reverse: *it's society as a mirror of television*."[9]

These theorists also observe that TV is "the emblematic cultural expression of what Jean-Paul Sartre has described as 'serial culture.' For Sartre, the pervasive effect of mass media . . . was to impose *serial structure* on the population," producing "seriality," as mass media's "cultural form."[10] The making of early television shows, therefore, conditioned viewers to accept a handful of sets, seen each week; to accept the same actors, pleasing not by being different or playing a different role each week but by being "themselves," being Ralph Kramden or Lucy Ricardo. Eight o'clock Tuesday night meant "The Milton Berle Show"; eight Sunday night meant "The Ed

Sullivan Show" and to a whole generation of children signified the end of
the weekend and the coming school week.

The postmodern generation grew up with television and the serial
structure it impressed upon the culture. As Robert Longo, an artist,
photographer, music video director, and director, recalled:

> And every day, I'd come home from school and either have cookies and
> milk and look at *Life* magazine or go downstairs and watch the Million-
> Dollar Movie. I saw *King Kong* 50 times. You could see *King Kong* at 9
> o'clock in the morning, 3 o'clock in the afternoon, 8 o'clock at night. I saw
> so many fucking movies. All those John Ford movies. I would come up
> from the basement only when my mother called me for dinner.[11]

In an article on the relationship between photography and cinema,
Rick Woodward discusses the influences on two young photographer-
artists, Cindy Sherman and Bruce Charlesworth:

> They are the media generation after Warhol. While Warhol's head swam
> with images from ads and cele-shots in *Life* magazine, Sherman and
> Charlesworth were raised on sitcoms, Disney, Fellini, Warner Bros. crime
> films on late-night TV, cheesy horror and suspense dramas, and soap
> operas. Warhol's . . . offspring, however, take a much more critical — bitter
> or funny — attitude toward the images that pervade our lives.[12]

Musician John Zorn recently released *The Big Gundown*, an album
which reinterprets several of Ennio Morricone's film scores. A second
album, *Spillane*, is a homage to the music of various film types (*film noir*,
African-American blues, and Japanese cinema). A writer suggests that
Spillane "might be the ultimate musical expression of what film means in
the modern imagination. Zorn's notes for *Spillane* say, 'I grew up in New
York City as a media freak, watching movies and TV and buying hundreds
of records. There's a lot of jazz in me, a lot of blues, a lot of movie sound-
tracks.'"[13]

Clearly, motion pictures, music, art, photography, and most of all
television have influenced each other and a whole generation of young
Americans. The popular and critical reception of Stanley Kubrick's *2001:
A Space Odyssey* when it was released in 1968 offers an example of this
generational break. A film critic for the *Minneapolis Tribune* wrote that

> listening to the audiences after the movie and reading most of the reviews
> only verify the opinion that we're still hung up on literary interpretation,
> even though we've been surrounded by various forms of this non-linear,
> nonsequential attitude . . . I have no doubts that persons under twenty-
> five who grew up on television images will understand *2001*. They've seen
> television commercials dealing with nothing but stomachs.[14]

Unfortunately, too many of the postmodern generation, the visually
literate generation that one critic calls the *cinemate* (as in *literate*) have *no*

Stanley Kubrick, shown here directing Dr. Strangelove, *was a strong influence on the young lions.*

other references except those they've gleaned from TV and film, especially the films of the lions. A scene in *King David* (1985) which featured the Ark of the Covenant elicited hoots of derisive laughter from a youthful audience. "That's from *Raiders of the Lost Ark*," one filmgoer shouted. Because "moving images impinge strikingly on the imagination, [the cinemate] tend to reproduce images they have seen—and not only in the dizzying recombination of old footage in anthology shows, worst moments, tributes to whomever, greatest hits, and 11:00 P.M. reruns."[15]

Since the cohorts of filmmakers who got their start in the seventies and eighties, including the young lions, are themselves part of the postmodern generation, we can label them as postmodern filmmakers, or even postmodern *auteurs*. But to do this, we must establish that there truly are clear links between these five young writer-producer-directors and the postmodernist culture of the fifties and sixties, as well as evidence that they have sufficient knowledge of earlier films, film styles, film genres, and film conventions to produce intentional or unintentional pastiches of them.

Postmodernism and the Young Lions

The childhoods of Francis Ford Coppola, George Lucas, and Steven Spielberg are typical of the childhoods of the postmodern *auteurs*. Brian

De Palma and Martin Scorsese are also children of the postmodern TV era, but the influences on them are less clear-cut, less intense, less obvious than with the other three.

Francis Ford Coppola

Francis Ford Coppola, the oldest of the five, was born in 1939, but he had access to many of the "toys" the others would later avail themselves of. Coppola recalled his childhood:

> My family had an 8mm projector, and a tape recorder, and let me play with them. I used to synchronize soundtracks to their home movies, and started a business of showing such films. I was about 8 or 9, and made a little money at it. Then I got polio and was in bed for about a year. I did a lot of work with puppets, and was given a 16mm film projector. I was fascinated with synchronizing sound and movies. I used to cut up the home movies and make stories out of them, with myself as the hero. But I was really just fooling around, and was more involved in the exhibition end.[16]

In addition to playing with his projector, his tape recorder, his ventriloquist's dummy (he also proudly possessed an autographed picture of Jerry Mahoney and Paul Winchell), and running his home movie exhibition business on 212th Street in Queens, New York, Coppola spent a great deal of time with that postmodern electronic blender called TV. As Coppola later admitted, "I watched television a lot."[17]

"I got immersed in a fantasy world," Coppola recalled many years later.

> The popular kid is out having a good time. He doesn't sit around thinking about who he is or how he feels. But the kid who is ugly, sick, miserable or schlumpy sits around heart-broken and thinks. He's like an oyster growing this pearl of feelings which becomes the basis of an art. I was funny-looking, not good in school, nearsighted, and I didn't know any girls.[18]

George Lucas

The singularly successful George Lucas is perhaps the best example of a young lion who grew up immersed in the postmodernist popular culture. Lucas, born into a bourgeois home in Modesto, California, in 1944, spent much of his free time in his room, where he could live out his fantasies. The following was apparently a typical afternoon for the teenage Lucas:

> Lucas got home from school around 3:00 P.M. and headed right for his room. He got out his collection of 45s and 78s (everything from Elvis Presley's "Hound Dog" to Chuck Berry's "Roll Over Beethoven") and played them, one after the other, for hours on end. Sitting on his bed, he read comic books, ate Hershey bars, and drank Cokes.[19]

When the Lucas family bought a television set in 1954, young George couldn't get enough of the old serials and adventure films KRON-TV, the nearby San Francisco station, showed — exciting cliffhangers with names like *Flash Gordon Conquers the Universe*, *Zorro Rides Again*, *Don Winslow of the Navy*, and *Manhunt of Mystery Island*. "Television had a lot of influence on Lucas' work. His attention to graphic design stems from years of watching TV commercials; so does his reliance on fast pace, action peaks, and visual excitement rather than content."[20]

Steven Spielberg

Steven Spielberg's childhood is closer to Coppola's than to Lucas' in that he was more a maker of his own films than a consumer of TV programs. Because a documentary on snakes had so frightened the 5-year-old, Spielberg's father wouldn't let him watch TV, eventually going so far as to rig the family setup with devices to tell if his son was cheating. Still, Spielberg recalled sneaking downstairs to watch "Science Fiction Theater" and the like after his babysitters fell asleep.[21]

When Spielberg was 12, his father received a movie camera for a Father's Day gift. Before long, the son had taken charge of the camera:

> My first real movie was of my Lionel trains crashing into each other. I used to stage little wrecks. My dad said, "If you break your trains one more time, I'll take them away!" So I took his camera and staged a great train wreck, with shots of the trains coming in different directions and shots of little plastic men reacting. Then I could look at my 8mm film over and over and enjoy the demolition of my trains without the threat of losing them.[22]

When Spielberg was 13, he won a Boy Scout merit badge for his three-minute 8mm film about the robbery of a stagecoach, starring one of his friends. At 16, he made *Fireflight*, a 150–minute science-fiction film which was an early version of *Close Encounters*. Like Coppola, this "weird, skinny kid with the acne," as he characterized himself, escaped into his own fantasy world, one fueled by the TV programs and movies he was finally allowed to watch.[23]

Brian De Palma

Unlike Coppola, Lucas, and Spielberg, De Palma's interest in film and mass media was slower to develop, and he has said he was "never a movie junkie." But growing up in Philadelphia and later New York City, De Palma *was* strongly influenced by TV, postmodernism's engine: "What is predominant in [New York City]," De Palma said, "is television. That's where all the networks are and Hollywood seems very far away."[24]

De Palma's childhood was a lonely one despite his being the youngest of three brothers. De Palma later confessed that he always felt that his two older brothers, Bruce and Barton, dominated him and that his mother ignored him in favor of them. One biographer insists that De Palma "describes himself, through the characters played by Keith Gordon [in *Home Movies* (1980) and *Dressed to Kill* (1980)], as an introverted, misunderstood, lonely, but intelligent teenager."[25]

Martin Scorsese

Because of his childhood asthma attacks, Martin Scorsese, like Francis Ford Coppola (polio) and Steven Spielberg (his nerdiness and inability to succeed at sports), was denied the opportunity to participate in many typical boyish activities. Born and raised in New York City's Little Italy, Scorsese instead attended film showings and old-movie retrospectives at the Thalia movie theater and the Museum of Modern Art with his father.[26]

"My father used to take me to see all sorts of films," he recalled. "From three, four, five years old, I was watching film after film, a complete range." After asserting that the youthful Scorsese believed he had to choose between two starkly conflicting careers — the priesthood or gangster — one biographical account of this period in his life continues:

> Instead, he became the perfect child of Hollywood. His mind filled with a rich store of images from musicals, Westerns, and gangster films; for each he knew the date, the stars, and even the director. When he grew up, he could fix those images and use them for his own films.[27]

Film School

Lucas, Coppola, Spielberg, De Palma, and Scorsese have been influenced by the culture of pastiche, recombination, and juxtaposition that so ubiquitously surrounds both producers and consumers of artistic texts, whether paintings, sculptures, photographs, novels, or films. But, unlike their readers, their audiences, the young lions have yet another layer, another veneer, of postmodern sensibility — one provided by the film-school experience. One of the key similarities in the young lions' backgrounds is the fact that they *all* attended film schools at one time or another, something few of their predecessors did.

The young lions, the film-school generation who began emerging from their film-school cocoons in the mid-sixties to insinuate themselves into the film business, have been called "the cinematic equivalent of the Paris writers' group of the 1920s." If this is an obvious exaggeration, it *can* be said that the University of Southern California (USC) gave Hollywood George Lucas; the University of California, Los Angeles (UCLA) produced Francis

Ford Coppola, whose film *You're a Big Boy Now*, served as his master's thesis; Martin Scorsese graduated from New York University; Steven Spielberg, after inventing his own film program there, emerged from Long Beach State and got a job at Universal Studios; and Brian De Palma, initially a maker of documentaries, was a product of Columbia University in New York City.[28]

As Pierre Maranda has written,

> Formal schooling structures the rational-response mechanisms of the young. It conditions a society's emerging generations to perpetuate the society: it conditions youth to think according to accepted paradigms — historical, aesthetic, social, religious, etc. It thinks these out for them. The set of rational-response mechanisms acquired through schooling and other intellectual activities (reading, conversation, etc.) defines in youth what Lacan has called their *organization intellectuelle* ("intellectual makeup"), which, it is hoped by the ruling classes, will become their emotional organization (*organisation passionnelle*) as well. Formal school is thus an important part of a society's survival mechanisms.[29]

This schooling is how societies — and complex industrial entities — not only survive the deaths of their individual members but (through the ongoing process of the replacement of the older generation by the new) maintain their original identity despite this constant renewal and deliver it to future generations.[30]

The older directors — Howard Hawks, Douglas Sirk, Vincent Minnelli, Orson Welles, Sam Peckinpah, Stanley Kubrick, John Huston, and even Jerry Lewis — came to filmmaking from acting, vaudeville, theater, radio, television, photography, and a multiplicity of fields; in other words, they were not products of film schools or a film culture. The previous generation of directors also grew up before the popular (read "youth") culture explosion of the fifties and the postmodernist trends of the sixties. They were makers of classical Hollywood films.

> For most of the sixties, movies were a business for middle-aged (or old) men: from 1957 to 1966, the Best Film Oscar went to movies directed by men whose average age was 52. Now movies are a young man's game: the average age of directors whose films have won the top Oscar over the last eight years [1972–1979] is 38. Of the twelve top-grossing films of 1978, only one (Blake Edwards' *Revenge of the Pink Panther*) was directed by a man who had made as many as three previous features. The five top-grossing films of all time — *Star Wars, Jaws, The Godfather, Grease*, and *Close Encounters of the Third Kind* — were all directed by men under 35. (We did say a young *man's* game.)[31]

If the film schools had been quietly graduating scholars and filmmakers for year after year to no effect, all that changed in the new-game seventies. "Francis Ford Coppola may have worked his way to the top like any old-fashioned craftsman (nudie movies, Roger Corman horror movies, the screenplays for *Is Paris Burning?* and *Patton*), but people remembered that his master's thesis at UCLA, *You're a Big Boy Now*, was distributed by Warner Bros."[32]

These new directors did not just study film; they immersed themselves in it; they learned it from top to bottom. "Someone who's been to film school has a kind of inverted pyramid of experience," Walter Murch says. "You are forced to do everything; and only gradually do you focus on one thing. Whereas, in the industry . . . if you enter as an assistant soundman, you become a soundman, and then, perhaps, a sound editor."[33]

If one accepts that postmodernist art *is* indeed primarily a pastiche, occurring in the case of film within mass culture, then to be capable of producing such pastiches, a director must have a solid understanding and appreciation of the original works he or she is replicating (while forgoing the traditionally serious approach of many of the originals). One way of acquiring this familiarity with film genres and conventions is to study film — in depth and all but indiscriminately.

Film schools, with their heavy diet of classic Hollywood cinema, are natural dispensers of film history. Just as the French critics of the fifties consumed a decade's worth of classic Hollywood cinema following the end of World War II, having been presented with an unparalleled opportunity to view an artificially compressed history of forties films, so did American film-school students consume fifty years of Hollywood film like so many potato chips, one after the other.

In film school, the young lions acquired a formidable knowledge of serials, B Westerns, jungle, and other adventure pictures — all of which had become "defamiliarized" genres (using a term utilized by neoformalists) for their youthful contemporaries and other moviegoers by the mid- to late seventies. Thus, the lions were well positioned to invoke these genres' long-lost stylistic and narrative elements for a postmodern generation that recalled them, if only vaguely.

Regarding George Lucas' days as a film student at USC, Dale Pollock has written, "Like a fat man who couldn't stop eating, Lucas gorged himself on movies."[34] Lucas said, "At USC we were a rare generation because we were open-minded. I was influenced by John Milius and his taste for Kurosawa and Japanese cinema. I liked documentaries by the Maysles brothers and Leacock and Pennebaker. But we also had guys there who did nothing but Republic serials and comic books. *I was being exposed to a whole lot of movies you don't see every day.*"[35] (Emphasis added.) Clearly, one possible effect of seeing so many films from different eras back to back, day in and day out, is to begin to experience a blurring of the lines between the styles, genres, techniques, and subjects — the very blurring between high and mass culture Jameson spoke of. Seeing *Citizen Kane* followed by *The Nutty Professor* followed by *Rio Bravo*, *The Rules of the Game*, and

Orson Welles, only 25 when he made Citizen Kane *was a hero to the young lions — indeed, to a whole generation of film-school graduates.*

What's Opera, Doc? can be simultaneously vertiginous and liberating: What's high art, Doc?

Perhaps because of this enthusiastic immersion in the films of older directors like Kurosawa, Lean, Hitchcock, Ford and Welles, the postmodern auteurs' film inspirations seem to have come less from literature, theater, and politics, those things which inspired many of their idols, than from the films themselves. Many years later, after the success of *Star Wars*, George Lucas, Paul Schrader, and Francis Ford Coppola met director Akira Kurosawa. Kurosawa told Lucas and the others, "If I think of John Ford as a father, I guess that makes you my children."[36]

John Wayne as Ethan Edwards in John Ford's classic 1956 Western The Searchers. *This is a seminal film for the young lions.*

Interestingly, the young postmodern directors should also acknowledge John Ford as their "father," especially when it comes to Ford's 1956 Western classic *The Searchers*:

> *The Searchers* relates not only to [Paul] Schrader but to John Milius, Martin Scorsese, Steven Spielberg, George Lucas, and Michael Cimino, not only to *Hardcore* but to *Taxi Driver, Close Encounters of the Third Kind, Dillinger, Mean Streets, Big Wednesday, The Deer Hunter, The Wind and the Lion, Ulzana's Raid*, and *Star Wars*. An obsessed man searches for someone — a woman, a child, a best friend — who has fallen into the clutches of an alien people. But when found, the lost one doesn't want to be rescued.[37]

The postmodern auteurs are emphatic about *The Searchers'* quality and about its impact upon them. Martin Scorsese says, "The dialogue is like poetry! And the changes of expression are so subtle, so magnificent! I see it once or twice a year."[38]

Adds Steven Spielberg, "*The Searchers* has so many superlatives going for it. It's John Wayne's best performance to date. It's a study in dramatic framing and composition. It contains the single most harrowing moment in any film I've ever seen. It is high on my twenty-favorite-films list." Spielberg has watched the movie over a dozen times, including twice during the filming of *Close Encounters of the Third Kind.*[39]

The first of the young lions to graduate from film school and get substantial work in Hollywood was Francis Ford Coppola. "I was the first film school graduate to make movies," he reflected in an interview. "I am a very successful amateur. I know more about every aspect of filmmaking, from photography to music — including writing and acting — than any other filmmaker in the world, and that's not a boast. Of course I still have to write my best film."[40]

"Also, through contacts at film school, notices on the bulletin board, I did get my job with Roger Corman," Coppola said. "Roger always had the policy of getting bright guys and girls from the colleges. He'd say to his secretary, 'Call up UCLA and get some film student who'll work cheap.'"[41]

Coppola's success at breaking into the film business directly out of film school electrified the others, especially George Lucas:

> You see, we were taught, it was the credo of film school that we had drilled into us every day — that nobody would ever get a job in the industry. You'll graduate from film school and become a ticket-taker at Disneyland, or get a job with some industrial outfit in Kansas. But nobody had ever gotten a job in Hollywood making theatrical films. Then Francis did it, clearly and indisputably, and this happened just when we were in school. He was about five years ahead of me, and he was working on his second film already, his first big feature.[42]

Lucas was never happier than during his years at USC, calling that period "a time when I really blossomed. When I went in there, I didn't know anything. The school helped me focus on film, and I loved doing that. They helped me become what I am today."[43]

Beginning in 1965, a new generation of USC graduates began emerging from the film school and moving almost immediately into the film industry. Besides George Lucas, this "USC Mafia" included writer-producer Hal Barwood and writer-director Matthew Robbins (screenwriters for *Sugarland Express* and *MacArthur*, director and producer for *Corvette Summer* and *Dragonslayer*); director Randal Kleiser (*Grease*, *Blue Lagoon*); writer-director John Milius (*Conan the Barbarian*, *Dillinger*, *The Wind and the Lion*, *Big Wednesday*); cinematographer-director Caleb Deschanel (*The Escape Artist*); Walter Murch, a sound editor (*Apocalypse Now*, *The Conversation*) and director (*Return to Oz*); producer Howard Kazanjian (*Return of the Jedi*); producer Bill Coutourie (*Twice Upon a Time*); director Robert Dalva (*Return of the Black Stallion*); producer Chuck Braverman (numerous TV specials and documentaries); writer-producer Bob Gale (*1941* and *Used Cars*); writer-director Bob Zemeckis (*Used Cars, Romancing the Stone, Who Framed Roger Rabbit?*); John Carpenter (*Halloween*); Willard Huyck, a director (*French Postcards*) and a writer (coscreenwriter of *American Graffiti* and *Indiana Jones and the Temple of Doom*); Dan O'Bannon, a writer (*Alien*) and director (*Return of the Living Dead*); composer Basil Poledouris (*Blue Lagoon, Conan the Barbarian*); writer David S. Ward (*The Sting*); writer-director W. D. Richter (*Buckaroo Banzai*); and sound wizard Ben Burtt (*Star Wars, Invasion of the Body Snatchers*).

Although some members think the superlatives about their group of USC graduates are overdone, they remain an impressive cohort. As writer-director John Milius says, "It's mostly a myth. But there was a definite . . . *thing* going on there."[44]

George Lucas, perhaps the foremost member of the USC group—which began calling itself "The Dirty Dozen" after the Robert Aldrich film—described the camaraderie among them:

> There was a sort of renaissance at that period at that school. There were about 30 or 40 of us, and we all liked each other. We were all very bright and ambitious; we were friends; we had no competitive drives with each other; we'd help each other on our movies. We had a lot of fun, and we've grown up together, and of that group, almost all have made it into the film business.[45]

George Lucas and all the other postmodern auteurs made lasting friendships, a network of connections that would play an important role in their later professional lives, as we shall see later. As Lucas recalled:

> It was an incredible period. . . . Everybody helped everybody; we were all friends. It spread, too. People got to know guys at UCLA, and it became a much larger community. We were like foreigners living in a strange country and all speaking the same language, all of us banding together to beat on the doors of Hollywood. We would share resources—if you needed something a friend would tell you who you could get it from. And we all looked at each other's work, mostly at student film festivals. That's how Steve Spielberg got to be a member of the group—he's working on a film with me now [*Raiders of the Lost Ark*]. He was at Long Beach State, but we met through film festivals.[46]

USC was *the* hot film school, certainly, but it was not the only one. In addition to Francis Ford Coppola, UCLA numbers among its graduates writer-director Paul Schrader (*Hard Core, Mishima*), writer-director Colin Higgins (*Foul Play, Nine to Five*), director Carroll Ballard (*The Black Stallion*), writer Nancy Dowd (*Slap Shot*), and Bill Kirby (*The Rose*).[47] And from the American Film Institute's production school came Terrence Malick (*Badlands, Days of Heaven*), Martin Brest (*Hot Tomorrows, Going in Style*), and David Lynch (*Eraserhead, The Elephant Man*).[48]

At the time Lucas and the others attended classes, USC "operated more along the lines of a trade school" whose "curriculum was specifically designed to train students to work in the movie business." Students were also encouraged to develop projects which reflected the classical Hollywood paradigm: a strongly plotted narrative film with invisible construction. James Foley, the director of *Reckless*, who attended USC in the seventies, substantiated this approach: "The kind of thing I was interested in was narrative, mass appeal filmmaking, and if that's what you wanted to do, you thrived at USC. If you wanted to do something else, you had a very hard time."[49]

Kevin Reynolds, who attended the film school in the late seventies, confirmed that the goal of the instructors at USC is practical, Hollywood filmmaking: "They want to teach you the kind of film that is made in the industry."[50]

If a young filmmaker's goal in the seventies was to go Hollywood to make the connections that would allow him or her to find a place in the industry, then USC was the place to be. "USC was how I cracked into the film business," says former student Robert Zemeckis, whose 1988 movie *Who Framed Roger Rabbit* is one of the biggest hits of all time. As Zemeckis told Stephen Farber,

> I made a student film that won a lot of awards, so I would just call the USC graduates and say to them, "I'm a USC student, and I made this student film. Would you take a look at it?" John Milius, George Lucas, Hal Barwood, and Matthew Robbins were all really receptive to SC film students. Milius liked my film, and then I sent him a script that Bob Gale and I had written. He asked us to do something for him. We ended up making a development deal for what turned out to be *1941*.[51]

Although some film educators believe that USC's "industry trade school" period is behind it, the bulletin for the School of Cinema-Television trumpeted this fact: "As of December 1983, 41 of the 42 all-time highest grossing films have USC alumni affiliated with them."[52]

Having examined postmodernism and the young lions' film school connection, we need to look closely at several theoretical constructs designed to examine the insertion and/or extraction of meaning in texts. We need to pursue the possible utility of auteur and reader-reception theories to the study of the films of the young lions.

Auteurism, Reader-Response Theory, and the Young Lions

If one insisted upon an absolutely purist application of both the auteur and reader-response theories, there could be no middle ground. This is because the first insists (in some interpretations) that a text's meaning is derived solely, or primarily from its "author." The second insists that a text's meaning is derived solely, or primarily, through the efforts of the "reader." As I use the terms in this section, however, I am allowing for a possible middle ground. I believe authors and readers share the burden of producing a text's meaning; thus, I am rejecting an either-or approach or definition of the two theories.

Auteurism can be reduced to a simple if admittedly oversimplified theoretical structure: Auteurism is a "concept which places the author as the source and center of the text."[53]

The primary initial proponents of the auteur theory in film were the writers of *Cahiers du Cinéma*, especially François Truffaut (*"la politique des auteurs"*), and the American critic Andrew Sarris, who rendered *la politique des auteurs* into "the *auteur* theory." According to the auteur theory, the author of a film (usually but not always the director) has complete control over the film (its images, camera angles and movement, lighting, dialogue, editing, sound) and uses that control to express his or her vision to produce a work of art which directly and indirectly (consciously and unconsciously) communicates "meaning" to the viewer, a meaning unchanged and unchallenged by the passage of time or presentation before audiences of different cultures.

There are problems with the auteur theory, however. As Stephen Crofts notes,

> Once the text has left its producer it is subject to the vicissitudes of the market, of critical assumptions and of cultural and historical variants in these factors. The films named as those of John Ford do not sell well in the USSR . . . and within any given culture and period, the meaning of, say, "Ford" which any given reader brings to any film by that name will vary according to his/her cultural, and particularly film-cultural, formation.[54]

Yet it is difficult to assert that authors do not have intentions, or that a study of their films will not reveal certain tendencies. If we accept the auteur theory on a limited basis — one that acknowledges that directors (and writers, producers, actors) *intend* certain effects, whether or not those intentions are realized — it can yield meaningful results. One can also argue, as Brian Winston has, that Truffaut and the young French critics and filmmakers who first espoused the auteur theory did so as a way of allowing critics and others to legitimize certain American directors and their films and study these popular movies as seriously as "high art" films. If one accepts this interpretation and application of the "theory," it loses some of its more debatable properties and offers critics another analytical tool with which to examine film. A "John Ford" film need no longer be approached as a monolithic entity to be correctly deciphered but a film which may or may not exhibit certain repetitive properties reflecting the conscious or unconscious hand of the director.

Literary critics, having already wrestled with the problems of authorship, were finding another source of meaning in the text in addition to, or instead of, the author:

> The reader is the space on which all the quotations that make up a writing are inscribed without any of them being lost; a text's unity lies not in its origin but in its destination. Yet this destination cannot any longer be personal: the reader is without history, biography, psychology; he is simply that *someone* who holds together in a single field all the traces by which the written text is constituted.[55]

This focus upon the reader and his or her reception and decoding of the text is the basis of reader-response studies. One of the pioneers of reader-response theory is Wolfgang Iser. Iser was one of the first scholars and researchers to credit the effect of a text (novel, poem, painting, film) not just to the work's author but also to the reader or decoder of that text:

> The phenomenological theory of art lays full stress on the idea that, in considering a literary work, one must take into account not only the actual text but also, and in equal measure, the actions involved in responding to that text. If this is so, then the literary work has two poles, which we might call the artistic and the esthetic: the artistic refers to the text created by the author, and the esthetic to the realization accomplished by the reader.[56]

Certainly, Iser recognized, the text is the "precondition" for the meaning the reader-viewer imposes upon it. The reader takes what the text offers to him and begins a process which "results ultimately in the awakening of responses within himself."[57]

The reader consumes the text, embedding it into his memory. Resident in memory, the text can then be called up at will to be measured against a new background, one which results in the reader now being able to make "hitherto unforeseeable connections." This very act of remembering, however, now means that original memory has been so distended and changed by the process that it can never reclaim its original configuration — because memory and perception are not the same thing. "Thus, the reader, in establishing these interrelations between past, present, and future, actually causes the text to reveal its potential multiplicity of connections. These connections are the product of the reader's mind working on the raw material of the text, though they are not the text itself — for this consists just of sentences, statements, information, etc."[58]

This juxtaposing of memory with new backgrounds is perhaps one of the key factors that make it possible for postmodern audiences to integrate so quickly the pastiche elements found in the films of the postmodern auteurs, films like *Star Wars*, *The Godfather*, *Close Encounters of the Third Kind*, *The Untouchables*, and *Raging Bull*.

For Iser, any single text has the potential to be read in many ways, and no single reading or reader is capable of realizing this multitude. Because each reader "fills in the gaps" that exist in any work by himself, he simultaneously creates his own version of the work and excludes the many other possible interpretations. Forced by the text to choose a meaning, the reader-viewer "implicitly acknowledges the inexhaustibility of the text"— the same inexhaustibility that compels his choice. This process of selection, of choice, Iser contends, proves that the "potential text is infinitely richer than any of its individual realizations."[59]

Iser compares the extraction of multiple meanings from a single text to the process of arbitrarily imposing images—constellations—upon stars whose positions are fixed. Just as the heavenly stars are fixed, so too are the "stars" in a literary work; it is the lines that can be drawn between them which are variable and which produce the near-infinity of meaning.[60]

Similarly, Robert Crosman, another literary critic, states:

> A poem really means whatever any reader seriously believes it to mean. . . . The number of possible meanings of the poem itself is infinite. And it is clear who is making these meanings—the reader, whether he be the author himself or anyone else.[61]

Authors—poets, novelists, sculptors, and filmmakers—may bring preconceived notions to creating a text by being a member of what Stanley Fish calls an "interpretive community."

> Interpretive communities are made up of those who share interpretive strategies not for reading . . . but for writing texts, for constituting their properties and assigning their intentions. In other words these strategies exist prior to the act of reading and therefore determine the shape of what is read rather than, as is usually assumed, the other way around. If it is an article of faith in a particular community that there are a variety of texts, its members will boast a repertoire of strategies for making them. And if a community believes in the existence of only one text, then the single strategy its members employ will be forever writing it.[62]

Lest those who interpret and employ Fish's theory of interpretive community differently be confused, I am enlarging his more restrictive interpretation of an interpretive community to posit the existence of many such communities—and suggesting that authors are routinely members of more than one community.

Fish's theories, if they are valid as I interpret and use them, offer much for my examination of the films of the young lions. It is quite possible that the five directors may belong to several "interpretive communities"—e.g., a postmodern (pastiche) interpretive community, a film-school interpretive community, and a "classical Hollywood" interpretive community.

Not unlike Fish, Hans Robert Jauss, theorizing that readers and audiences operate on the basis of a "horizon of expectations," dismisses much of the basis for the auteur theory as originally delineated: the idea that an author's work is timeless, capable of exactly the same sort of reading and decoding by audiences of different cultures, epochs, values, and histories. The reconstruction of the horizon of expectations, on the basis of which a work in the past was created and received, Jauss writes,

> brings out the hermeneutic difference between past and present ways of understanding a work, points up the history of its reception – providing both approaches – and thereby challenges as platonizing dogma the apparently self-evident dictum of philological metaphysics that literature is timelessly present and that it has objective meaning, determined once and for all and directly open to the interpreter at any time.[63]

Jauss' horizon of expectations is less effective, however, in subtly directing the scholar away from the text and toward the reader and the history of reception than is Fish's interpretive strategies and communities. In addition to concentrating upon how a writer's, poet's, or director's work has been received, Jauss' horizon of expectations "not only follows the fame, image, and influence of a writer through history but also examines the historical conditions and changes in his understanding."[64]

Commenting upon Jauss' writings, another critic notes that this idea of a horizon of expectations allows Jauss

> to theorize the relationship between works appearing simultaneously but received in different ways – some as "fashionable," others as "outdated," still others as "before their time," and so on. Such labels are a way of designating the degree to which a given work meets, disappoints, or anticipates the reading public's horizon of expectations at a given time.[65]

It is apparent that Jauss' theory has much import for the way the young lions' films have been and continue to be received critically, popularly, and financially (essentially the same as popularly). Have they coincided with the viewers' horizon of expectations all of the time, most of the time, or only occasionally?

Finally, Susan Suleiman sums up the value of reader-response theories:

> We might find in today's hermeneutic controversies support for an idea which is gaining ground in both linguistics and literary study ... namely, that interpretation is a communal, context-specified act, the result of what Stanley Fish calls shared interpretive strategies and what Jonathan Culler calls reading conventions. And by this view ... each variety of audience-oriented criticism might fruitfully ... study ... the multiplicity of contexts, the shared horizons of belief, knowledge and expectation, that make any understanding, however fleeting, of minds or of texts, possible.[66]

Reader-response theories, then, offer a way to integrate postmodernism, the postmodernist generation – both producers and consumers and the techniques and the exposure to classical Hollywood filmmaking that the postmodern auteurs learned in film school. And just as importantly, they point to the final element needed to analyze the films of the young lions: the classical Hollywood cinema.

The Young Lions and the Classical Hollywood Cinema and Its Paradigms

Stylistic factors can explain the most

> specific and interesting aspects of Hollywood filmmaking. The . . . classical norms depended upon models of storytelling drawn from literature, theater, music, and the visual arts. After 1917, the principle of using narrative logic to control systems of space and time became central. . . . The classical style was critical in reinforcing both economic practices . . . and ideological/signifying practices. . . . Within the mode of production, the tensions of standardization and differentiation, the increase in specialization, and the tendency of Hollywood's institutions to focus energy and capital toward a controlled uniformity all crucially depended on the norms of the classical style.[67]

The classical style as defined by Bordwell, Staiger, Thompson, and others, then, is primarily concerned with telling a story, but telling it "realistically" and concealing artifice through techniques of narrative continuity and "invisible" construction (lighting, editing, shot–reverse shot, framing, camera movement, acting, makeup, musical cues, set and costume design, etc.). Standardization and other industrial practices soon guaranteed that each Hollywood film, while "unique," was a part of the paradigm. Bordwell, especially, stresses the use of the word *paradigm* when addressing this idea:

> My emphasis on norms should not be taken to imply an iron-clad technical formula imposed upon filmmakers. Any group style offers a *range* of alternatives. Classical filmmaking is not, strictly speaking, formulaic; there is always another way to do something. . . . A group style establishes what semiologists call a paradigm, a set of elements which can, according to rules, substitute for one another. . . . The style remains a unified system because the paradigm offers *bounded* alternatives.[68]

What makes all this even more striking with regard to my thesis is the way the classical Hollywood paradigms mesh smoothly with reader-response theory: "If classical cinema makes the screen a plate-glass window, it is partly because . . . the viewer, having learned distinct perceptual and cognitive activities, meets the film halfway and completes the illusion."[69]

As early as 1918, according to Helen Starr, the moviegoing public was sophisticated enough at "reading" films and screen direction (things like an actor exiting out a door on the right and being seen entering a room in the next scene from the left, as if completing the action) that editors could use that sophistication to save themselves production costs, as in a battle scene:

> We cut the picture so that it seemed as if thousands took part — first a long shot of the seventy [total soldiers] fighting amid battle smoke on one side, then closer shots of a dozen or two soldiers running in from the right, another dozen running in from the left, another long shot of the seventy soldiers but now wearing the uniforms of the enemy and fighting on the opposite side, then back to a shot of the hero and his forces and so on throughout the picture. It was just a matter of reverse camera shots and joining them together so carefully that any audience would be deceived.[70]

Kristin Thompson observes, "From a very young age we see and hear a great many artworks and come to understand their conventions. We are not born understanding how to follow plots, how to grasp filmic space from shot to shot, how to notice the return of a musical theme in a symphony, and so on."[71] It is the young lions' film-school experience that has most joined them to the tradition of the classical Hollywood cinema since USC, UCLA, and the other universities not only firmly taught the basics of filmmaking but also helped to transmit the industry's dominant standards to students eager to break in what had been a closed shop.[72]

By the seventies, when films like Spielberg's *Sugarland Express*, Coppola's *The Conversation*, and Lucas' *American Graffiti* had appeared, some scholars, including Thomas Elsaesser, called for a recognition that a "new" Hollywood had appeared. Others saw this "new" Hollywood as something else — the international art cinema stylistically assimilated by the industry to produce a new Hollywood superficially different from the old but remarkably intact nonetheless.[73]

Chapter 2
Francis Ford Coppola

Francis Ford Coppola was born April 7, 1939, in Detroit, Michigan. His father Carmine was for many years a flutist with Arturo Toscanini's NBC Symphony Orchestra; his mother, Italia, the daughter of Neapolitan musician Francesco Pennino, was at one time an actress (she appeared in several Vittorio de Sica films).[1]

Coppola grew up on Long Island, in Bayside, Queens, and later Great Neck. As a boy, he played the tuba and loved playing around with gadgets and mechanical toys. By the time he was 10, he was adding sound to his parents' home movies.

Polio made Coppola, already an introspective child, even more reliant upon himself and his inner resources. Once he had recovered from polio (which also affected Harry Caul in *The Conversation*), he was sent away to a military school. An unwilling cadet, Coppola made pocket money "by writing love letters for his fellow cadets at the price of a dollar per page."[2]

Like several other young lions (Lucas and Spielberg especially), Coppola was not popular. "I was funny-looking, not good in school, near-sighted, and I didn't know any girls," Coppola recalled. "My mother called me the affectionate one of the family. My older brother was handsome, brilliant, the adored one of any group. I really took up writing to imitate him."[3]

"When I was a kid," Coppola told Brian De Palma, "I was one of those guys like I was describing [the kind of technical freak who's president of the radio club]. In fact, my nickname was 'Science.' You know, 'Hey, Science, come over here and tell him about induction coils.' And I was president of the radio club."[4]

Much of Coppola's early life was apparently colored by his father's sense of failure. As one biographer notes, Carmine Coppola was "always the interpreter, never the composer. 'Our lives centered on what we all felt was the tragedy of his career,' [Coppola] told *Playboy*. 'He was a very frustrated man. . . . He felt that his own music never really emerged.'"[5]

In 1956, Coppola was accepted at Hofstra College (now Hofstra University). Although he was attracted to film, Coppola decided the best way to prepare for filmmaking was to get a solid grounding in theater and stagecraft first.

> When I was about eighteen, I became very interested in Eisenstein. . . . I read all of his work and went to see his films at the Museum of Modern Art. And I was really dying to make a film. . . . I went to theater school, and worked very hard. I directed lots of plays and I studied theater. . . . I wanted to be very well rounded, very complete, to have that . . . background, because Eisenstein had started like that.[6]

Coppola, shrewdly for his age, had decided not to go into film immediately for fear that the medium would "seduce" him:

> I think most young filmmakers in the schools get so hung up — handling film is so much fun, so exciting — *that they tend to bypass content and acting. . . . They just go into technique.* So I really tried to stay away from film for four years, just so I would have something to bring to it.[7] [Emphasis added.]

As a freshman, Coppola was cast in several small roles as an actor and helped design and light several student productions. As he told Brian De Palma,

> I became attracted to the theater because it fulfilled the two poles of my life: one was stories, and the other was science. I was just as much attracted to the theater because of its technical aspects — light dimmers, sets, etc.[8]

After Coppola became president of Hofstra's drama society, he staged a play based on H. G. Wells' "The Man Who Could Work Miracles" and wrote and produced a musical comedy. It was at Hofstra that Coppola first met actor James Caan, who would appear in *The Rain People* and achieve stardom as Sonny Corleone in *The Godfather*. Coppola also made friends with Robert Spiotta, later the head of American Zoetrope.[9]

Coppola would later say of his years at Hofstra:

> Hofstra was very influential in my life. I went from being an average student to being at the center of college theater. It was the first time I had the real responsibility of running my own show. I was relatively as powerful there as I am now in the larger world.[10]

In 1960, fresh out of Hofstra, Coppola enrolled in UCLA's graduate film course. Coppola discovered that it was strongly vocational, despite the fact that few film school graduates were known to have "made it." He described the atmosphere:

> It's very informal, very loose, primarily production workshops, but there *are* classes. It's separate from UCLA — we worked out of little wooden bungalows and never really saw kids from the main school at all. When I went there it was very depressing — the guys were much older and it was

a very negative kind of group, everyone was moping and saying, "Well, they'll never let us make films anyway.... Hollywood's all full of sell-outs."[11]

Bright, ambitious, and aggressive, Coppola saw few other students who possessed his desire to succeed. Too many of them, he believed, "stood around talking very impressively about how lousy Hollywood films were and how *they* could really make great films." But talk was all they did.[12]

Coppola's drive to make it commercially did not sit well with some of the other students: "The day I got my first job as a screenwriter there was a big sign on the bulletin board saying: '*Sell out!*' Oh, yes, I'm the famous sell-out from UCLA," he recalled. "There was open resentment. I was making money. And I was sort of *doing* it. I was already doing what everybody was just talking about."[13]

The atmosphere at UCLA was apparently far different than the one Lucas was to encounter at USC; indeed, Coppola's experience, told to an interviewer, was almost entirely 180 degrees from Lucas' and *may* be responsible for his later playing "Godfather" to Lucas and other young film-school grads and his creating American Zoetrope:

> I was disappointed in film school. I had thought about it when I was very young, and the whole time I was an undergraduate ... I was looking forward to film school. When I got there [however] ... it was nowhere as much fun or as satisfying as the theater experience had been. I found that the other students were not really interested in film as a more complete humanistic art form.... They didn't seem to have any breadth or depth to them. I was at UCLA film school from about 1960 to 1962, and I barely had two friends in that time. There was none of the camaraderie that I had imagined in high school in my *La Boheme* imagination. My fantasy was you're working on the films and drinking wine at night, and there are beautiful girls who are working on the films and you're all in it together. It wasn't like that. It was very lonely.[14]

While Coppola was still at UCLA, he saw a want ad on a bulletin board and was hired by producer-director Roger Corman to write the English translation of a Russian SF movie, *Battle Beyond the Sun*. Coppola schemed to catch Corman's eye:

> I tried to impress Roger. I'd deliberately work all night so when he'd arrive in the morning he'd see me slumped over the moviola. He started to see me as an all-purpose guy. Roger was always really nice to me. He'd pay you nothing to do a film, but your success then was your own and he never had any ties on you. I always felt grateful to him, and I like him a lot.[15]

Eventually, Corman made the young UCLA graduate his assistant. While Coppola was dialogue director on *The Tower of London*, Corman asked him to recommend a sound man for his next picture. Coppola seized his chance:

I said, "Look, Roger, I can do the sound." So I became sound man on *The Young Racers,* and then its second-unit director. I shot all of the racing footage. Then Corman let me do my own picture. I told him a zingy horror scene and he said, "Well, okay Francis, can you make it for $20,000?" I said yeah, and raised another $20,000 from an English producer named Raymond Strose.[16]

Raymond Strose believed he was buying the rights to a horror film that was already in production. As Coppola told an interviewer,

I sold the English rights for a movie which did not exist to [Strose]. And with the $20,000 he paid me and the $20,000 Roger put up, I was able to direct my first feature film [*Dementia 13*] — based on a script it had taken me three nights to write. I think it showed promise. It was imaginative. It wasn't totally cliche after cliche. Very beautiful visuals . . . it had some of the nicest visuals I've ever done.[17]

"When Corman heard about this [second $20,000]," Coppola said, "he wanted to withdraw the initial production money, but I had put it into another account, remember. We were young and making a feature film," he said, adding, "It was the only film I ever enjoyed working on."[18]

After Coppola won the Samuel Goldwyn writing award at UCLA, he was hired as the "house writer" for Seven Arts. Writing as many as three finished scripts a year (and working on numerous others), including *Is Paris Burning?* and *Patton,* Coppola "started getting horny to direct a film."[19]

You're a Big Boy Now

Working on his own screenplay, Coppola chanced upon a novel entitled *You're a Big Boy Now* by an English author, David Benedictus. When Coppola discovered that the novel and his screenplay were covering much of the same ground, he bought the book and merged it with his screenplay. Coppola knew that anything he wrote while working for Seven Arts would legally belong to the studio. However, anything he bought with his own money would be his. Seven Arts correctly assumed that they owned Coppola's screenplay, but they were not ready for what happened next. "I told the company, 'I own the book on which the screenplay is based. Consequently, I own half and you own half — so let's get together.'"[20]

The way Coppola learned to grasp the reins of commercial filmmaking, first with *Dementia 13* and then with *You're a Big Boy Now,* is in many ways more fascinating than these rather modest films themselves. From the beginning, Coppola understood the film *industry,* understood its commercial and paradigmatic nature.[21]

As with many of his later films, Coppola adapted someone else's original material to the screen. One recent study of Coppola's career

Francis Ford Coppola's directorial style in You're a Big Boy Now *(1966) was compared unfavorably with Richard Lester's* The Knack *and* It's a Hard Day's Night.

noted that in *Big Boy* "he shamelessly pirated narrative ideas from David Benedictus' novel, while in no way attempting to embrace the vision of the book."[22]

Even if true, Coppola's "piracy" of the book's narrative nature went undetected; as he himself notes, however, he was accused of copying another filmmaker's style: "One of the great pities was that I had written *You're a Big Boy Now* before Dick Lester's *The Knack* came out and yet everyone said it was a copy. It was definitely influenced by *A Hard Day's Night*. But it was all there already before I even saw *Hard Day's Night*."[23]

Unlike Lucas, who had his best experience making *THX 1138*, Coppola got little pleasure from making *Big Boy*. "I didn't enjoy doing the film," Coppola said later. "I was scared.... I was in New York and it was a real union crew, and I had a limited schedule."[24]

Diane Jacobs' assessment of the film is a good one:

> [*You're a Big Boy Now*] is ... an energetic *potpourri*, brandishing exuberance, prodigy, and a consummated mastery of craft — but little that could be construed as innovative or profound.... Coppola's camera is as little inclined toward *verité* as his literary mind is suited to the anarchic syncopations of such early De Palmas as *Hi Mom!* and *Greetings!* What it demonstrates instead is a poised camera ... and the capacity to fashion a series of congruent story lines.[25]

Finian's Rainbow

In 1968, Coppola was offered the job of directing his first really big Hollywood film, a musical based on the successful 1947 Broadway musical that mixed leprechauns and race relations, *Finian's Rainbow*. Coppola thought it over and accepted because he remembered the show. As he put it, "It was a very romantic idea, like wouldn't my father be happy if I did a big musical?"[26] Coppola did a quick uncredited rewrite of the screenplay and was hoping to shoot on location in the South.

"It was basically a cheat," Coppola later said of *Finian's*. "The score was great, but we improvised dance numbers. We were competing with *Funny Girl*; they rehearsed musical numbers for two months."[27] *Finian's* low budget allowed Coppola just over three weeks of rehearsal and three months of shooting, very little time for a complicated musical.

After confrontations with the choreographer, Hermes Pan — (hired at Fred Astaire's insistence) Coppola soon felt himself in over his head. He fired Pan and staged most of the numbers himself. "I was faking it," he later admitted. No choreographer, Coppola's efforts were no better than Pan's.[28]

Coppola was astounded to learn that Warners loved the completed movie and wanted to showcase it: "[Warners] decided to blow the picture up to 70mm and make it a roadshow picture. And when they did that, they blew the feet off Fred Astaire when he was dancing. No one had calculated the top and bottom of the frame."[29]

Coppola shot each scene as many as eight times, each take different. Rather than trying to match the picture, he simply jump-cut the shots together, giving the scenes a disjointed kinetic energy if nothing else. And like the director of a live-on-tape TV soap opera that forges ahead regardless of mistakes or miscues, Coppola rammed his way through the

Finian's Rainbow, a backlot-bound musical starring Fred Astaire and Petula Clark, cut the feet off the great dancer when it was blown up to 70mm for roadshow performances.

scenes involving the child actors and extras. Despite his later disavowals of the film and his lack of resources, Coppola also admits that he had the sort of totalitarian power during the filming of *Finian's* that the director of any major Hollywood film enjoys: "I had my way, within the limitations of time and money," he said. "I was very responsible."[30]

Effectively washing his hands of *Finian's*, Coppola began working on *The Rain People* and (as he would later do with *The Conversation*) left the completion of the editing of the film to Joe Landon, the film's producer.[31] Coppola took with him his new assistant, a young USC grad and Warners intern who worked on *Finian's*, George Lucas.

Lucas recalled their meeting on *Finian's* set:

> Warners had just been taken over by Seven Arts and the place was desolate. They were making one film — and that was *Finian's Rainbow*. "Look, kid" [Coppola told Lucas], "help me. You come up with one good idea a day and you can actually do stuff for me."[32]

Both young filmmakers found a kindred spirit in the other because they were bearded film-school graduates and they were the only two people on the film under 40.

Runaway wife Shirley Knight picks up James Caan, a hitchhiker, in The Rain People, *a film notable for introducing Coppola to Caan and George Lucas and leading to Coppola's establishing American Zoetrope in San Francisco.*

The Rain People

The Rain People grew out of a short story Coppola wrote for a creative-writing class while he was at Hofstra. "It was first called *Echoes*," Coppola said, "and it was the story of three housewives—a newly married one, an older woman, and one who has a few kids. All go off in a station wagon, and leave their husbands."[33]

Although Coppola didn't know Shirley Knight, he admired her work and thought her an actress of substance. He met her at a film festival where she was crying because someone had apparently said something rude to her. Coppola went up to her and said, "'Don't cry, I'll write you a movie.' And she said, 'You will? That's sweet.' And I did. I went back and took out this old college draft and decided to make it one character."[34]

With the $80,000 he'd been paid to direct *Finian's Rainbow*, Coppola bought some sound and film equipment, convinced Warner Bros. to bankroll his "road" film, gathered up George Lucas and Walter Murch and a crew, and set off across the country to shoot the film. Like the silent filmmakers of the teens, Coppola decided to incorporate actual events that occurred along the way, including a parade in Chattanooga, Tennessee.[35]

During the course of the three-month filming schedule, Coppola faced two problems that had a direct bearing on the film's ultimate success, or lack of it. First, he had difficulties working with Shirley Knight and slowly began moving the focus of the story away from her character to James Caan's brain-damaged football player. "I started to throw more weight to Jimmy Caan's character. That is definitely the flaw in the film," Coppola admitted. "I chickened out, partly because I didn't have enough time."[36]

The other problem was one that would confront Coppola again and again: how to end the film satisfactorily. Coppola's ending is neither jarring nor illogical, but it leaves his female protagonist with nowhere to go after all that time on the road. She has escaped her husband but not the trap of the stereotyped role of the nurturing female. It was perhaps this lack of catharsis that led to audiences staying away from Coppola's dark and downbeat vision.

Still, for all his departures from the norms of Hollywood filmmaking, Coppola's film shows the difficulty the young lions (and every director) faced in attempting to eschew the classical Hollywood style. Like his protagonist, Natalie, Coppola could not simultaneously escape the paradigms of classical storytelling and expect to attract a mass audience.

American Zoetrope

The weeks on the road making *The Rain People* allowed George Lucas time to convince Coppola that San Francisco (not far from Modesto) would be ideal for the small independent studio they hoped to create under Coppola's leadership. "We wanted a little studio where we could mix and edit our films," Lucas said later. "We moved up in April 1969."[37]

Coppola constructed a small studio in a loft building. With somewhere between $100,000 and $500,000 worth of cameras, editing machines, and other basic equipment, Coppola, Lucas, and a few of their friends and colleagues established American Zoetrope. The dream was to provide a base for young independent filmmakers like themselves.[38] Coppola, ever the family man, was going to provide a home for a family of like-minded young filmmakers. Located several hundred miles up the coast from the frenzy of Hollywood and its studio-factories, Zoetrope would become an oasis of independence and creativity: "Shangri-Coppola," in Steven Spielberg's memorable phrase.[39]

Perhaps Coppola wanted to create the same atmosphere that Lucas and the others had known at USC but which seemed to have passed him by at UCLA. But perhaps he simply wanted to be a modern mogul.

Zoetrope's roster was full of young lions:

Coppola was president, George Lucas vice-president, and Mona Skager (Coppola's associate producer beginning with *The Conversation*) secretary and treasurer. The [original] group . . . included John Milius . . . Willard Huyck and Gloria Katz (screenwriters for *American Graffiti* . . .), and Matt Robins and Hal Barwood (screenwriters for *Sugarland Express* . . .). All of them, along with Lucas, were part of the class of 1967 at USC. Carroll Ballard (*The Black Stallion*) . . . attended UCLA with Coppola.[40]

"The studios had hired us, but we were aliens," George Lucas remembered. "We had no connections in the business, no family, we were all young and had just gone to film school so we knew how to help each other the way we had in film school."[41]

George Lucas was the first batter up to the box. With *Finian's Rainbow* yet to be released, Coppola announced *THX 1138*:

George is just going to direct it in his own way. It's all based on my strength now. Let's say *Finian's Rainbow* is a big flop. It's going to hurt George more than anybody. I'm saying, "If you want me, you've got to give George Lucas his break." Well, if suddenly they don't want me, then George has got a problem.[42]

With the failure of *THX* and American Zoetrope, Coppola needed to make some money fast. Fortunately, he was offered a directing assignment almost immediately. It was to turn a best-selling novel about the Mafia into a modestly budgeted, modern-dress film.

The Godfather

I always wanted to use the Mafia as a metaphor for America [Coppola said]. I feel that the Mafia is an incredible metaphor for this country. Both . . . have their hands stained with blood from what it is necessary to do to protect their power and interests. Both are totally capitalistic phenomena and basically have a profit motive. . . . Of course that is a romantic conception of the Mafia.[43]

The Godfather and *The Godfather, Part II* are arguably Coppola's best films. They are also inexorably bound to his postmodern upbringing and influences, his knowledge of popular genres and popular narrative construction, his film-school education, and his use of classical Hollywood methodology and techniques.

Despite Coppola's uneven commercial record, Paramount Pictures' Robert Evans offered him the job of directing the film to be made from Mario Puzo's novel. Coppola had several things going for him: His previous movies had been mostly low-budget affairs, and *Godfather* was originally planned as a relatively inexpensive modern dress film; he was young; and, most important of all, he was Italian. His hiring helped quiet

The older generation gives way to the new in Coppola's The Godfather. *The aging Vito Corleone gives advice to his son Michael, soon to be the new Don.*

some of the protests coming from Italian-American groups concerned about the film's impact on their image.[44]

After reading the book and determining that it possessed sufficient potential to justify his taking on the assignment, Coppola professed himself shocked by Puzo's contemporary script and suggested that he produce a script more like the novel, set in the forties and showcasing the family.[45] Coppola and Puzo rewrote the script, each taking half; then they switched halves and rewrote the other's work.[46] "It was my intention," Coppola said, "to make this an authentic piece of film about gangsters who were Italian, how they lived, how they behaved, the way they treated their families, celebrated their rituals."[47]

Coppola's crew, unimpressed with their 31-year-old director, were openly contemptuous of his abilities at the beginning of filming. When Coppola would tell cinematographer Gordon Willis how he wanted to shoot a scene, the veteran Willis would respond, "Oh, that's dumb," Coppola recalled. Coppola fired the troublemakers, made his peace with Willis, and kept his job. "I had to hang in. Everything was at stake."[48]

Coppola turned what had been planned as a quick commercial gangster film into a stately, paced, well-filmed epic. As Coppola recalled, "I love the look of this film. I shot it somewhat like a forties film. No zoom shots.... There's plenty of violence. Yet the film style is simple, almost tableaux. Light and dark is a motif throughout. We juxtapose incredibly dark images with very light images, which is a theme of the story — a warm, generous godfather who's also a murderer."[49]

In addition to forgoing zoom shots, Coppola and Willis also eschewed rapid cutting and extreme close-ups (by the early seventies, a staple of television, with its smaller screen, that was infiltrating film). Coppola and his four editors cut the film in a "'legato' rather than a 'staccato' rhythm, enabling him to build tension gradually and effectively over the picture's three-hour labyrinthian development."[50]

Robert B. Ray has brilliantly analyzed *The Godfather* in light of his provocative theory, which posits that in the late sixties and early seventies Hollywood came up with a new type of film — the "corrected" genre movie. The corrected genre film provided traditionalists with all the action they could ask for, and enough self-awareness to mollify more iconoclastic viewers and critics.[51] According to Ray, *The Godfather's* success depended among other things, on its ability to maintain an ideal balance between "reassuring conventionality and disquieting revisionism."[52]

Ray also notes how Coppola is able to maintain audience identification with his "outlaw" heroes (the protagonists of what Ray has identified as a cycle of "Left" movies, such as *Easy Rider* and *Butch Cassidy and the Sundance Kid* [both 1969]) by several traditional means. First, by using subjective point-of-view (POV) shots which, figuratively, forces the viewer to see events through the eyes of the outlaw protagonists; second, by placing the protagonists in conflict with a corrupt establishment, thereby justifying their violence and outlawry.[53]

If, as Coppola has stated, one of his purposes in making *The Godfather* was to expose the hollowness of modern capitalism, his traditional narrative construction and complicitous point-of-view shot selection permits (directs?) us to identify with the Corleones, with criminal acts and murder.

McCluskey, the corrupt police captain, is symbolic of the venal establishment which confronts and opposes the Corleone family. Rather than being repulsed by his violent murder by Michael, audiences cheered his demise.[54] The murder itself, which is secondary to the revenge killing of Sollozzo, the drug dealer who had the Don shot, follows the classic shot-reverse shot pattern (except for two carefully considered "objective" shots), thereby placing the viewer in Michael's shoes as he kills McCluskey and Sollozzo.

By our gleeful "participation" in Michael's murders, not only of McCluskey and Sollozzo but also of the heads of the Five Families at the end, we have indicted ourselves and revealed our inner desires for power and revenge. "[*The Godfather*] shrewdly touches contemporary nerves," one reviewer wrote at the time of the film's release. "Our society is pervaded by a conviction of powerlessness. *The Godfather* makes it possible for all of us, in the darkness of the movie house, to become powerful. It plays upon our inner fantasies not only on the criminal inside each of us but on our secret admiration for men who get what they want, whose propositions no one dares turn down."[55]

The Godfather's opening shot, we quickly learn, is a POV shot from Don Corleone's perspective. While there are numerous narratively "objective" shots during the wedding (scenes in which the Don is not present), the identification is with Don Corleone. After a POV shot of his attackers rushing toward him, the assassination scene is shot from an unmotivated overhead angle (similar to the one Hitchcock used in *Psycho* to transfer the narrative from Marion Crane's POV to Norman Bates'). Then, in the hospital, during a standard shot-reverse shot between Michael ("I'm with you now") and the wounded Don, Coppola privileges Michael's POV at the expense of the Don's. From now on, the audience's sympathies will lie with Michael; the Don is almost as absent from the rest of the film as the murdered Marion Crane is from the remainder of *Psycho*.[56]

One of the elements that made *The Godfather* so palatable to the mass audience, presumably, was the lack of focus on real crime. "The film is so constructed that we are not even allowed to consider the nature of the Corleones' business," one critic observed. "There are no victims! We are never allowed to see the real human cost of the family business. We see no prostitutes, no junkies, no victims of extortion, or robbery; none of the actual human effects of the decisions and actions taken by these families."[57]

What Coppola leaves us with is a (more or less) kindly old gentleman who occasionally uses a little force to correct injustices either ignored by the system or imposed by it. Those who oppose the godfather are invariably venal and corrupt, while those he helps are victims who have no other recourse in light of the system's failures to protect them. And while the Don gives well-reasoned orders (rough up the undertaker's enemies, don't kill them), he is primarily seen as the wise and loving head of his family: dancing with his daughter, buying fruit, playing with his grandson.[58]

One of the strengths of the film, and perhaps one of the main reasons it appealed to so many people not normally disposed to attend a "crime" movie, is that *The Godfather* is as much about family as about anything. In addition to a wildly romanticized portrait of a criminal family, it contained one of the finest depictions of an Italian-American family ever put on film, a portrait linked, ironically, with the Mafia stereotype. One needn't be an Italian-American to identify with the Corleones and their traditional family values, their touching, hugging, loving family. If you *are* Italian-American, the scenes between the Don and his family have special import.[59]

In constructing a "corrected" genre film, Coppola was able to work both sides of the street, so to speak, and make a film that worked on multiple levels: a basic crime-genre level and a more sophisticated and "artistic" level. Any immense popular *and* critical success must contain levels of meaning, levels of narrative accessible to different audiences. Coppola had done the same thing in his script for *Patton*: he'd constructed it so that either an antiwar or a pro-war reading was possible. Similarly, one of the horizons of expectations that many people presumably and understandably brought to *The Godfather* was that it was a "gangster" film. If that was what they went prepared to see, their expectations were clearly met. Another horizon of expectations that intellectuals, especially Marxists like critic John Hess, brought to the film was that it exposed the corruption in American life so often covered up.

"If [*The Godfather*] offered enough action to attract the naive filmgoer," Robert B. Ray argues, "it also offered enough ideological criticism of that action to please the ironists."[60] "We had been sure of the square audience," wrote Mario Puzo, ". . . and now it looked as if we were going to get the hip avant-garde too."[61]

That the film supports these various readings is easily demonstrated:

> In juxtaposing Connie's wedding with Don Corleone's murder plans, a christening with Michael's scheming, a religious festival with Vito's first murder, *The Godfather* implicitly demonstrated, to those so disposed to think about such things, that American society functioned on two levels: an ideologically whitewashed exterior and a foundation of predatory violence. For those not so predisposed, these sequences merely represented particularly gripping instances of Classic American narrative cinema.[62]

"I was disturbed that people thought I had romanticized Michael, when I felt I had presented him as a monster at the end of *The Godfather*," said Coppola.[63] Although Coppola laments that the popular audience had missed his point, one can honestly ask *which* point? As Robert B. Ray observes, "*The Godfather*'s failure to become the subversive movie of Coppola's designs reconfirmed the *Cahiers du Cinéma* point that an effective ideological critique occurs primarily at the level of style." Just as *The Godfather* (and *The Godfather, Part II*) indicts the system for hiding its corruption beneath a surface layer of respectability, so too do Coppola's traditional methods of assuring audience identification all but guarantee that its subversive message will be forgotten as viewers are swept up in the Corleone family epic.[64]

The Godfather's richness allows for many correct readings, and it is a reflection of its intertextual sophistication that it is open to so many readings — as a crime drama, a family epic, a critique of American society, a commentary on the relationships between men and women. And ultimately it remains a classical Hollywood film whose narrative thrust and crosscut editing are closer to the Hollywood paradigms represented in the work of John Ford or D. W. Griffith than they are to the disruptive patterns of a Jean Luc Godard or Alain Resnais.

As for Coppola, as he said in 1974, "I went from being an eccentric runaway and offbeat filmmaker whose tastes ran to arty films that didn't make much money to one of the top five most sought, highest paid directors in the world."[65]

The Godfather, Part II

Even though he had attempted to withstand the pressure from Paramount to make a sequel to *The Godfather* and had suggested Martin Scorsese as a possible director, Coppola eventually gave in. Working with Puzo again, he even cowrote the script in three months.[66] Since *The Godfather* had earned over $85 million in U.S.-Canada rentals (the worldwide box-office gross was $285 million), a sequel, according to the usual formula, could be expected to earn approximately two-thirds of the original's box-office take (ultimately *Godfather II* had rentals of $30 million).[67] Paramount had helped finance and distribute the commercially risky *The Conversation* following *The Godfather*'s success, so Coppola may have reasoned they would do the same for his next "artistic" project if he made *Godfather II*. Shrewdly, Paramount let Coppola see a script for what was then called *The Death of Michael Corleone*. The message to Coppola was "Make the film the way you want to make it, or watch someone else ruin it."[68]

The other reasons Coppola may have had for agreeing to do the second film were more complex. First there was the challenge of equaling or topping the quality of the first film; second, Coppola saw *Godfather, Part II* as more than a mere sequel. As he said, "It was an opportunity to make

2. Francis Ford Coppola

a serious continuation of the first film."[69] Coppola also saw an opportunity
to correct a moral imbalance in the first film:

> I felt that *Godfather* had never finished; morally, I believed that the Family would be destroyed, and it would be like a kind of Gotterdammerung. I thought it would be interesting to juxtapose the decline of the Family with the ascension of the Family; to show that as the young Vito Corleone is building this thing out of America, his son is presiding over its destruction.[70]

Finally, there was perhaps the best reason of all for making *Godfather, Part II* — the chance to roll the dice again, the opportunity to take a big risk and beat the odds:

> You see, I could make five failures ... and I'd still be the guy who directed *The Godfather*. There's only one way to undo that fast, and that's to attempt to make another *Godfather*, and fail. In other words, this movie is the riskiest thing I could do. If it bombs, then people would look at the first *Godfather* and say it was all Brando, or whatever. If I took my career to an insurance actuary, he'd tell me to lay off the sequels if I wanted to stay healthy.[71]

Stung by the criticisms that he romanticized the Mafia and the Corleone crime family in the first film, Coppola wanted to make sure that no one missed the point this time. Puzo, who worked on the script with Coppola, disagreed:

> But the concept of power desolating someone, the way they showed it in the picture ... I think is just baloney. I would have showed Michael at the height of his power, everybody around him. Everybody loves him. . . . Everything is great with him. He's the only one who knows what's happening to him. That's a different concept. . . . I would have done it differently. It was too pointed a moral. It was almost like saying, "Look, we want to show you that we don't think the Mafia are good guys. This is how bad they are, and this is what evil leads to." It was too much on the nose, too blatant. I think they should have been more subtle about it.[72]

Another of Coppola's decisions was controversial — his idea to contrast the story of the young Vito Corleone (Robert DeNiro) with the story of Michael (Al Pacino):

> I decided to make a film about a man obsessed with his father's success on the eve of his own failure. A story of succession, juxtaposing the father and the son at approximately the same ages; the father in his rise and the son in his fall. And that's hard to do. So, for a long time there, I had two films that didn't make sense together. They were shot in a different style; they had a different smell to them. My friend George Lucas told me, "Francis, you have two movies. Throw one away. It doesn't work." But I had this hunch that if I could ever make it work, it could be fantastic. And finally, I made it work. So what was thought to be the weakness of the movie is really its strength.[73]

In an acting tour-de-force, Robert DeNiro portrays the young Vito Corleone in Coppola's superlative sequel, The Godfather, Part II.

Coppola is half correct. The use of the two intertwined stories is both *Godfather, Part II's* great strength and its weakest point. Where *Godfather* almost magically balanced, and obscured, its postmodern-intertextual elements to achieve enormous popular and critical success, *Godfather, Part II's* "corrections" (as Coppola deemed his harsh portrayal of Michael) were too overt for the film to achieve anywhere near the commercial success of *Godfather.*[74]

Although each story has approximately six segments, the total time devoted to each is skewed toward Michael and the "modern" story. The film begins with a 10-minute sequence set in Sicily and is followed by a 33-minute segment set in 1958. While nominally contrasting with Vito's story, this sequence seems really meant to demonstrate the slow diminishing of the warmth and ethnicity of the Corleone family seen in the wedding sequence in *Godfather.* Ostensibly doing everything for the Family, Michael is blind to the real effects of his dehumanized and ultimately self-destructive manipulations.

Another 16-minute young–Vito segment is followed by the longest single segment in the film, a 50-minute modern sequence. The Vito and

Michael segments continue to alternate, the modern story always longer. The film ends with three short scenes: Michael at a family gathering in 1941; Michael as a child with his father in Sicily; and a shot of Michael sitting alone in half shadow, pondering his life.

Coppola uses settings and color to deepen the contrast between the two stories. Vito's world, whether in Sicily or Little Italy, is full of life, vitality, and rich colors. Michael lives and operates in sterile surroundings like Nevada and Miami, and the colors in his scenes are muted and washed out. Perhaps the best example of this can be seen in two short juxtaposed sequences in the middle of the film. After his brutal killing of Fanucci, Vito returns home, picks up his infant son, and whispers to him, "Michael, your father loves you very much." After a slow fade to black, the scene shifts to Michael's gloomy Tahoe residence — abandoned toys rusting in the snow.

Godfather, Part II demanded that the viewer be at least aware of the first film, even if he had not seen it. Michael's character had to grow organically and logically from his character in the original yet make sense. Similarly, since Brando did not return as the younger Vito, Robert DeNiro's portrayal was complicated by the fact that he not only had to use gestures and voice patterns that mirrored Brando's but also had to suggest these characteristics in their developmental stage. "Both these borrowings," writes Robert B. Ray, ". . . clearly revealed the sequel's overt intertextuality, and thus, by implication, the inherent artificiality of the cinema itself, a world where characters grow not from 'life,' but from other fictions."[75]

Coppola also used *Part II* to explore further the parallel he saw between organized crime and big business. In his *Playboy* interview, Coppola discussed his beliefs concerning American business' role in crime:

> *Playboy*: As far as we know, A.T.&T. hasn't killed anyone in pursuit of its business.
> *Coppola*: Who says? Who says?
> *Playboy*: Have you got anything on A.T.&T.?
> *Coppola*: A.T.&T. I don't know about, but I.T.T. in Chile? I wouldn't bet my life that it hadn't. And it's not just business. How about the Yablonski murders in the coal miners' union. That was just the union equivalent of a Mafia hit. How about politics? . . . What's the difference between the United States putting a guy like Trujillo in power so our companies can operate in the Dominican Republic, and the Mafia handing the Boston territory to one of its *capos*?[76]

Coppola sends Michael and his partners — mafiosi like Hyman Roth (Lee Strasberg), politicians, and representatives of worldwide conglomerates like ITT — to Cuba where they agree to work with the Batista government in pillaging the country. Their agreement is symbolized by Roth's cutting up a cake decorated with the outline of Cuba. But before the deal can be realized, "superior" forces, revolutionaries fighting for principle rather than money, overthrow the government. Michael is allowed a vision of this future when he sees a guerrilla blow himself and an army officer up with a grenade rather than be captured.

If *Godfather* was justly famous for Coppola bravura crosscutting between his godson's baptism ceremony and the almost ceremonial killing of his enemies, *Part II* goes even further to juxtapose violent acts and religious ceremonies and celebrations. Vito's brother is killed during the opening funeral procession in Sicily; Fanucci is brutally dispatched while a festive religious procession fills the streets below, teeming with life; Don Ciccio's revenge murder is followed by a beautiful tableaux of Vito and his growing family outside a church.

The film's intent, argues John Hess, is to condemn the Church as one more empty capitalist institution, capable of control but not comfort: "But by juxtaposing it with its opposite — murder, hatred, brutality — Coppola implicated the Church in this activity. By showing the Church's inability to comfort anyone, Coppola shows its impotence. It is one more bourgeois ideal that does not work."[77]

As with *Godfather*, Coppola wanted *Godfather, Part II* to reflect the classical style of filmmaking he learned in film school:

> I have certain prejudices about how films are made. I feel, for example, that nowadays all movies are shot too close, and it's getting worse. You go to the movies and you're looking at people's heads. I saw *Jesus Christ Superstar*, which was a musical, and most of the time I was looking at their noses or their chins. It's a prejudice about what's being done wrong. I really went out of my way in *Godfather II* — to cut most of the people at their knees.[78]

Apocalypse Now

> My film is not a movie; it's not about Vietnam [said Coppola]. It *is* Vietnam. It's what it was really like; it was crazy. The way we made it was very much like the way the Americans were in Vietnam. We were in the jungle, there were too many of us, we had access to too much money, too much equipment; and little by little, we went insane. I think you can see it in the film. As it goes up the river, you can see the photography going a little crazy, and the director and the actors going a little crazy.... I thought I was making a kind of war film, and it was no longer a war film. Then, as Marlon (as Kurtz) says, "It struck me like a diamond bullet in my head" that I wasn't making the film. The film was making itself; the jungle was making the film, and all I did was do my best.[79]

John Milius, who wrote the original screenplay, discussed the film's origins:

> The original started at cinema school. George Lucas and I were great connoisseurs of the Vietnam War.... I wanted to go to Vietnam but I had asthma.... I was the only person I knew who *wanted* to go into the army.

George and I would talk about the battles all the time and what a great movie it would make. I had the title to call it, *Apocalypse Now*, because all these hippies at the time had these buttons that said, "Nirvana Now," and I loved the idea of a guy having a button with a mushroom cloud on it that said "Apocalypse Now," you know, let's bring it on, full nuke. Ever hear that Randy Newman song "Let's Drop the Big One Now"? That's the spirit that it started in right there![80]

Coppola gave shape to the project by suggesting that they base the screenplay on Joseph Conrad's novella *Heart of Darkness*. "Francis paid for [the *Apocalypse Now* script] under his Warner Bros.–Zoetrope agreement, paid George Lucas and me to direct and write it, respectively," Milius recalled. "Then they were very discontented with George because of *THX* — they didn't like it very well — and then they became discontented with Francis, and threw him out, and argued over the orphaned projects. . . . [Warners] didn't want to make it, but they didn't want to let it go, either. And Francis wanted to keep it."[81]

Milius completed the script in late 1969 and rewrote it in 1975. Since Lucas was tied up with the making of *Star Wars*, Coppola felt he had to make the film himself. He reportedly told Milius, "I've got to do this picture. I consider it the most important picture I will ever make. If I die making it, you'll take over; if you die, George Lucas will take over!"[82]

At one point, Milius was furious about what Coppola intended to do with the film:

Basically, [Coppola] wanted to ruin it, liberalize it, and turn it into *Hair*. He sees himself as a great humanitarian, an enlightened soul who will tell you such wonderful things as he does at the end of *Godfather II* — that crime doesn't pay. . . . We may have come up with some great statement at the end of *Apocalypse* to the effect that war is hell. . . . Francis Coppola has this compelling desire to save humanity when the man is a raving fascist, the Bay Area Mussolini.[83]

A first glance at *Apocalypse Now* suggests that like *Godfather* films, Coppola's intent was to construct the film so that it could be read two ways — first as a traditional war movie filled with all the action, violence, and spectacle, and second as a social commentary on the American involvement in Vietnam and its relationship to our political and cultural values.

"New Hollywood cinema consists of gangster and outlaw films, thrillers, Westerns, musicals, science-fiction films, comedies, and an occasional melodrama," argue David Bordwell and Janet Staiger. "*Apocalypse Now* is primarily and almost entirely a war movie."[84] While their assertion seems sensible, other critics have dismissed *Apocalypse Now*'s war-movie credentials. Gilbert Adair suggests the film is not what it appears to be: "If, from its opening shots, *Apocalypse Now* reveals the influence of thrillers and fantasies, Samurai films and even Westerns, one genre to which it bears little resemblance is the traditional war movie."[85]

Similarly, several perceptive analyses of *Apocalypse Now* argue that because of its structure, dialogue, characterization, use of genre formulas, and social analysis, the film is really a version of the traditional hard-boiled detective story. The unlikely plot (whatever one says of *Apocalypse Now*, plausibility is not its strong suit) and the film's narrative and moral ambiguity are characteristic of the American romantic tradition, especially when the work deals with large and troubling challenges to our fundamentally optimistic mythology. As Robert B. Ray has observed, Hollywood filmmakers traditionally made socially "dangerous" themes commercially acceptable by converting their troubling problems into more easily digestible individual melodramas.[86]

Thus, just as *Casablanca* "displaced" American fears about the dangers of entering World War II by transforming the core of the story to one focusing on Rick's hesitation about helping Victor Laszlo escape, so too does *Apocalypse* displace American fears about our culpability in Vietnam by focusing primarily on individuals: Willard's mission, Kilgore's blood-and-guts excesses, and Kurtz's madness. A reading of the film that includes criticism of our involvement in Vietnam and of our cultural blind spots is both possible and accurate, but the structure that supports these readings is genre — more specifically, the hard-boiled L. A. detective novel and film genres. John Hellmann argues that the "use of the hard-boiled detective formula [is] the structural, stylistic, and thematic center of the film."[87]

Victoria Geng points to Willard's voice-over narration in the film as paradigmatic of *Apocalypse Now*'s detective-genre elements:

> Willard talks in the easy ironies, the sin-city similes, the weary, laconic, why-am-I-even-bothering-to-tell-you language of the pulp private eye.... Our first look at Willard is the classic opening of a private eye movie: his face seen upside down, a cigarette stuck to his lip, under a rotating ceiling fan . . . and then the camera moving in a tight closeup over his books, snapshots, bottle of brandy, cigarettes, Zippo, and, finally, obligatory revolver on the rumpled bedsheets. This guy is not Marlow. He is a parody — maybe a self-created one — of Philip Marlowe, Raymond Chandler's L.A. private eye.[88]

"There are important similarities, reflecting their common source in quest/myths, between *Heart of Darkness* and the hard-boiled detective formula," writes Hellmann. "Both have isolated protagonists on a mystery/adventure who are in the employ of others while actually preserving their personal autonomy of judgment . . . [and] the protagonist encounters revelatory scenes of the depravity of his society in the course of his journey."[89]

Willard's journey is a classic hard-boiled detective formula: the morally ambivalent hero's journey is as much an investigation of society (in the film, the army) and a peculiarly American idealism (the philosophical

killer, Colonel Kurtz) as it is the unraveling of a mystery. As Hellmann
says,

> The river journey in *Apocalypse Now* is full of allusions to southern
> California, the usual setting of the hard-boiled genre, with the major
> episodes of this trip through Vietnam centering around the surfing, rock
> music, go-go dancing, and drug-taking associated with the west coast
> culture of the time. As a result, the river journey drawn from *Heart of
> Darkness* takes the detective and the viewer, not through Vietnam as a
> separate culture, but through Vietnam as the resisting object of a
> hallucinatory self-projection of the American culture.[90]

In his voice-over narration, Willard says of Kurtz, "There is no
way to tell his story without telling my own, and if his story is really a
confession, then so is mine." This suggests that like many hard-boiled
detective stories, the story Willard relates is a flashback to events that have
already happened. Supporting this reading are the film's images to come
that pass before Willard's (and our) eyes as Jim Morrison sings "This is the
end."

Another of the genre's formulas is that in his investigation the detective
unearths so much official and social corruption and decay that he finds it
difficult to judge the criminal harshly and may even understand and identify with him. As Willard says in his voice-over, "If that's the way Kilgore
fought the war, I wondered what they had against Kurtz. It couldn't be just
insanity and murder. There was enough of that to go around." And again:
"Charging a man with murder in this place is like handing out speeding
tickets at the Indy 500."

That Willard's and the film's investigation is really one of our
American culture is beyond question: we learn little or nothing about Vietnam or its people. The few Vietnamese in the film are seen as passive
onlookers (overwhelmed by the wash of our onrushing technological self-
involvement) or victims. *Apocalypse Now* says no more about Vietnam
than does the ideologically troubling *The Deer Hunter*.

The Vietnamese soldiers are spoken of with respect, but we only *hear*
about them and their supposedly superior motives (like the rebels in *Godfather, Part II*, they are superior because they are fighting for a cause they
believe in). After the troubling USO experience, Willard says, "Charlie
didn't get much USO. He was dug in too deep. . . . He had only two ways
home—death or victory." The American leadership in Vietnam is not far
removed from the bumbling Batista government in Cuba seen in *The Godfather, Part II*. As Willard observes, "The war was being run by a bunch
of four-star clowns who were going to give the circus away."

Willard's confrontation with Kurtz in a compound consisting of Cambodian temples and holy places is true to the formula, argues George
Grella:

> The bizarre cults and temples lend a quasi-magical element of the Grail
> romance to the hard-boiled thriller — the detective knight must journey to
> a Perilous Chapel where an ambivalent Merlin figure, a mad or evil priest,
> presides. His eventual triumph over the charlatan becomes a ritual feat,
> a besting of the powers of darkness.[91]

Despite the film's attempt to reduce the larger issues of our involvement in Vietnam to the paradigm — to an individual melodrama — the
characters are underdeveloped and full of contradictory impulses and actions. As one critic writes, "The biggest nonentity of all, sadly enough, is
Willard. The narration — alternately sensitive, psychopathic, literary,
gung-ho and anti-war — is self-contradictory and often at odds with
Willard's behavior." Further, "The journey into America's Viet Nam madness — not to mention the journey into Willard's and Kurtz's souls — reaches
its dead end in a quagmire of freshman English class recitations."[92]

Apart from *Apocalypse Now*'s genre elements, Coppola, many critics
have suggested, was incapable of infusing his film with any substantial intellectual depth — perhaps reflecting his postmodern and film-school background:

> *Apocalypse Now* suggests the work of a twenty-year-old film-school stu-
> dent, who, brought up on the conventional realism and pseudo-realism of
> Hollywood and TV, has just breathlessly discovered modernism.
> Although not twenty years old but nearing forty, Coppola piled into T.S.
> Eliot and *The Golden Bough* as if he were the first person who had ever
> read them, and this gives his film an unmistakably sophomoric, not to say
> semi-educated, quality.[93]

Another critic also sees little beyond Coppola's gestures toward deeper
meaning:

> Kurtz quotes from T. S. Eliot's *The Hollow Men*.... In a rather too art-
> fully composed still-life shot, his bedside reading is exhibited: Jesse L.
> Weston's *From Ritual to Romance*, Sir James Frazer's ... *The Golden
> Bough*, obviously designed as pointers to guide the spectator toward a
> true understanding of his impending assassination. For when Willard at
> last "terminates" Kurtz, the act is intercut with the ritualized felling of an
> ox, thus taking on overtones of parricide, both Oedipal and an-
> thropological, the killing of the father, the destitution of a chief whose eb-
> bing powers demand that he willingly sacrifice himself in favor of a
> younger, stronger man. But these mythic resonances never seem more
> than "token," planted mainly to bolster a sagging narrative, an impression
> reinforced by Coppola's uncertainty as to how the film should end."[94]

Indeed, Coppola's intercutting of the natives' sacrificial killing of a
water buffalo and Willard's murder of Kurtz is more a postmodern auteur's
intertextual quote — both self-reflexive and historical — than a mythic sym-
bol. It strongly recalls *Godfather*'s juxtaposition of the baptism and the killing of the heads of the Five Families and a scene in Eisenstein's (Coppola's

Harry Caul (Gene Hackman), a surveillance expert, becomes paranoid when he realizes he is the target of wiretaps. (Courtesy Steve and Nancy Gould.)

idol, you'll recall) *Strike* where the massacred workers were also juxtaposed with the slaughter of an ox.[95]

As was becoming his habit, Coppola had no ending for his film. Nothing suitable occurred to him during the shooting, so when Brando arrived, Coppola allowed him to improvise. As Richard Grenier notes, "They shot it. Coppola rewrote it. Brando improvised. Coppola rewrote. They

Coppola (right) discusses a scene with Marlon Brando, playing the mad Colonel Kurtz in Apocalypse Now.

shot. They improvised, rewrote, shot, improvised, rewrote, shot. Thus was filmed a crucial, climactic scene for the 'Film of the Decade.'"[96]

Coppola recalled the angst of finding an ending in his *Rolling Stone* interview:

> I thought the film should end with a choice, which was: "Should I be Kurtz? Or should I be Willard?" But I think what happened is that it was abrupt, that maybe I didn't have enough material to really extend it, as I would have had I known that was where the movie was going to end. And maybe his going down, and taking Lance by the hand, getting in the boat and going— It's not the same though. At the end, when the face comes on and you hear, "The horror, the horror," that's an echo of a warning rather than a real choice. Oh, fuck.... The ending of this movie has tortured me for five fucking years. I know this is the more popular ending, but *that* was *my* ending. But I can't fool around. If the picture doesn't get some form of popular support—I mean the first couple of weeks it'll do very well, but if doesn't begin to attract people ... although I think it will.[97]

Thus, Coppola, the self-proclaimed artist, was willing to give up the ending he preferred—Willard standing on the temple steps, unsure what choice to make and saying quietly, "The horror, the horror"—in order to ensure his film's commercial viability.

The patrol boat enters Colonel Kurtz's Cambodian compound in Apocalypse Now.

Like *The Conversation, Apocalypse* was praised for being an "art" film when it was really just another genre film — a very good genre film, certainly. The film is stunningly photographed by Vittorio Storaro, and it arguably gives the viewer more of a sense of the madness and chaos of the Vietnam War than any other film about the war made to that point. The set pieces — Kilgore's helicopter attack on the Viet Cong village, the Playmate USO show, the surrealistic imagery of the Do Lung Bridge, the arrival at Kurtz's compound — are examples of bravura filmmaking, brilliantly staged and directed. The slow series of dissolves that open the film are a direct result of Coppola's film-school sophistication. The straight cut had been used extensively since the late fifties (see Kubrick's *Paths of Glory* for an example of a film that eschewed dissolves), but with *Apocalypse Now*, Coppola helped return the dissolve to the filmmaker's toolbox.

Like so many of the other young lions, however, Coppola cannot resist inserting self-reflexive "in" jokes and references. Harrison Ford's Colonel Lucas and G. D. Spradlin's General Corman are multi-level jokes. "Lucas" and "Corman" refer to George Lucas and Roger Corman, but the actors playing them have other resonances: Harrison Ford played a similar aide in *The Conversation,* and G. D. Spradlin was the corrupt senator in *Godfather, Part II.* Many of the other actors are members of Coppola's extended professional family. Robert Duvall (Col. Kilgore) was in Coppola's *The Rain People, The Conversation,* and both *Godfather* films, and played the title role in *THX 1138,* produced by Coppola and directed by George Lucas. Marlon Brando (Colonel Kurtz) *was The Godfather,* of course. Frederic Forrest (Chef) was in *The Conversation* and would appear in many of Coppola's subsequent films, most notably in *One from the Heart.* The MC at the Playmate show was played by Bill Graham, a famous San Francisco music promoter. Coppola himself played the documentary filmmaker seen filming one of Colonel Kilgore's landings, and both Coppola and his father, Carmine, are credited with the music. (Eleanor Coppola may play an un- credited photojournalist.)

Coppola's knowledge of pop culture was reflected in the rock music played in the film, from The Doors' *The End* to *Susie Q.* There is a knowing reference to Charles Manson, further underscoring the film's indictment of California culture.

After the film was released and deemed a success, Milius retracted his earlier negative comments about Coppola:

> I love *Apocalypse Now....* That one movie justifies my career. I feel I really did something worthwhile by writing it. Even though I share credit (with Coppola) and I didn't direct it, it's a real piece of me. Francis is the best of us all. He has the most talent and the most daring. There are a lot of faults in Francis, but I think that he's the leader.[98]

One from the Heart

After the physically and emotionally draining experience of filming *Apocalypse Now* in the jungles of the Philippines, Coppola yearned for a less strenuous production. Fred Roos, longtime Coppola producer and associate, recalled that while they were in the bush, he and Coppola "got to thinking there must be an easier way to make movies than going out into a jungle every time, both figuratively and literally." But that sort of control could be had only one way — on a sound stage.[99]

So in March 1980 Coppola used some of the money that was flowing in from *Apocalypse Now* to buy and modernize the 60-year-old Hollywood General Studios.[100] The earlier incarnation of Zoetrope Studios had lacked sound stages or a backlot of its own.[101] Coppola hoped to produce the sort of popular genre films that the old studios specialized in. "We wanted an old-fashioned studio," said a former Zoetrope executive, "[to make] the kind of movies we think people have been yearning to see. People are sick of watching actors walking around New York talking about their personal relationships."[102]

Coppola, who gave the studio streets names like Akira Kurosawa Avenue, Sergei Eisenstein Park, and Alexander Korda Boulevard (*Thief of*

Bagdad was shot there in 1940), planned "a studio that is civilized, pro-artistic, and also makes money.... From the idea through the writing, casting, acting, and post production, it will be an all resident motion picture company, a team, a happy artistic community."[103] Unfortunately, the studio's first production was *One from the Heart*.

Calling the film "a simple little love story," Coppola nonetheless decided to go for a technologically complicated approach, labeling it "a theatrical reality."[104] "The long takes and elaborate tracking movements pointedly remind the viewer that what is on display is contrivance," writes Jeffrey Chown. "Rather than cut from a scene of Hank to a scene of Frannie, Coppola used a scrim-light effect where the foreground darkens as the background lights up and the camera dollies forward. The theatrical element and the artificial sets are thus emphasized."[105]

Art designer Dean Tavoularis recreated the famous Las Vegas strip on the Zoetrope lot. Built on two sound stages, Zoetrope's "miniature" strip is one reason the budget ballooned to an estimated $23 million. "A foot-high replica of the Dunes Hotel sign alone uses 1,600 neon light bulbs and costs $11,000," marveled one account. "A stylized jungle set of Bora-Bora is constructed for a fantasy sequence, along with a replica of the Vegas airport lobby."[106]

Why all this attention to set design? "I'm on the side of the audience. I want to make a film about love that *feels* like it. It's going to be a fluid, romantic film. Sweet. The sets themselves will be emotions."[107]

Coppola's self-rapture about the film was just beginning:

> I wanted to take a fable-like story and treat it almost the way Disney would approach a story in his animated films. Treat it with very expressive sets and lighting and music that heighten the story. If we had made the movie in Las Vegas, it would have been just another relationship movie set on a real location with people jumping in and out of cabs, talking about their love affairs. I wanted to do something people hadn't seen before.[108]

Critic Sheila Benson wrote that *One from the Heart* seemed to come "from the same artistic impulses that inspire airbrush art, three-dimensional pop-up greeting cards, and the delicately beautiful new neon that illuminates L.A. shops. It is post-Warhol, where everything is 'pretty,' all slickness and sleekness, and it cherishes its surfaces even more because of the hollowness they cover."[109] In other words, *Heart* is a postmodern pastiche that lacks a — well, a heart. It is Coppola the technician winning out over Coppola the writer, or Coppola the humanist.

Jeffrey Chown says there is "one very basic thematic issue about the film, which is that *One from the Heart* is not a 'boy gets girl' fantasy romance.... The thrust of *One from the Heart* is to *undercut* the fantasy romance contained in Hank chasing Leila and Frannie being chased by Ray, not to make it our main concern."[110] Chown is correct, but where he sees Coppola's disdain for adhering to the expected conventions as brave, I see it as ill-considered and confusing to audiences. Further, the two "common" everyday lovers at the center of the film are just that: too common and everyday for audiences seeking romantic escapism. Those who came to see *One from the Heart* were presumably upset to learn that their horizon of expectations would not be catered to as the film's advertising and posters seemed to promise. Coppola bet his studio on a fool's gamble: that he could make a $26-million nonnarrative art film in the guise of a tender romantic fable. Audiences wanted real romance and a real story, not set design and theatrical audacity, and Coppola crapped out.

As David Ehrenstein saw it, Coppola's error was believing that he could film anything and audiences would respond positively:

> Coppola embodies the new hubris. A perfectly respectable, highly successful mainstream craftsman in the George Stevens–William Wyler mold suddenly declares conventional narrative of no further interest to him. Possessed of enormous technical skill, he embarks on a project that will allegedly wed the glories of the past to the brave new world of gimmickry of the future. The result — *One from the Heart* — is exactly what might be expected from a filmmaker working in an area in which he is no way suited: a ribbon of visual tricks wrapped around a virtual void.... What is *One from the Heart* if not *Cleopatra* all over again? The difference is that this time only one showman was involved; Coppola was Mankiewicz, Skouras, Zanuck, and Liz Taylor all in one. And not in the name of commerce, mind you, but in the name of Art.[111]

The Cotton Club

Following *One from the Heart* by two years, *The Cotton Club* was important to Coppola's career if not his wallet.[112] It was not the box-office success he needed, but it partially restored his reputation as a gifted director.

The story of two love affairs, one white and one black, the film is structured similarly to *Godfather, Part II* with its alternating Vito-Michael storylines. The device is less successful, even though, as in *Part II*, the "main" story (concerning the white couple) is given much more screen time than the secondary story (concerning the black couple). Combining the two is a third story involving Dutch Schultz, Lucky Luciano, and the Harlem rackets. The gangster story even contains its own "couple": Cotton Club owner Owney Madden (Bob Hoskins in a wonderful performance) and his prognathous henchman Frenchy (Fred Gwynne).

In an otherwise wonderful sequence involving tap-dancer Sandman Williams (Gregory Hines) teaching his sister a time step, Coppola inexplicably cuts to close-ups and reaction shots, even cutting to the dancers' shoes while they dance. Just as *Finian's* Fred Astaire lost his feet when that film was blown up to 70mm, Hines and company lose theirs to ineptitude.

One from the Heart *was stylized, a triumph of technology and ultimately an over-produced and overdirected failure for Coppola.*

Coppola redeems himself with the final bravura sequence, however. Despite its similarity to the endings of *Godfather* and *Apocalypse Now*, *Cotton Club*'s crosscutting of Sandman Williams' magnificent solo dance with the killing of Dutch Schultz is stunningly photographed. Also, with William Kennedy as a cowriter of the screenplay, Coppola rediscovered traditional storytelling, producing a film with the strongest narrative structure since the two *Godfather* films. Working again with a genre that he knows like the back of his hand (and with Mario Puzo contributing via the original story), Coppola recaptured some of his early zest and enthusiasm. Coppola's mise-en-scène is evocative and supportive of the story in ways the gigantic sets and sound stages dwarfing his underdeveloped story and characters in *One from the Heart* could never be. His people are human again, not just types or collections of gestures and mannerisms as they were in *Apocalypse Now*.

Tucker: The Man and His Dream

Tucker: The Man and His Dream, Coppola's most recent full-length film (he contributed the weakest segment to a three-part film called *New*

Coppola (left) joined Woody Allen (center) and Martin Scorsese (right) in the tripartite New York Stories *(1989). Most critics assailed Coppola's segment as the weakest. (Courtesy of Steve and Nancy Gould.)*

York Stories) is paradigmatic of Coppola's career. It showcases many of his strengths while revealing that he still retains many of his old weaknesses. *Tucker* is the film that Coppola wanted to make for well over a decade. Numerous articles on Coppola mentioned the director's desire to create a film about the maverick carmaker:

"The company's next film project will be *The 1948 Tucker*, written, produced, and directed by Coppola and starring Marlon Brando as automotive rebel Preston Tucker, with the rest of Detroit as villains" (1974).[113]

"Coppola's next personal movie will be *Tucker*, a script he was been working on for fifteen years. 'American products used to be the best in the world. *Tucker* is about that period in American history when making the best car became irrelevant'" (1976).[114]

"[Coppola] will make a movie musical about [Preston] Tucker after *One from the Heart* that will portray the hero as a brave visionary who is cruelly squashed by the major auto companies" (1981).[115]

At the time of *Tucker*'s release, many articles mentioned the obvious parallels between Preston Tucker and Francis Ford Coppola. Asked by Jill Kearney if the Tucker story was "an allegory for the rise and fall" of Zoetrope, Coppola replied:

Well in my own little company there were by accident lots of parallels to the Tucker story. It was a family operation without a lot of dough behind it, and gathered together a lot of very talented individuals who fought for the right of the company to exist and to get to a point where it could compete. Usually you're knocked off before you can compete — and probably so you won't compete. ... Basically, I failed on a financial level because everyone knew, including myself, that I didn't have enough money to launch the kind of program I was launching, unless I was very, very lucky right in the beginning. I was like Tucker in the personality flaws. ... My attitude was, well, just because I don't have enough money to survive for three or four years no matter what, that doesn't mean that we shouldn't attempt it.[116]

Like many projects that take years to be realized, *Tucker* seems to be not quite worth the wait. Still, the film is brash, and glossy — fast-paced entertainment. Coppola had designer Dean Tavoularis build the marvelous sets as he did for *One from the Heart*. Unlike *Heart*, however, both the sets and Coppola's "theatrical reality" worked much better this time, proving the well-worn theory that *everything* in a film works better when you have a good script and fully realized characters. Unfortunately for Coppola and *Tucker*, the only underdeveloped character in the movie happened to be Preston Tucker (Jeff Bridges). Beset by petty bureaucrats and scheming auto executives, Coppola's Tucker smiles his way through a roller-coaster ride of highs and lows, never really letting us see what drives him. He punches a wall once and throws a telephone, but that's the extent of his anger at the establishment that shatters his dream.

When Coppola has Tucker on the phone to his wife and you realize that (through intense lighting and deep focus) they're physically in the frame together, it's an exhilarating device that doesn't come off as forced as Coppola's similar scrim-lighting scene changes in *Heart*. Similarly, it seems a reflection of the movie's vitality when Tucker strides forcefully from one set into the midst of another, whether literally or by means of an artfully concealed cut on the action. Unlike *Heart*, *Tucker*'s self-consciously theatrical devices work because they're not all the movie has going for it.

Like the two *Godfather* films, *Tucker* is about two of Coppola's favorite themes: the family and big business. While neither theme is clearly limned by the story or Coppola's handling of it, the postmodernist-nostalgic director is clearly having a ball plunging us into late forties pop culture: "Tiger Rag" ("Hold that tiger!") on the soundtrack, the wide lapels on the suits and the narrow brims on the hats, the moviehouse showing *Incendiary Blonde*, the existence of real *service* stations, and the parade of Tucker Torpedoes at the end.

In *Tucker*, Coppola has come home. He even worked with one-time protégé George Lucas. "I was very anxious to collaborate with George

[Lucas] and have George pull me down to a scope and kind of film that had a chance of being successful, and paying for itself. So we put it into a format that was ... like a Frank Capra film."[117]

Lucas played the role for *Tucker* that Coppola had played for the younger man's *THX 1138* nearly twenty years earlier: he served as the film's executive producer, thereby helping Coppola to get the film made by showing his willingness to subordinate his gambler's instincts to the caution and tightfistedness of a proven commercial winner—*Howard the Duck* notwithstanding. "I started out as his creative assistant," Lucas says, "and I guess that's still what I am, when it really comes down to it. It's just that now I'm helping to fund him, and then he was helping to fund me."[118] Lucas also reined in Coppola's showman's flair and more flamboyant impulses as thoroughly as the more conventional business executives tried to do with Tucker. The film is therefore both "safer" and less satisfying than it could have been. Although *Tucker* was a critical and in many ways a personal success and vindication for Coppola, it was a financial failure, costing $23 million to make, returning rentals of only $10 million.[119] Still, as *Tucker* makes clear, it's the dream that counts, not the result.

Francis Ford Coppola's immense talents seem to lie squarely in the area of the genre film, whether a "corrected" genre film (in Robert B. Ray's usage) or not. While no more subscribing to the notion that Coppola is a genuine auteur than I do, Jeffrey Chown used the words *Hollywood Auteur* in the title of his recent book on Coppola. Presumably, Chown meant that as the filmmakers of the previous generation were supposed to be able to do, Coppola could take someone else's creative base or structure—usually in the form of a story, screenplay, or idea—and make a wonderful and unique film from it. Coppola's films seem to work best when he works in genres that allow him the freedom to expand their boundaries, like the two *Godfather* films. He is less successful creating conscious "art."

Writes Leo Braudy:

> I have been recounting those elements in Coppola's films that lend themselves to an allegorical reading of his own relation to Hollywood and his past masters: a deep homage along with a simultaneous effort to replace them with his own aesthetic family—his father the composer, his sister the actress, and of course all his friends and coworkers at the (now defunct) American Zoetrope. Always there is a dream of camaraderie, and invariably that dream turns sour. . . . Coppola is committed to storytelling and narrative of an older sort, in accord with his commitment to genre and family ritual as structures of feeling that he wishes would still retain their ability to compel belief. But Coppola's commitment is undermined by his general unwillingness to question his own role as the director and *Wunderkind* who will pull all this together and make it work.[120]

Finally, John Milius argues for Coppola's importance to the other young lions:

> He subsidized us all. . . . He is responsible for a whole generation; indirectly, he is responsible for Scorsese and De Palma. You cannot overemphasize the importance he has had. If this generation is to change American cinema, he is to be given the credit, or the discredit.[121]

Chapter 3

George Lucas

George Lucas is emphatic: "I don't like the word *art* because it means pretension and bullshit, and I equate those two.... Art is for critics, for somebody ... who spends his time figuring it out and doesn't really do anything else. Well, that's for them; I'm a craftsman. I don't make a work of art; I make a movie."[1]

> I'm more drawn to Flash Gordon. I like action adventure, chases, things blowing up, and I have strong feelings about science fiction and comic books and that sort of world. Some of my friends are more concerned about art and being considered a Fellini or an Orson Welles, but ... I just like making movies.... If I wasn't a filmmaker, I'd probably *be* a toymaker. I can sit forever doodling on my movie. I don't think that much about whether it's going to be a great movie or a terrible movie, or whether it's going to be a piece of art or a piece of shit.[2]

Lucas makes films to see them realized, he says. "For me it's like sculpture or painting. I come up with an idea that I think will make a great image or a great scene and then I go out and make it happen. I do it partially because I think it will be good for the story; and I do it partially because I want to see that scene re-created from what was in my head; and I do it partially just from enjoyment."[3]

George Walton Lucas, Jr., was born in Modesto, California, on Sunday, May 14, 1944, the son of George W. Lucas, the owner of a stationery store, and Dorothy Bomberger Lucas. "I was as normal as you can get," Lucas recalled. "I wanted a car and hated school. I was a poor student. I lived for summer vacations and got into trouble a lot shooting out windows with my BB gun."[4]

While Lucas was not a social failure, some of his classmates remember him as a "nerd," sort of a combination of *American Graffiti*'s klutzy, bumbling "Toad," the drag-racing John Milner, and Curt, the soul-searching high school graduate unsure of his future.[5]

Lucas agreed with this assessment:

> I started out . . . as Terry the Toad, and I think everybody sort of starts out as Terry the Toad. And I went from that to being John. I had a hot car, and I raced around a lot. Finally I got into a very bad accident and almost got myself killed . . . [and] I became much more academic-minded. . . . I decided to give up cars and go to junior college, try to get my grades back. So for the next two years, while I was at junior college, I more or less was Curt. I was thinking about leaving town, and I had a lot more perspective on things.[6]

The near-fatal auto accident altered the course of Lucas' life, and he began to rethink his future.

> The accident made me more aware of myself and my feelings. *I began to trust my instincts.* I had the feeling I should go to college, and I did. I had the same feeling later that I should go to film school, even though everybody thought I was nuts. I had the same feeling when I decided to make *Star Wars,* when even my friends told me I was crazy. These are just things that have to be done, and I feel as if I have to do them.[7] [Emphasis added.]

Since he had never been the best of students in high school, Lucas' decision to study film came as a shock to everyone he knew. "All my friends thought I was crazy," Lucas remembered. "I lost a lot of face because for hot rodders the idea of going into film was really a goofy idea." But when the former car- and motorcycle fanatic finally discovered film, he "really fell madly in love with it, ate it and slept it 24 hours a day. There was no going back after that."[8]

The film program Lucas decided was best for him was the one offered by the University of Southern California. At that time, before its illustrious and successful graduates like Lucas showed the way into the industry, USC may have operated like a trade school, but it was a trade school whose instructors cautioned its students that they would have little opportunity to use what they learned: "The instructors would walk in and say, 'Good morning, this is editing, and although we're here to teach you the fundamentals of editing, you'll never use them because you'll never get into the upper echelons of the industry,'" recalled Howard Kazanjian, USC alumnus and Lucas associate.[9]

"The department (instructors) never taught us much, other than the basics," Lucas remembered. "They opened the door, but we had to go inside and find out for ourselves. We students were learning things infinitely faster than the classes were teaching us. You had to in order to keep up with what was going on."[10]

Given USC's trade-school approach, Lucas and the other members of his film-school generation were immersed in the techniques of film editing, cinematography, lighting, animation, directing, acting, staging. Lucas also

Although George Lucas paid homage to Akira Kurosawa films like The Seven Samurai, *he captured their scope but only rarely their humanity. (Courtesy of Steve and Nancy Gould.)*

began to watch films with a passion, the films of directors he considered especially "cinematic": Jean-Luc Godard, Richard Lester, Orson Welles, Stanley Kubrick, and most important, the great Japanese director Akira Kurosawa. Lucas admired Kurosawa's "formal Japanese sense of composition and texture" and later attempted, whenever possible, to work such elements into his own films — as in the triumphant victory celebration that ends *Star Wars*.[11]

Ironically, this scene, showing Luke Skywalker, Han Solo, and Chewbacca walking between ranks of cheering rebels to receive their medals, has been singled out by many critics as closely resembling the march of Hitler, Himmler, and Lutze to the Nuremberg memorial monument in Leni Riefenstahl's Nazi propaganda film *Triumph of the Will*. While some might find such a film quote distasteful, Lucas apparently has no qualms about embracing that film's images if not its values — lending credence to charges that he is more concerned about the *look* of his films than their content. It is *because* of his postmodernist preoccupation with borrowing and juxtaposing various film styles, including Riefenstahl's powerfully realized images, that Lucas is able to so blithely appropriate anything and everything, regardless of its ideological origins.

Was this scene from Lucas' Star Wars *a joyous affirmation of righteous victory — or a naïve young filmmaker's unthinking tribute to the Nazi propaganda film* Triumph of the Will?

Similarly, it seems that the lessons Lucas learned from Kurosawa were technical and visual ones, not dramatic or human ones. A great visual stylist, Kurosawa is nonetheless a filmmaker more concerned with matters of substance than surface — honor, love, hate, revenge, and sacrifice — as films like *Rashomon* (1950), *Seven Samurai* (1954), *Throne of Blood* (1956), *Kagemusha* (1980), and *Ran* (1985) testify. As a child of the postmodernist age, however, Lucas appears to have been less interested in Kurosawa's moral and psychological themes than with his stylistic strengths.[12]

David Johnson, one of Lucas' USC instructors, recalled that Lucas' "forte was designing and constructing film stories, but his attitude was 'Let someone else work with the people.' Look at his student films — they're all about things and facts. People are just objects."[13]

If Lucas' filmic instincts were toward the mechanical, he nonetheless was initiated into a network of people with but one thing on their minds — film. As Lucas later recalled:

> When we were in film school everyone cooperated; there was a lot of cross-pollenization between UCLA and USC . . . I don't think it had ever happened before — there's more of a tendency for people to be sort of rah-rah and form little groups of us against them. That was when I got to know Bill Norton, who's doing *More American Graffiti* for me now. His father was a writer, and he was a UCLA classmate of Gloria Katz, who married my good friend from USC, Bill Huyck (both of whom screenwrote on *American Graffiti*). [And] everybody helped everybody; we were all friends. . . . And we all looked at each other's work, mostly at student film festivals.[14]

If Lucas and the other young lions were making contacts that they would draw upon once they became professionals, they were also, arguably, limiting their college experiences to just one discipline — films and filmmaking. "At USC the film school is so separate from the rest of the campus," remembers Kevin Reynolds, a USC alumnus. "It's sort of a world unto itself. Everyone knew everyone else in the film school. We really didn't have anything to do with anyone outside that environment."[15] Thus, instead of mixing with students and intellectuals of all stripes — philosophers, English majors, business students, historians, Marxists, or conservatives — Lucas and his friends seemed content to define a single area of interest and focus on it to the exclusion of other, presumably enriching, experiences.

Lucas began in animation but soon moved on to photography and then editing. He made the next logical leap because of frustration: "I was going to be an editor, but I sort of got tired of directors telling me how to cut stuff . . . so I said I'm just not going to take this anymore; I'm just going to become a director. So I became a director out of self-defense as an editor."[16]

Using a cast and crew supplied by the U.S. Navy, Lucas wrote and directed *THX 1138:4EB (Electronic Labyrinth)* in 1967 and won first prize at the Third National Student Film Festival. Another of his films, *6–18–67* (Lucas had a thing for numbers), was a documentary about the making of *MacKenna's Gold*.

As Dale Pollock has observed of Lucas' leaving film school for the vicissitudes of finding a (supposedly nonexistent) real job in Hollywood, "His timing was right. The average age in the Hollywood labor force was fifty-five, and there was no one to replace them. 'A bit of history opened up like a seam, and as many of us who could crammed in,' Lucas says. 'Then it drifted back closed again.'"[17]

Despite how it turned out, the timing didn't seem all that fortuitous to Lucas at the time:

> I had a Samuel Warner scholarship, which paid me about $80 a week to go to Warner Bros. and watch them make movies. . . . But the day I arrived at Warner's was the day Jack Warner was leaving, because they had sold the studios to a big corporation . . . so I couldn't be assigned to the story department. They were only making one movie, *Finian's Rainbow* (1968), so that's where I ended up.[18]

Finian's Rainbow introduced Lucas to its director, Francis Ford Coppola, an older film-school graduate who was soon to be Lucas' friend and mentor. Lucas recalled their instant affinity: "Everybody in the industry was then over 50 years old, but there we were — both in our 20s, both bearded, and both from film school. We immediately became very close. I was essentially an editor and a cameraman, while Francis is a writer and director — more into actors and acting."[19]

When Coppola went on the road to make *The Rain People* (1969), Lucas went along, and in addition to helping in numerous ways (assistant art editor, assistant cameraman, etc.) he ended up making a documentary, *Filmmaker* (1968), on the movie's production. What's notable about that fact is that as with *6–18–67*, Lucas again shot a film about the making of a film — another example of his self-reflexive interests.[20]

Wanting a studio of their own, a place to make the sort of films that *they* wanted to make, Coppola, Lucas, and several of the other young lions founded their own production entity, American Zoetrope. As Audie Bock noted, "Coppola was able to talk Warners into a deal backing five or six pictures for American Zoetrope, giving the unknowns a chance. The theory was that if one film in ten succeeded it would pay for all the failures. The first bona-fide American Zoetrope film in this package was Lucas' *THX*, a science-fiction caper shot in the Bay Area subway system before it was put into operation, and a film for which Lucas feels a deep affection. But Warners hated it."[21]

THX 1138

With Francis Ford Coppola's backing at American Zoetrope, Lucas turned his award-winning student film *THX 1138:EB* (1967) into his first full-length feature. Coppola was a stern taskmaster and told Lucas that he was going to have to learn to write and write well if he was to be a first-rate director. "He forced me to write the script for *THX 1138*, and the first draft was pretty awful," said Lucas. Since writing the screenplay took him a year, Lucas began working on a script about the Vietnam War with fellow USC graduate John Milius.[22]

Lucas shot the film in San Francisco, using the Bay Area Rapid Transit System's (BART) partially constructed tunnels for the exciting and visually thrilling final chase sequence. Although he had assisted Coppola as an all-around "gofer" and extra technician on *The Rain People* (1969), directing *THX 1138* was his first real experience with a professional crew. It was both eye-opening and reassuring. "'They still put the film in backward and screwed up,'" Lucas marveled. "'Only in the professional industry, you pay for it — enormously. What a realization that was for me and my friends.'"[23]

"Once I started directing, I realized that I really didn't enjoy it. I didn't enjoy it because of the fact that it isn't hands on. I like hands on. I like to actually cut the film. *THX* was the best experience I had. I was the editor. I actually was the director of photography, the lighting cameraman, so it was like a hands-on movie."[24]

Because of his hands-on self-sufficiency, Lucas' quiet determination and emotionless approach to directing his first feature did not endear him to his cast and crew. "I'm not very good with people, never have been," Lucas admitted. "It's a real weak link for me."[25]

THX 1138 begins with George Lucas' first postmodern quote: a short sequence from Buck Rogers, a 1939 serial starring Buster Crabbe. The space-opera hero is engaged in freeing the twenty-fifth century from the rule of a tyrant named Killer Kane.

THX is, for Lucas, relatively original. The parts that are not—the present projected into a grim future where individualism is devalued, sex is forbidden or regulated (Orwell's 1984), or drug use is mandatory (Huxley's Brave New World)—have lost their once shocking and visionary air. It is possible, certainly, that some viewers (but presumably these are the very moviegoers unlikely to go to see a modern SF fable) are unfamiliar with the conventions of this type of tale (which in SF is known as an "if this goes on . . ." story) and would accept it as original. Lucas' original touches, then, lie not in his use of familiar SF themes but in his mise-en-scène, the way his images, sounds, sets, and striking tableaus combine to produce a compelling portrait of sterility and hopelessness.

THX 1138 is not only the title of the film but the name of Lucas' eponymous hero. THX (Robert Duvall) lives with LUH 3147 (Maggie McOmie). After THX stops taking his mandatory medication, he and LUH engage in illegal sex. When THX's supervisor, SEN 5241 (Donald Pleasence), reports him, he is found guilty of "drug evasion" and "sexual perversion." Imprisoned in the White Limbo, THX escapes with SEN (whom he reported because SEN wanted to live with him) and another inmate, an electronic hologram called SRT (Don Pedro Colley). The last third of the film is devoted to THX's efforts to escape from the underground city.

When the film was labeled cold and sterile, Lucas angrily pointed to the tender love scenes between THX and LUH as revealing his warmer side.[26] While Lucas is correct to call attention to such sequences, the overall tone of the film is arid and impersonal, one of smothering blandness. Despite his love scenes with LUH, THX is not a fully developed character (one of Lucas' weaknesses in film school), and the viewer watches his efforts to escape the stifling bureaucracy with dispassionate interest—rather as one might watch a laboratory rat's attempt to escape from a maze.

If characterization was Lucas' weak point, his strength in THX 1138 is his technical proficiency. His images are startling and remarkable; his sound montaging and layering of voices, intercoms, and police transmissions (created for the most part by Walter Murch) add tremendously to our appreciation for what a cold and inhumane civilization this is. As one review noted, Lucas "holds us with endless frames of austere beauty, his white-suited citizens, their heads floating like pink balloons, somnambulating down empty, purest-white corridors."[27]

Several scenes of THX in detention profit enormously from this visual

Lucas' first filmic vision of the future was a cold and sterile one. Here THX 1138's robot policemen enforce a dehumanized society's sanctions. (Courtesy of Steve and Nancy Gould.)

and aural sophistication. While THX, dressed entirely in white, huddles fearfully in the middle of an all-white cell, we hear the voices of unseen technicians dispassionately discussing the proper level of electrical manipulation of THX's muscles; as they blandly discuss power levels, THX is alternately twisted like a pretzel and unknotted like a rope. Their discussion entirely technical, the two men never acknowledge the pain and suffering they are casually putting THX through.

Apart from the bows to *Buck Rogers* (acknowledged) and to Huxley and Orwell (unacknowledged), *THX's* postmodern components are primarily technical: the set design, the use of TV images, Murch's impressive sound montages, and the film's low emotional quotient. Lucas put images at the center of his film, not compelling human feelings. Even the powerful final scene, the shot of a now-free THX standing silhouetted against a massive yellow sun, was chosen for its visual rather than its emotional or symbolic impact. When a friend asked Lucas and Murch about the significance of the final sunrise, the two men just looked at each other before Lucas answered, "Well, it's just a sunrise."[28]

Even though Lucas made the film for approximately $750,000, getting remarkable quality on screen for that expenditure, the film was only desultorily promoted by Warners and didn't make a profit. "*THX 1138* is the first San Francisco–produced feature to do well at the box office [*sic*]; but, characteristically for these times . . . the distributors thought they had a disaster on their hands and didn't even have a poster ready when the film first opened. They probably still don't understand it."[29]

The distributors were not the only ones who didn't understand the film: neither did the mass moviegoing audience. If one accepts that the ideal interpretive community (using Stanley Fish's words) for *THX* was presumably SF-literate teens and adults, one must also accept that this is a numerically insignificant audience (in terms of a semi–mass medium-like film), an audience incapable on its own of making a hit out of such a "sophisticated" text.

"And then came Black Thursday," Lucas said. "That was what we called it. Francis had borrowed all this money from Warner Bros. to set [American Zoetrope] up, and when the studio saw a rough cut of *THX* and the scripts of the movies we wanted to make, they said, 'This is all junk. You have to pay back the money you owe us.' Which is why Francis did *Godfather*. He was so much in debt he didn't have any choice."[30]

His feelings bruised and believing himself at least partially responsible for the demise of American Zoetrope, Lucas knew what he had to do next:

> After *THX*, I realized I had to make entertaining films or back off and release through libraries. I didn't want to struggle to get $3,000. It was too limiting, like giving a painter one brush, a piece of cardboard, and tubes of black and white paint. You can do it, but . . . I didn't want to be a self-indulgent artist, and I didn't want my wife to support me forever. I started on the road to make a rock 'n' roll cruising movie, determined to master that trade.[31]

American Graffiti

> *THX* is very much the way that I am as a filmmaker [said Lucas]. *American Graffiti* is very much the way I am as a person — two different worlds, really.[32]

Lucas had spent three years of his life on *THX 1138* and felt that he had little to show for it; his wife, Marcia, a film editor, was still supporting the two of them. His next film had to be carefully considered.

> I thought, "Well, I'll do the rock & roll movie—that's commercial."
> Besides, I was getting a lot of razz from Francis and a bunch of friends who
> said that everyone thought I was cold and weird and why didn't I do
> something warm and human. I thought, "You want warm and human, I'll
> give you warm and human." So I went to Gloria [Katz] and Willard Huyck
> and they developed the idea for *American Graffiti*, and I took the twelve-
> page treatment around.[33]

Unfortunately for Lucas, none of the studios he approached would touch the film after the nonperformance of *THX*. Finally, David Picker, the head of United Artists, listened to Lucas' pitch and agreed to make the film; indeed, UA went so far as to sign a two-picture deal with Lucas: *American Graffiti* and a science-fiction film Lucas was calling *Star Wars*.[34]

But when Huyck and Katz had a shot at directing their own film, Lucas went with another friend to write the script. Lucas soon regretted his decision when the script the man turned in was a formula piece of hack work, a typical "teen" film. As Lucas recalled,

> The man had put in playing chicken on the road instead of drag racing.
> That was my life. I spent four years driving around the main street of
> Modesto, chasing girls. It was the mating ritual of my times, before . . .
> everybody got into psychedelia and drugs.[35]

Making *American Graffiti* also gave Lucas an opportunity to showcase the music that he loves—rock and roll. "George wrote the script," said Walter Murch, "with his old forty-fives playing in the background."[36] "Making *Graffiti* I could sit down at my Steenbeck [editing machine] and play all this rock 'n' roll all day; that was my job in editing. The editors were cutting the scenes and I was putting in the rock 'n' roll, saying, 'Wow, that's really great!' It's like carving something; it takes shape, and it's a lot of fun. It's kind of therapy."[37]

By the time Lucas had something to show them, however, United Artists was no longer interested in his script or film. So Lucas shopped the script around again, and Universal agreed to produce the film if Francis Ford Coppola agreed to act as the producer. As Lucas says, "You could see the way they were thinking: 'From the man who brought you *The God-father.*' Anyway, Francis said sure."[38]

Once Universal agreed to make *American Graffiti*, Lucas realized he needed more help with the underdeveloped script. As before, he turned to Willard Huyck and Gloria Katz. While stressing that Huyck and Katz didn't alter his basic structure, Lucas says that they did

> improve the dialogue, make it funnier, more human, truer. And they also
> wrote in the Steve and Laurie relationship. They took those scenes and

made them work. So though they improved it . . . it was basically my story. The scenes are mine; the dialogue is theirs. But . . . of course, they completely changed some scenes, and others were left intact.[39]

Since Lucas says he writes what he knows, he admits that three of the four male characters are in one way or another based on him.

Because the film is a fond reminiscence of Lucas' teenage years spent cruising Modesto's main drag, he says, one reason he made it was so that his father wouldn't think he'd wasted those years. "I can say I was doing research, though I didn't know it at the time." While Lucas insists that many of the movie's incidents are things that really happened to him or his friends, he also concedes that "they've also been fantasized, *as they should be in a movie*. They aren't really the way they were *but the way they should have been*."[40] [Emphasis added.]

American Graffiti takes place during one incident-filled night which the characters spend cruising the streets of Modesto, California, and listening to the rock and roll music played by a mysterious disc jockey called the Wolfman. Curt (Richard Dreyfuss) is poised to leave for college in the East, and he vacillates over whether to go or to stay.

Complicating his decision is his obsession with a mysterious blonde woman (Suzanne Somers) in a T-Bird who mouths "I love you" at him. John Milner (Paul Le Mat), who's been out of school for a few years, is a mechanic and the local drag-race champion. He tells Curt to seize his chance and leave, or end up like him, facing endless challenges to his deuce coupe's supremacy.

Steve (Ron Howard), the popular class president, is going with Curt and wants to date other women while he's apart from his steady girlfriend, Laurie (Cindy Williams). Laurie is outraged by Steve's proposal, and they spend the night sparring over it. Steve leaves his "boss" car in the care of the nerdy Terry (Charles Martin Smith). Terry, who normally drives a motor scooter, is thrilled to have access to Steve's car and picks up a bleached blonde named Debbie (Candy Clark).

The film ends with John winning his race with rival Bob Falfa (Harrison Ford) when Falfa's car crashes. Terry has found a girl and has also found some self-respect. While Steve decides to stay by Laurie's side, Curt leaves on the plane for the East, seeing the T-bird far below on the highway.

"The whole film is essentially a teenage fantasy," George Lucas says about *American Graffiti*. "It's not really the way it is. That one night is really a year's cruising. It's purposely done that the kids get the better of the authority figures. That's part of a teenage fantasy. How often do you really get the better of an adult when you're a kid?"[41]

While the film garnered mostly favorable reviews, not everyone was enamored by Lucas' accomplishment. After the release of *Star Wars*, one

Lucas' 1973 monster hit, American Graffiti, *starred, from left to right, Ron Howard, Candy Clark, and Charles Martin Smith. Smith played Terry the Toad, a character not unlike George Lucas during his high school years.*

critic berated *Graffiti* as "a look at the early sixties seen through the eyes of someone who has seen too many Roger Corman films about that period; Lucas does not provide any insight or perceptive observation on that era. Like *Star Wars*, its characters are one-dimensional cartoons, and the situations arbitrarily arranged for the easiest possible laughs and responses."[42]

Like a number of critics writing during the height of the feminist movement, James Monoco criticized Lucas' lack of well-defined female characters comparable to the fleshed-out male characters in the film: "Where are the bookworm, the best friend, and the talent? The blond fantasy makes a mysterious appearance, but where is the female equivalent of

Curt? *American Graffiti* has a distinctly male point of view that is, moreover, adolescent. It gives us the nostalgia; it doesn't give us a more reasoned explication of our untenable situation at seventeen."[43]

Lucas later admitted that "the largest real criticism about that [the end titles telling the male characters' fates] has been that we didn't tell about the girls. But Women's Lib has really evolved since the film was finished a year ago January. It was going on, but it wasn't as militant then."[44]

In Lucas' defense, one can note that *American Graffiti* is concerned with *his* recollections of his high school and cruising years, not anyone else's. Understandably, Lucas' focus is on a fondly remembered male world. Still, it is rare for any of the lions' films to contain strong and realistic female characters. Since so many of their films have been aimed primarily at the adolescent male audience, this has been a positive factor for the box office if less so for women's rights.

Although Lucas left out strong and believable women characters, he did not forget to include several self-reflexive or private jokes about himself, his friends, and their films. John Milner's deuce coupe's license plates read *THX 1138*, and Milner's character and name are based on Lucas' good friend John Milius. The movie theater in the film is playing *Dementia 13*, Francis Ford Coppola's first film. Lucas cast fellow USC alum Fred Roos in a small part, and Johnny Weissmuller, Jr., who appeared in *THX* as a robot cop, also had a small role as a hood.[45]

Lucas' decision to allot $80,000, roughly 10 percent of *Graffiti's* budget, to pay for the music rights to 41 rock and roll classics was a brilliant stroke. Reviewers and critics praised the music track's nostalgic energy, and its amazing ability to complement the on-screen action.[46] "Walter Murch did the sound montages, and the amazing thing we found was that we could take almost any song and put it on almost any scene and it would work," Lucas remembered. "All good rock 'n' roll is classic teenage stuff, and all the scenes were such classic teenage scenes that they all just sort of meshed, no matter how you threw them together."[47]

After observing that *American Graffiti* is ostensibly set in the sixties, one writer called the film "the quintessential fifties nostalgia movie—a comprehensive recreation of the world of sock hops, drag races, cherry cokes, and Eisenhower complacency."[48] *Graffiti* seems to be firmly entrenched as that type of pastiche movie Frederic Jameson identifies as the "nostalgia film." Indeed, Jameson singles it out as a prime example.[49]

Lucas is impatient with the nostalgia label. "I didn't have the west or gangsters, or anything, so I used what I grew up with. I'm doing what filmmakers have always done.... It's just that now they've made it a classification, so any time you do a film that's five years in the past, it's a nostalgia film."[50]

One article on *American Graffiti* as a nostalgia film observes that the movie reflects Lucas' familiarity with pop culture, especially cruising and rock and roll:

> This verism pertains to surface details only, elements such as dress, cars, settings, etc., for what is being enacted on the screen is often ... wish fulfillment expanded to the magnitude of myth. Lucas makes a distinction between the realism of *Graffiti*'s style and the unrealistic nature of many of the characters' actions. ... The obsession with period detail which is so characteristic of nostalgic art serves to further confuse the viewer's clouded memory of his clumsy teenage years. ... It never really happened.[51]

Some critics have observed that *American Graffiti* contains superficial similarities to *High School Confidential, Rock Around the Clock*, and "Nicholas Ray's template for the high school film, *Rebel Without a Cause*." John Milner's climactic drag race looks not unlike a similar scene in *Rebel*. Whether Lucas' quotes were intentional or not, he was learning the power of nostalgia.[52]

American Graffiti became a giant hit and thrust Lucas into a charmed circle, one composed of hot young directors with sure commercial instincts. Still, the experience had been neither pleasant (Universal cut several minutes of insignificant footage out against Lucas' will) nor easy. Lucas made the film for several reasons. One was simply that people had told him it couldn't work. Lucas' response to that could serve as his credo: "I did it because I didn't believe what they said. You just have to be stubborn and bull-headed, and move forward no matter what you're up against."[53]

Star Wars

While George Lucas and John Milius tried to put together *Apocalypse Now*, Gary Kurtz traveled to the Philippines to arrange things and check locations. Their version of the film was to be "a low-budget, documentary-style [cheap and cheesy, to use Lucas' words] film" costing about $2 million and ready to be shown for the nation's bicentennial. When difficulties loomed, another of Lucas' ideas looked more promising—an SF film called *Star Wars*.[54]

Lucas told one interviewer:

> Rather than do some angry, socially relevant film, I realized there was another relevance that is even more important—dreams and fantasies, getting children to believe there is more to life than garbage and killing and all that real stuff like stealing hubcaps—that you could still sit and dream about exotic lands and strange creatures.[55]

"*Star Wars*," he revealed to another interviewer, "came out of my desire to make a modern fairy tale":

> In college I became fascinated by how culture is transmitted through fairy
> tales and myths. Fairy tales are how people learn about good and evil,
> about how to conduct themselves in society. Darth Vader is the bad
> father; Ben Kenobi is the good father. The good and bad mothers are still
> to come. I was influenced by the dragonslayer genre of fairy tale—the
> damsel in distress, the evil brothers, the young knight who through his vir-
> tue slays the dragon.[56]

What Lucas discovered was that modern kids lacked the sort of fantasy
life he had grown up with, had taken for granted:

> [Kids] don't have westerns, they don't have pirate movies, they don't have
> that stupid serial fantasy life that we used to believe in. It wasn't that we
> really believed in it. . . . Look, what would happen if there had never been
> John Wayne movies and Errol Flynn movies and all that stuff that we got
> to see all the time? I mean, you could go into a theater, not just watch it
> on television on Saturday morning, actually . . . sit down and watch an
> incredible adventure . . . a real Errol Flynn, John Wayne—*gosh*—kind of
> adventure.[57]

Lucas also believes movies should offer more responsible images and
role models to kids:

> Film [is] an extremely significant influence on the way our society
> operates. The influence of the church . . . has been usurped by film. Films
> and television tell us the way we conduct our lives, what is right and
> wrong. When Burt Reynolds is drunk on beer in *Hooper* and racing cops
> in his rocket car, that reinforces the recklessness of the kids who've been
> drawn to the movie in the first place and are probably sitting in the theater
> drinking beer.[58]

"As a kid, I read a *lot* of science fiction," Lucas remembered,

> but instead of reading technical, hard-science writers like Isaac Asimov,
> I was interested in Harry Harrison and his fantastic, surreal approach to
> the genre. . . . *Star Wars* is a sort of compilation of this stuff, but it's never
> been put in one story before, never put down on film. I wanted it to be
> an adventure in space, like *John Carter of Mars*. That was before *science*
> fiction took over, and everything got very serious and science oriented.
> *Star Wars* has more to do with disclaiming science than anything else.
> There are very elaborate Rube Goldberg explanations for things. . . . It's
> not based on science, which bogs you down.[59]

"I didn't want to make a *2001*. I wanted to make a space fantasy that
was more in the genre of Edgar Rice Burroughs; that whole other end of
space fantasy that was there before science took it over in the fifties. Once
the atomic bomb came, everybody got into monsters and science and what
would happen with this and what would happen with that. I think
speculative fiction is very valid but they forgot the fairy tales and Tolkien
and all the *real* heroes."[60]

Star Wars has been called a new myth for the seventies, a myth whose time has come — or an old myth that has simply come back in a new form:

> The life of myths consists in reorganizing traditional components in the face of new circumstances or ... in reorganizing new, imported components in the light of tradition. More generally, the mythic process is a learning device in which the unintelligible — randomness — is reduced to intelligibility — a pattern: "Myth may be more universal than history."[61]

After Lucas completed editing *American Graffiti* in early 1972, he began working on *Star Wars*, writing in the morning and using his afternoons to research fairy tales, mythology, and social psychology. Through his research, Lucas discovered Joseph Campbell's *The Hero with a Thousand Faces*, the seminal 1949 work detailing the universality of the myths that permeate our society and our lives. Campbell told an interviewer after the release of the *Star Wars* trilogy, "I was invited by George Lucas to his place in San Rafael to see all his films. He told me that it's my books, particularly *The Hero with a Thousand Faces* ... that lie behind his *Star Wars* films. I see Lucas continuing a major concern of modern life and shifting from the world of literate minds to the popular masses who seem to me to be running the world."[62]

The *Star Wars* trilogy follows Campbell's standard path of the mythological adventure of the hero — *separation, initiation, return* — which *Hero* calls the Monomyth (a word Campbell appropriated from James Joyce's *Finnegans Wake*).[63] In the Monomyth, "a hero ventures forth from the world of common day into a region of supernatural wonder: fabulous forces are there encountered and a decisive victory is won: the hero comes back from this mysterious adventure with the power to bestow boons on his fellow man."[64] Society demands a continuous rebirth to offset the frequent reminders of death which surround and enervate us. By successfully completing his wondrous journey of transfiguration, the hero shows us the marvelous gift of life ever renewed.

Although both myths and dreams originate in a fantasy world of our subconscious minds' making, the patterns of myths, unlike dreams, are consciously controlled. And as Campbell notes, "Their understood function is to serve as powerful *picture language* [emphasis added] for the communication of traditional wisdom."[65]

Other filmmakers and studios, unaware of Lucas' reliance on Campbell's work, thought the success of *Star Wars* and its sequels was due only to the marvelous special effects. They did not understand that Luke's breaking through personal limitations is his and our agony of spiritual growth. The wave of derivative films which followed brimmed with special effects —

George Lucas created a new mythology with the last film he directed, 1977's Star Wars.

laser guns, spaceships, exploding planets, and strange creatures. What their makers failed to recognize was the mythic depth of Lucas' seemingly simple saga; they saw only the surface and therefore their films were usually artistic and financial failures.

Once he had the backing of Fox, Lucas completed writing the script of *Star Wars*, filling the SF-fantasy film not only with consciously mythic elements but also with the sorts of derring-do swashbuckling adventures that had so strongly influenced him as a child. Lucas modeled his unseen emperor on Ming the Merciless, from Alex Raymond's *Flash Gordon* strips. "I loved the Flash Gordon comic books," Lucas recalled. "I loved the Universal serials with Buster Crabbe. After *THX 1138* I wanted to do Flash Gordon and tried to buy the rights to it from King Features, but they wanted a lot of money for it, more than I could afford then."[66]

As he began writing the script, Lucas pulled out ideas from everywhere. When his sound editor on *Graffiti*, Walter Murch, asked for R2-D2 (reel 2, dialogue 2), Lucas put the abbreviation in his notebook. Lucas got the Jawas from *THX*. "They were the shell dwellers, the little people that lived underground in the shells. And in a way, part of *Star Wars* came out of me wanting to do a sequel to *THX*. Wookies came out of *THX* too." Lucas was riding in a car with DJ friend Terry McGovern, who said, "I think I just ran over a Wookie back there." Lucas asked, "What's a

Wookie?" "I don't know," replied McGovern, "I just made it up." "That's great," said Lucas. "I love that word. I'm going to use that."[67]

Lucas threw everything from his readings and his childhood into his *Star Wars* drafts. "*Star Wars* is a combination of *Flash Gordon, The Wizard of Oz*, the Errol Flynn swashbucklers of the '30s and '40s and almost every western ever screened — not to mention the *Hardy Boys, Sir Gawain and the Green Knight* and *The Faerie Queene*," *Time* magazine noted. "It's the flotsam and jetsam from the period when I was twelve years old," Lucas said."[68]

When Alan Ladd, Jr., saw a rough assembly of footage — lacking special effects, music, sound effects, and dialogue redubbing — he nearly closed down the film. Lucas convinced him the 40-minute version he saw was not how the finished film would look, and Ladd kept mum about what he'd seen when he went before Fox's board to give them a progress report.[69]

When George Lucas invited his Hollywood friends to see a rough version of the film, "They all thought it a disaster," he remembers. Fortunately for Lucas and the rest of us, those most critical of the film had seen it minus John Williams' heroic score. Lucas' friend Carroll Ballard saw *Star Wars* before and after the music had been added. "It was a mind-boggling difference," he recalled. "It gave the hokey characters a certain dimension."[70]

John Williams has written of his music for the film:

> When I thought of a theme for Luke and his adventures, I composed a melody that reflected the brassy, bold, masculine, and noble qualities I saw in the character. I think of Ben Kenobi's theme as reflecting both him and, also, the Jedi Knights and the Old Republic that he remembers. It also serves to represent the Force. . . . It has a fairy tale aspect rather than a futuristic aspect. I think the use of all these themes and the orchestrations give the score a kind of classic operatic quality.[71]

Williams' score helped "sell" *Star Wars*, and George Lucas knew it. As Lucas said, "I was very, very pleased with the score. We wanted a very sort of Max Steiner–type, old-fashioned, romantic movie score . . . [and] I really expected to get devastated in terms of people saying, 'Oh, my God, what a stupid, old-fashioned thing and how corny can you get?'"[72]

On May 1, 1977, Lucas scheduled a Sunday-morning sneak preview of *Star Wars* at the Northpoint Theater in San Francisco. The theater was filled with Lucas' friends and an audience abuzz with anticipation; rumors of the film's quality had circulated among hardcore SF fans. When the opening crawl ended and the *Star Destroyer* passed overhead on the screen — the Dolby soundtrack rocking the theater — the audience went berserk.

When *Star Wars* opened in 92 theaters on May 25, 1977, there were already lines — the word from the preview had gotten out. *Star Wars* grossed more than $525 million, returning rentals of $193,500,000 to Fox and Lucasfilm. *Star Wars* is second on the all-time film rental champs list in *Variety* (as of January 1989), behind only *E.T. The Extra-Terrestrial*.

Lucas assumed (correctly, I believe) that his audiences had the same familiarity with older films and cinematic conventions and genres that he had. According to producer Gary Kurtz, *Star Wars'* story "advances, not by any orthodox storytelling, but by telling the audience what to expect. It depends on their cine-literacy."[73]

If the sixties are the time of the great postmodernist break, then Lucas' preteen and teenage audiences are as much attuned to his postmodernist genre mixing as he and his fellow film-school graduates. It can be argued that the movie-literate (the *cinemate*) audiences of today *complete* the lions' films by recognizing the elements borrowed from other films. A reader of the text, however, need not recognize *all* of the borrowings — it's enough that she recognizes *some*.

One writer has observed that the growth of cinema-literacy reflects "in some sense the rise of the availability of classic films . . . and even of the lightweight foreign films that now regularly play many major cities, notably New York. *The taste for old films came from the 'Million Dollar Movies' filler on TV during the Fifties,* while foreign films were created as a market by the skin they showed."[74] (Emphasis added.)

Postmodern filmmakers, like Lucas and the young lions, rely on what Jane Feuer calls a metatext. Feuer quotes James Bond scholar Tony Bennett's thesis that the metatext is composed of elements usually ignored by the traditional researcher in favor of analysis of the "primary" text (e.g., reviews, "fan mags," interviews, fashion systems, and the general knowledge of the subject or genre). Bennett calls these texts "'hermeneutic activators,' popular readings of popular texts located within critical apparatuses."[75]

Bennett also takes account of what Pierre Macherey has called the encrustations that build up around a text, which involves the recognition that the text is often inseparable from those encrustations. If this is so, then such "hermeneutic activators" as science-fiction novels and films, serials, B movies, Westerns, and so forth constitute a part of the text of *Star Wars*. This is *Star Wars'* metatext and one reason why *Time* called the film "a subliminal history of the movies."[76]

Reviewers, certainly as fluent with the popular culture mix that makes up *Star Wars'* metatext as filmgoers, were quick to pick up on Lucas' homages, especially to Kurosawa's films. Kurosawa's *The Hidden Fortress* (1958) concerns a perilous journey by a young princess and her loyal general (in early drafts of *Star Wars'* script, young Luke Skywalker was originally a Jedi general in his sixties). They are assisted by two bumbling misfits (clearly the inspiration for R2-D2 and C-3PO).

Since Lucas himself admitted that *Star Wars* has a lot of material "taken from Westerns, mythology, and samurai movies,"[77] let us catalog some of the sources he so consciously and effectively mined. Lucas lovingly recalls Tarzan movies (Luke and Leia's rope swing across a steel canyon), B Westerns (Han Solo's character, his gunslinger garb, and his shoot-out with a bad guy in the Cantina), *The Wizard of Oz* (a trio of unlikely heroes, including one covered in fur [the Cowardly Lion/Chewbacca] enters the Witch's castle/*Death Star* to rescue Dorothy/Leia), *Forbidden Planet* (C-3PO's humanlike personality is not unlike Robbie's; also "hyperspace"), *Silent Running* (Huey, Dewey and Louie, the little chirping and twittering "droids" who predate R2-D2), and just about any World War II or Korean War aerial dogfight movie ever made, for the final attack on the *Death Star*.[78]

As producer Gary Kurtz explained,

> Before the storyboards were done, we recorded on videotape any war movie involving aircraft that came up on television, so we had this massive library of parts of old war movies — *The Dam Busters* [quite similar, actually, to Luke and the others' "bombing" run], *Tora!, Tora!, Tora!, The Battle of Britain, Jet Pilot, The Bridges at Toko-Ri, 633 Squadron* and about forty-five other movies. We went through them all and picked out scenes to transfer to film to use as guidelines in the battle.[79]

When the similarity of the final awards scene to a scene in Leni Riefenstahl's *Triumph of the Will* was pointed out to Kurtz, he said, "I can see why people think that."[80]

Lucas' interpretation has a defender in Denis Wood, however: "This is no fascist hegemony establishing its reign, tens of thousands of massed identities under the booming sky of home. This is a small group of uncertain future of many kinds of peoples under the ground of a far-off foreign place."[81]

One sharp-eyed critic pointed out the similarity between the scene in John Ford's *The Searchers* when Martin discovers his family's ranch house burned to the ground and the one in *Star Wars* where Luke Skywalker finds his uncle's moisture farm destroyed by Imperial troops. He also notes that "the Tusken Raiders' intrusion into the left foreground of the frame as Luke and C-3PO fly through the countryside in search of R2-D2 is a shot right out of *Fort Apache*."[82]

In a harshly negative review of *Star Wars*, Terry Curtis Fox assays the same scene, comparing it unfavorably to Ford's original:

> When it comes to extending the genre, Lucas hasn't done a thing. Consider Luke's return from the desert to find his surrogate parents blown away by an Imperial raiding party. The shot itself is a direct quote from *The Searchers* and ... a particularly relevant quote at that. Martin Pauley's

George Lucas studies a camera angle for one of the Star Wars *sequels as producer Gary Kurtz (left) looks on.*

> discovery of his massacred family . . . forces Pauley to begin the redefini-
> tion of family which lies at the heart of that film. But . . . the death of
> Luke's "family" causes neither pain nor a confrontation with difficult deci-
> sions. Rather than raising problems, it solves them. With his old surrogate
> parents conveniently killed off, Luke can follow his new surrogate father
> to the ends of the universe. Between good and evil is an easy choice.[83]

Fox misses the point. Lucas is uninterested in "extending the genre"; he
is content merely to replicate the scene visually. As one critic observed, "In
Star Wars, George Lucas doesn't work *within* or even *on* genre. He *plugs
in* genre, flashing its proven elements at us as though they were special
effects."[84]

Still, another critic contests Fox's analysis of the moisture-farm scene
and writes that he misses

> both the new nature of his relationship to [Aunt Beru and Uncle Owen]
> and the logic of the story. Owen and Beru are killed by the identical net
> of circumstances that led Luke to Kenobi in the first place: one without
> the other is inconceivable. But it was this very meeting that exposed their
> true natures. . . . Not only not mother and father, they have denied him
> his past . . . kept him in servitude . . . and lied to him about Obi-Wan
> (probably dead) *and* Ben (just a crazy old man) Kenobi. . . . It is not true
> that they freed him from making a difficult decision. He'd already made
> that: to stay on the farm.[85]

While directing *Star Wars*, Lucas fought with cinematographer Gil Taylor, the English crew, the money people at 20th Century–Fox, and the film's special-effects wizard, John Dykstra. After one particularly rancorous shouting match between Lucas and Dykstra, Lucas was hospitalized for chest pains.[86] When the film was completed, Lucas vowed that that was it for him and directing:

> I dislike directing. I hate the constant dealing with volatile personalities. Directing is emotional frustration, anger, and tremendously hard work — seven days a week, twelve to sixteen hours a day. For years my wife asked why we couldn't go out to dinner like other people. But I couldn't turn it off. Eventually, I realized that directing wasn't healthy for me.[87]

Lucas has said that making *Star Wars* satisfied his dream of directing a big Hollywood movie. "I wanted to learn it. I wanted to say, 'I've done it, I did it once.'" Lucas now gets to do the fun part, while the director has the terrible part: "The fun part is coming up with the designs for the creatures or the equipment, designing the toys and editing. I have the advantage now of being able to cut the film and not have the director telling me that it can't be that way, because I'm the boss."[88]

Although no longer directing, Lucas did not give up writing films or serving as an executive producer for films produced under the Lucasfilm, Ltd. banner. And Lucas' derivative ways continued after *Star Wars*. Both of that film's sequels reveal Lucas' tendency to borrow liberally from other films — including *Star Wars* itself (like the original, *Return of the Jedi* features a scene similar to the Cantina "Monster Rally," a crucial light-saber duel, and an attack on another *Death Star*).

Willow, Lucas' summer 1988 release, while doing okay business, rang up reviews as withering as any *Howard the Duck* received. Most of the naysayers like David Ansen were quick to point out Lucas' kitchen-sink theory of fantasy filmmaking: Throw in "every legend, myth, fairy tale and old movie known to man."[89] Lucas raided *Star Wars* (for C-3PO and R2-D2, Han Solo, and Darth Vader), the Conan films, *The Wizard of Oz*, the story of Moses in bulrushes from the Bible, *Snow White and the Seven Dwarfs* (note especially Jean Marsh's similarity to that film's evil queen), *The Living Daylights* (for the escape down a snowy mountain slope on a shield), and on and on.

Like the other lions, George Lucas is not only a child of the postmodern era and a film-school graduate but a man who's never grown up. And as such, he hasn't anything original to say. A master of technique, of cranking out thrill machines, Lucas is no master of subtlety. Lucas *still* cannot handle people or human emotions, something which may not matter to his fans since Lucas knows what his audiences want and gives it to them. As one interviewer has noted, "[Lucas] is simply one of the lucky ones — like Alfred Hitchcock, Preston Sturges, and David Lean — whose vision, however lightweight, coincides with the inner needs and unspoken desires of his customers."[90] I disagree slightly. Lucas' "vision" doesn't just coincide with his viewers'; it is the *same* as his viewers'. Lucas' audience has shared his horizon of expectations; they have subscribed to his popular culture interpretive community. But they are growing older and putting childish things behind them. Lucas, creating rides for Disneyland and Walt Disney World, is not.[91]

Among the other young lions, one can see a moderating of their original pastiche approach to filmmaking. Francis Ford Coppola, Martin Scorsese, and even Brian De Palma have begun to rely less on recycling the stuff old dreams were made of and making quasi-original and adult-oriented films. Steven Spielberg, Lucas' collaborator on the Indiana Jones films, is also beginning to address, with varying degrees of success, less childish concerns with films like *The Color Purple* and *Empire of the Sun*.

Lucas, however, seems content to continue making the sorts of movies he would have done anything to see as a 12-year-old boy. While there is nothing wrong with this, Lucas is probably on a road to nowhere — or, given his recent disappointments, to another *Star Wars* trilogy (itself probably a road to nowhere).

George Lucas *is* a brilliant filmmaker. And the films he makes are fine family fare: full of wonder and (relatively) free of violence. It is perhaps time, however, for this multitalented artist to forget about comics and serials, and grow up.

May the Force be with you, George.

Chapter 4
Brian De Palma

Brian De Palma was born in Newark, New Jersey, in 1940, the son of an orthopedic-surgeon father and a would-be opera singer mother, and the youngest of three sons. When De Palma was 5, his family moved to Philadelphia where he grew up. He attended Friends Central, a Quaker school.[1]

De Palma would later trace his lack of concern about the blood spilled in his films to his father's profession and his childhood proximity to it. In addition to working in a hospital laboratory, De Palma was allowed to see his father's surgical training films at home and to watch his father operate. "My father is an orthopedic surgeon," De Palma said, "so I guess I have a high tolerance for blood, gore, I'd guess you'd call it. I've seen my father amputate legs and open people up. So I was used to that at a young age."[2]

"My father's life was elsewhere; he was rarely home," De Palma told Georgia A. Brown. As for his mother, she "was absorbed with my oldest brother. He was her genius. My brothers and I were isolated from each other, although today my middle brother and I are friends. He's a painter." When Brown said to De Palma, "I thought *you* were the genius," he replied, "Never in my family. Even today, I could get my picture on the cover of *Time* and I don't think my mother would notice. My father was the great doctor, my mother was the opera singer, my oldest brother the genius, my older brother the artist — what did that leave me? I was the public relations man."[3]

Concerning his relationship to his family, "See *Home Movies*; it's all there," says De Palma, directing those curious about his childhood to the character of Denis Byrd, played by Keith Gordon.[4] "I've always thought that the Keith Gordon characters were stand-ins for him," says a woman friend of De Palma's, "the insecure outsider who wants to save the girl but fails."[5]

"I was one of those science types who was always up in his room with all these parts," De Palma says, recalling yet another Keith Gordon role, the computer-nerd son in *Dressed to Kill*.[6]

De Palma attended Columbia University where he eventually earned a B.A. Although he was majoring in physics, he soon found himself intrigued by the arts:

> I was interested in theater first, because I had a way of approaching that. They were doing plays at Columbia and I had been doing skits and things in high school, so I knew something about it. I had a lot of scientific training. I used to win science fairs and build computers and things. I was much more of a scientist than an artist.[7]

At Columbia, when De Palma could not realize his new ambition to direct in theater, he turned to film:

> I started making movies when I was at Columbia University.... I was with the Columbia Players, and I had a background in photography. I was obsessed with the idea of directing the Players. But they wouldn't let undergraduates direct them, so ... I figured I'd go out and direct movies instead. I bought a Bolex 16mm movie camera ... for about $150. I hocked everything I had and used my allowance ... to finance a long, forty-minute short called *Icarus*. It was pretentious and disastrous, but it was a beginning.[8]

For the naive boy from Philadelphia, his experiences at Columbia were liberating. "It was wild," he recalled. "Anything was possible. People weren't so willing to follow a set course. You wanted to make movies, you got a camera and did it. Basically we were putting together films of our lives."[9]

De Palma quickly switched majors, leaving physics and science behind for theatre arts. His old background was quite useful, however: "I have a very good scientific background.... I know all about sound, optics, and cameras. I was going to be a physicist. I did all the work on my shorts, all the shooting, all the cutting, put all the sound in."[10]

After making *Icarus*, "I made another film called *660124, The Story of an IBM Card*, which was pretentious but a little better, technically," De Palma said. "Then I finally made a short called *Wotan's Wake*,[11] which won a lot of prizes. It won the Rosenthal Award, and all the awards that were available to short films in 1962-63."[12]

It was while he was a student at Columbia that De Palma discovered the films of Alfred Hitchcock. He likened watching Hitchcock's films to going to suspense school:

> It was like suddenly finding someone who is speaking your language and realizing there is a vocabulary. You begin to be aware of a very grammatical use of the camera.... I began to realize why Hitchcock engages you so strongly; you were in the same position as the character. You saw the same information the character saw.[13]

Another strong influence was Stanley Kubrick. De Palma has spoken often of how Kubrick's films, like *Lolita* and *2001*, have been poorly received

In Get to Know Your Rabbit, *De Palma directed not only Tom Smothers (right) but the great master of film Orson Welles (center). (Courtesy of Steve and Nancy Gould.)*

critically at first, only to be declared masterpieces later. And De Palma admits to being inspired by other directors as well. "Godard's a terrific influence, of course. If I could be the American Godard, that would be great."[14]

De Palma also credits the influence of documentary filmmakers, especially the Maysles (*Gimme Shelter, Grey Gardens*). "The Maysles have made some of the most important films in the last decade," De Palma said in 1977.

> I think the documentary background gives you a sort of contemporary conception of reality the dramatic background doesn't necessarily give you; you have a little more of an ear for what people perceive as real. The documentary reality and the television reality have more or less given us a whole new conception of what we consider real. To people who come before that tradition, it might look a little hokey today, like naturalism or all the stuff that came out of group theater.[15]

After graduating from Columbia in 1962, De Palma went to Sarah Lawrence College on an MCA (Universal Pictures) writing fellowship. He

Robert DeNiro ponders conscription in De Palma's youth comedy Greetings. *(Courtesy of Steve and Nancy Gould.)*

received his M.A. in theatre arts in 1964. "And I got involved in making movies. I collaborated with a teacher [Wilfred Leach] and a very wealthy girl, who put up $100,000, and together we created a 35mm black and white feature called *The Wedding Party*."[16] *The Wedding Party* was completed in 1963; however, it was not released until 1969, after the success of *Greetings*.

Once De Palma began making Hollywood films, he comfortably settled into the thriller genre mode, and his biggest successes were genre films. As De Palma once said,

> The reason that I like the genre is because you can work in a sort of pure cinema form. That is why Hitchcock likes it too. It's all images, and your story-telling is entirely through images and not people talking to each other. Films with endless jabber make me sleepy. I strongly believe there are reasons for genre forms and there are reasons that make them work. And if you ignore all the tenets of the form you are going to have something else which isn't going to be that genre. But if you are going to avoid telling stories, then you had better come up with another way to make a movie last 90 minutes because it becomes difficult any other way.[17]

With the melding of his various influences—Hitchock and Kubrick films, the documentary style, the impact of television, and his scientific interests—De Palma became a postmodern filmmaker. A premier director of genre films, be began his long practice of shamelessly borrowing or paying homage to the films and filmmakers he admired.

Hi, Mom!

Brian De Palma's *Greetings* was playing to good crowds in New York City, and it was while he was watching people standing in line to get into the film that his gaze wandered to a nearby building. Looking at the blank windows facing the street, De Palma mused what might be going on behind the panes. From that speculation came the basic idea for *Hi, Mom!* (1970), a nominal sequel to *Greetings*.[18]

The film, alternately brilliant and amateurish, ultimately failed to work because of its tripartite construction. *Hi, Mom!* opens with Jon (Robert DeNiro), the voyeur from *Greetings*, getting money from a producer to produce a homemade porno film shot by aiming a camera through the windows of his neighbors. This amusing low-key story is superseded—indeed overwhelmed—by the middle story about the staging and televising (on NIT, National Intellectual Television) of a play called *Be Black, Baby*. The third sequence follows Jon and his boring life with Judy (Jennifer Salt), a woman he used to peep on. Jon rebels by blowing up his building, saying "Hi, Mom!" into a TV camera.

In the *Be Black, Baby* middle section, De Palma has black actors wearing whiteface paint the audience's faces black and then proceed to threaten and abuse them. The result is powerful, unsettling, and somewhat sinister; it blurs the line between the theater (and film) audience and the "reality" they are confronting.

"I was trying to show how you lie with documentaries," De Palma said, explaining why he made the *Be Black, Baby* sequence.

> Those ridiculous documentaries you see on . . . television . . . about oppressed blacks made by white middle-class filmmakers. The fact is that the blacks are being oppressed by . . . that class, yet these people are running around saying: "Don't worry. It's all going to be okay. Here are your food stamps."[19]

De Palma also wanted to make the audience confront the fact that they were watching a film: "First of all, I am interested in the medium of film itself, and I am constantly standing outside and making people aware that they are always watching a film. At the same time I am evolving it."[20]

In Hi, Mom! *De Palma's 1970 semisequel to* Greetings, *Robert DeNiro (right) and a troupe of black actors threaten and abuse a white middle-class audience attending the play* Be Black, Baby. *(Courtesy of Steve and Nancy Gould.)*

"Unfortunately, *Hi, Mom!* is too unintegrated; it doesn't work," De Palma admitted.

> Like *Greetings*, it is a contemporary statement of what was going on in my life.... From *Dionysus in 69* I had learned so much about the documentary reality of that type of theater, so I wanted to show in *Hi, Mom!* how you can really involve an audience. You take an absurd premise—"Be Black, Baby"—and totally involve them and really frighten them at the same time. You suck 'em in and annihilate them. Then you say, "It's just a movie, right? It's not real." The "Be Black, Baby" section of *Hi, Mom!* is probably the most important piece of film I've ever done. It also ran away with the movie, destroyed the ending. It became so strong that nobody could go anywhere after that.[21]

Actually, De Palma had somewhere to go—Hollywood. *Easy Rider* had just stunned middle-aged studio executives, and opened their eyes to the money to be made in the "youth" market by hiring young iconoclastic directors like De Palma. In Frank Lovece's words, De Palma "got a one-way ticket to Producerville."[22] Unfortunately, his first Hollywood film, *Get to Know Your Rabbit*, was a flop, and it was not until 1973 that he would make *Sisters*.

Sisters

Sisters was the first film in which De Palma began his trademark copying of Hitchcockian themes, styles, and music. But the inspiration for the film came from elsewhere:

> In 1966 I saw an article in *Life* magazine about a pair of Russian Siamese twins.... At the end of the article there was a picture of the two girls sitting on a couch and the caption said that apart from the fact that they were joined together at the hip both girls were physiologically normal, but as they were getting older they were developing psychological problems. One ... had a very surly, disturbing look on her face and the other looked perfectly healthy and smiling. And this strong visual image started the whole idea off in my mind.[23]

De Palma's *Sisters* (1973) contains many borrowings from Hitchock's *Psycho*. They include an insane killer who, by reason of possession by a dead "other," may or may not be morally responsible for the killings — or may be conveniently using that "other" to avoid assuming the guilt for his mad acts. The atmospheric score is the result of De Palma working with Hitchcock's musical collaborator, Bernard Herrmann.

De Palma speaks of another plot device lifted from *Psycho*:

> I am also a great admirer of Hitchcock and *Psycho*, and there are a great many structural elements here that are in all of Hitchcock's movies: introducing a character and then having him killed off early in the film; switching points of view: taking the person who sees the murder and then involving him in solving the crime.[24]

De Palma carefully follows two of Hitchcock's rules for suspense films: The police and other authorities are ineffectual or indifferent, and there is a seemingly important clue which turns out to be nothing more or less than a "MacGuffin." When asked why his characters don't go to the police, Hitchcock said, "Because it makes a boring movie."[25]

As for the MacGuffin, Hitchcock has said:

> In any spy story you have to say to yourself, what are the spies after?... We always called this thing the "MacGuffin" because actually, when you come down to it, it doesn't matter what the spies are after. The characters on the screen worry about what they're after, but the audience don't care because they only care about the safety of the hero or heroine.[26]

In *Sisters*, the MacGuffin is the sofa in which Emil (William Finley) and Danielle (Margot Kidder) have hidden a murdered body. Although the private detective figures out that the sofa must contain the body, he also believes he can identify the killer by noting who finally takes possession of the sofa. The futility of his quest, continued long after Danielle has killed Emil and been arrested for his murder, is underscored by the film's last scene

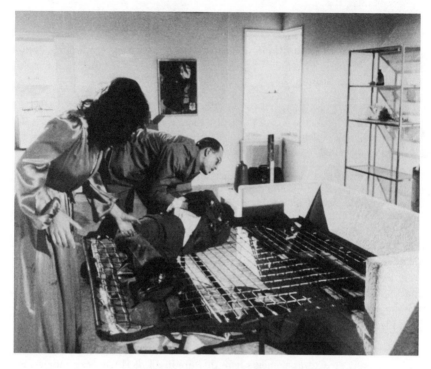

Sisters (1973) marked the beginning of De Palma's borrowings from Hitchcock. The body hidden in the sofa bed is De Palma's version of Hitch's "MacGuffin" — a device which drives the plot but ultimately has little to do with the story.

as Larch (Charles Durning), disguised as a telephone lineman, patiently waits at a Canadian railroad depot for someone to claim the sofa.

It was De Palma's film editor, Paul Hirsch, who first conceived the idea of using Bernard Herrmann to write the musical score. Like many directors, De Palma believes he can gauge a sequence's effectiveness best when it is accompanied by music, even temporary tracks which ultimately will not be used in the final version. Hirsch used a lot of Herrmann's music over the footage. As De Palma recalled, "We used the violins from the *Psycho* murder scene; *Marnie* over some of the love stuff on the boat; the whole *Vertigo* dream score over our dream sequence. And suddenly all this stuff we'd been looking at silently took on a very ominous dimension; it became scary and disturbing."[27]

Like many others, De Palma had assumed that Herrmann had died or retired. What he discovered was that Herrmann was alive and living in London. De Palma had Herrmann flown in to view a rough cut of the film. Unfortunately, De Palma did not realize that Herrmann hated to hear his music played under other films. As De Palma recalled ruefully,

> When he first came to look at *Sisters* I put his music in it all the way through — you know, *Vertigo, Psycho, Marnie,* and whatever else I had. He heard it and went into a rage! "Turn it off, turn it off!" "But Mr. Herrmann...." "Turn it off! How can you play that while I'm listening to the film. I don't want to listen to that — oh, don't do that!" He didn't want to hear his music played with the wrong movie. When he first heard *Obsession* he said, "It's a great movie and I can hear the score." He was looking at it and he heard the music in his head.[28]

After De Palma removed the offending tracks, Herrmann grudgingly viewed the film. Herrmann pronounced that the experience had reminded him of the first time he'd seen *Psycho*. Flattered and encouraged, De Palma asked Herrmann to score *Sisters*.[29] The experience of working with the aging and increasingly touchy composer was a trying one, De Palma later admitted.

Among other things, Herrmann belittled De Palma's proposed opening sequences. "That's terrible!" Herrmann shouted. When asked by De Palma what the problem was, Herrmann said, "Nothing happens in this movie for forty minutes!" De Palma explained that was the whole idea, "like *Psycho*, where the murder doesn't happen until about 40 minutes into the picture." "YOU are not Hitchcock," Herrmann shouted. "For Hitchcock they will WAIT!" De Palma admitted the truth of Herrmann's objection: "Because it's a Hitchcock movie you KNOW something is going to happen."[30]

When asked if it bothers him to be accused of ripping off Hitchcock, De Palma replied:

> It doesn't bother me. You can reinterpret good material in different ways, into your own framework. If you have a style of your own and individuality, you'll take good things from other people and make them better. Great artists have done it.[31]

De Palma got twice the self-reflexive bang for the buck by not only using a *Psycho*-recalling psychiatrist to comment upon the Blanchion twins' case but also giving him the name Doctor Milius, after writer-director John Milius.

Rushed into release, *Sisters* did not do well commercially and only later found the audience it deserved. No matter, De Palma was off to another project, one that couldn't miss: a rock music remake of *The Phantom of the Opera*.

Phantom of the Paradise

De Palma described to John Coates the origin of 1974s *Phantom of the Paradise*:

> I was sitting around one night with a young NYU film student and a friend

The master of the macabre, Alfred Hitchcock, in a publicity still for The Birds.

of his, talking about ideas for movies. We were all into the idea of rock music, and one of the kids came up with the idea of the Phantom of the Fillmore. I said, "That's terrific!" The notion of a contemporary opera house being haunted by a ripped-off composer was very appealing. I wrote the first treatment for Filmways in 1969. I had the idea that rock was developing as a Grand Guignol.[32]

De Palma insists that his film was planned as more than a simple remake of one of the three earlier versions of *Phantom of the Opera* (1925, Lon Chaney; 1943, Claude Rains; 1961, Herbert Lom): "I never had any intention of simply remaking *Phantom of the Opera*," De Palma said. "I took its idea of a composer having his music ripped off, endeavoring to kill the people who are massacring his music and putting on the girl he loves to sing it the way he wants it to be sung."[33]

De Palma had long admired the horror genre and German expressionism, especially *The Cabinet of Dr. Caligari*. "In *Phantom of the Paradise* I was trying to find a new way to enter that world," he says. "I thought the rock world is so stylized and expressionistic to begin with, that it would be a perfect environment in which to tell old horror tales."[34]

Gerrit Graham as Beef, Phantom of the Paradise's *dead-on parody of rock superstars that may have been too uncomfortably real for teen audiences to accept. (Courtesy of Steve and Nancy Gould.)*

As for Beef (Gerrit Graham), *Phantom's* strutting androgynous glitter rocker, De Palma has said, "Well, generally, the glitter rock world [was the model for Beef]. You have to laugh at it, it seems to me; I mean, you can't really identify with that world: all these pubescent kids arriving in glitter, jeans, and heels a foot high: those unisex outfits. It's so bizarre I find it hard to understand just where it comes from. Maybe it's just a matter of putting on makeup at a certain age—I don't know."[35]

Phantom has at least one clear-cut Hitchcockian moment, a parody of the famous shower sequence from *Psycho.* Beef, the singer who is to sing the phantom's songs instead of his young protégée Phoenix (Jessica Harper), is taking a shower and rehearsing one of his songs when through the shower curtain we can see the phantom (William Finley) entering the bathroom. Suddenly the phantom slices an opening in the shower curtain with a large knife and . . . plunges a plumber's helper over the hapless Beef's mouth. "Never sing my music again!" he hisses.

Speaking about the *Psycho* shower homage, De Palma said, "You're playing with a movie sensibility all the time. You set up your audience in one direction, then hit them in another, with the last thing they'd expect. The director always has to be a bit of a magician, pulling a cigarette out of the air or a rabbit out of a hat. It's like Welles says, it's an illusionary thing, you constantly have to surprise them."[36]

Another Hitchcockian moment occurs when De Palma's camera describes a 360-degree circle around Winslow Leach (the name is a salute to Wilford Leach, De Palma's old teacher) as the budding composer rapturously plays one of his compositions for Swan (Paul Williams). This 360-degree pan is one of De Palma's signature devices.

De Palma's Orson Welles-*Citizen Kane* tribute is in the form of an opening narration which tells of a rich and seclusive magnate who's "built his own Xanadu" in the form of the Paradise, a rock theater. Just as Kane married Susan Alexander and built her the Chicago Opera House, Swan (Paul Williams) wants to showcase Phoenix in his own "opera" house.

When interviewer John Coates suggested to De Palma that *Phantom* indicated a fondness on the director's part for genre films, De Palma replied, "That's because I like stylization. I like fantasy; I like science fiction; I like creating worlds. And rock presented the possibility of creating a whole new fantastic world."[37] For De Palma, *Phantom* offered yet another opportunity to demonstrate his postmodernist tendencies toward pastiche and parody.

A $1.3 million independent production, *Phantom of the Paradise* was picked up by 20th Century–Fox for $2 million and then marketed to the rock-concertgoing teenage market — which stayed away in droves. The film was a major flop after being projected to gross $35 million. In hindsight, it seemed unlikely that the very kids whose music and lifestyles were being parodied and mocked would embrace such a cynical and on-target skewering of the object of their affections.

After his 1985 mob comedy *Wise Guys*, starring Danny DeVito and Joe Piscopo, failed, De Palma compared its lack of box-office success to *Phantom's*: "When you mix genres," he said, "you get into big trouble."[38]

For his next outing, De Palma would reembrace Hitchcock with a passion. The film was *Obsession*.

Obsession

Lacking the graphic violence of *Sisters* and his later films like *Dressed to Kill* and *Scarface*, *Obsession* (1976) is one of De Palma's earliest "adult" films, albeit yet another paean to Hitchcock. The film's primary inspiration is obviously *Vertigo*, even though De Palma and scriptwriter Paul Schrader took only that film's central premise.

Originally called *Deja Vu*, and then *Double Ransom*, the film is De Palma's clearest use of the theme of doubling. In *Sisters*, the Siamese twins were the deadly doubles; in *Phantom of the Paradise*, the doubles were Winslow-phantom and Swan, the corrupt rock impresario. In *Obsession* there are seemingly two of everything: two business partners, two kidnappings, two

William Finley's phantom, robbed of his voice and his songs, makes music again through electronics in Brian De Palma's Phantom of the Paradise. *(Courtesy of Steve and Nancy Gould.)*

ransoms, and two identical (for all practical purposes) wives. Michael Bliss makes much of the fact that the title was once *Double Ransom*, "itself suitably ambiguous since 'double' may refer to the two attempts at ransoming or the attempts to ransom the two Courtlands: Elizabeth and Amy."[39]

De Palma, never one easily to forgo a favorite device, here uses his 360-degree pan (from *Carrie* and *Phantom*) at several key moments: at the film's beginning, taking us from 1959 to 1975 ("today" in the film) and at the end when Michael (Cliff Robertson) and Amy (Genevieve Bujold) are reunited as father and daughter.

The "obsession" of the film's title is Michael's attempt to restore the vision of his first wife, Elizabeth, by marrying her double, Sandra (really Amy, his daughter). Here too, De Palma and Schrader closely follow Hitchcock's *Vertigo* by recreating Scottie's obsessive, and unquestioning, remolding of Judy into Madeleine. In both films, the male characters are so guilt-ridden and full of wishful determination that they never stop to wonder about the unusual resemblance of another woman to the one they lost.

De Palma spoke dispassionately about cutting out much of Paul Schrader's original ending (at Bernard Herrmann's suggestion), which elongated the story time by an additional 10 years:

De Palma's ill-fated couple in Obsession: *Elizabeth and Michael Courtland (Genevieve Bujold and Cliff Robertson). (Courtesy of Steve and Nancy Gould.)*

I felt it was much too complicated and wouldn't sustain, so I abbreviated it. Robertson is arrested at the airport and goes into a mental institution for ten years. He gets out, grabs a gun and goes to Florence, goes in the same church, *again* Genevieve Bujold is there! But she doesn't recognize him as she's been in a catatonic state since her attempted suicide. The nuns at the clinic she's in want to try out a new form of hypnotherapy in which they reenact the kidnapping a *third* time! Bujold thinks it's the first, and Robertson thinks it's the second . . . and it's then she says, 'Daddy, daddy' . . . as Robertson opens the suitcase with the money finally in the right place. It was an interesting sequence, but it just wouldn't have worked. It made Schrader very unhappy: he thought I'd truncated his masterpiece. He's never been the same since.[40]

Home Movies

In 1980's *Home Movies*, De Palma decided to try an audacious experiment — to make a low-budget independent film totally free of Hollywood influence, hoping to "start off" new directors like Terry Melick who'd told De Palma he'd been inspired to be a director by seeing *Greetings*.[41]

De Palma also wanted to repay a debt:

> [Sarah Lawrence College] was a great place for me to get started, so I felt very close to the school. I always wanted to do something to pay back the help.... I called Wilfred [Leach] and said I'd really like to teach a course in low-budget filmmaking. And for the course we would make a low-budget film.[42]

De Palma outlined the film's plot to Gerald Peary:

> The story is about a young kid, Denis Byrd, whose older brother, James, teaches a course in Spartanetics, a wilderness type of course. Denis has a love affair with James' fiancée and gathers divorce evidence on his father, Dr. Byrd, by following him around at night taking pictures of his various rendezvous with a Swedish nurse.[43]

De Palma later admitted to Peary that "there are a lot of autobiographical things. The Byrds are somewhat reminiscent of my own family, the brother and the parents."[44] In reality, the Byrd family seems to be much more than "somewhat reminiscent" of De Palma's family situation. Mrs. Byrd (played by Mary Davenport of *Sisters*) is histrionic and selfish, thinking only of herself and her favored older son, James (Gerrit Graham), a snobbish puritan who's given up most pleasures of the flesh. The father (Vincent Gardenia) is a doctor whose interests, mainly seducing young women, lie outside the family.

Denis (Keith Gordon) is, in the words of "the Maestro" (Kirk Douglas), "an extra in his own life." Like De Palma, he is largely invisible in his family of self-centered prima donnas. Despite his mother's lack of maternal attention toward him, Denis vows to catch his father on film in the act and "be the hero of this family just once!" De Palma's revenge is two-edged: not only does he portray his family background in a wickedly savage manner, but he also gets to attribute to James many of the characteristics his critics have reputedly found in De Palma and his films — misogyny, coldness, and calculated manipulation of others through a combination of intimidation and self-proclaimed authority.

Eventually, after an apparently tragic ending (Kristina [Nancy Allen], James' fiancée, is struck by an ambulance and seemingly killed), Denis takes control of his life and following the Maestro's advice, makes himself a star in his own life. It is a case of art imitating life: if De Palma is still not a "star" in his family, especially to his mother, he has painstakingly made himself a star in his life.

The film, more interesting than funny, was not a success. It did not, as De Palma hoped, "start a whole new generation of low-budget filmmakers."[45]

Dressed to Kill

De Palma enters Hitchcock's world again in *Dressed to Kill*, and the parallels to *Psycho* are striking. In both films the female "star" of the film is killed off in the first third of the picture by an insane murderer who commits his crimes dressed as a woman; the killer is identified through the efforts of a male-female pair of amateur sleuths who are not a romantic couple; and the crime is "explained" by a psychiatrist who really explains nothing.

"Take *Dressed to Kill*," says De Palma. "That has a great idea that's taken from *Psycho*. You take a character, a leading cast member . . . and you bump her off 30 minutes into the movie. The audience can't believe you're bumping her off. You don't want your audience to know where the story is going."[46]

De Palma showed Dr. Elliott (Michael Caine) in a split-screen shot watching a show about transsexuals while the audience simultaneously saw the blonde they imagined to be the killer (she's really a policewoman). This deception convinced the audience that the killer couldn't be Elliott, but De Palma refused to admit to any "cheating" and compared the scene to *Psycho*:

> Why is that any worse than having *Psycho*'s Mrs. Bates stuffed in a rock-
> ing chair in a window? Or having this loud conversation between Norman
> and his mother, where he must be shouting at the top of his lungs in order
> that Marion hears? I think people get confused a lot in *Dressed to Kill*; I've
> read a lot of reviews in which people believe that Bobbie gets knocked
> down by that cabbie.[47]

The museum scene, where Kate (Angie Dickinson) follows a mysterious stranger, has been compared to a similar one in *Vertigo*, and Peter's spying and eavesdropping recall both *Vertigo* and *Rear Window*. There is even a reference to *North by Northwest* where the innocent bystander, the prostitute played by Nancy Allen, is found holding the murder weapon in her hand.

Besides taking elements from Hitchcock films like *Psycho*, *Rear Window*, *North by Northwest*, and others, De Palma plunders his own films,

In Home Movies, *Kirk Douglas (left) plays "the Maestro" to Denis Byrd (Keith Gordon), "an extra in his own life."*

especially *Carrie*. Both films begin with dreamy, steamy shower sequences, and both end with a shocking, unexpected final twist which turns out to be a nightmare: Carrie's arm shooting up from the grave to grab Sue Snell, and Dr. Elliott's return as Bobbie to slit Liz's throat with a razor.

De Palma insists that the horrific fate visited upon Kate in *Dressed to Kill* is simple genre justice. "Angie plays a woman who cheats on her husband," De Palma says. "If I respect and love my wife and I have a sexual encounter, I am going to feel guilty and punish myself. Angie feels this way. But then people say it's *me* punishing her. What's true is that the audience has a good time seeing 'sin' and then they get the relief of punishment."[48]

When Georgia A. Brown suggested that many people viewed De Palma as a misogynist, he replied, "I've always had a feminine point of view in many ways. My point-of-view characters are usually women. You know, I took a degree at a woman's college, and I had a tremendous understanding of what it was to be a woman. In Hollywood, a woman is a piece of meat. It's *worse* than any Bob Guccione fantasy you might have. That's not my world; I'm appalled by it."[49]

As for the violence in his films, especially violence directed against women, De Palma said:

You try to deal with things that an audience can identify with on a visceral
level.... People say, "Why do women get slashed in his films, what does
he have against women?" I just think that when women are in a perilous
situation, audiences identify with them more than men because they look
more helpless. People say, "Well, he's out to kill women," but when you
have a man walking down a dark hall you don't care as much if somebody
jumps out and kills him or threatens him.[50]

"I was expecting to get totally roasted for *Dressed to Kill*," De Palma
admits. "Because it's similar to *Psycho*. But I was amazed at the kind of very
good reviews that I got and the tremendous media hype and response that
came out on the film."[51]

Dressed to Kill was De Palma's most successful film to date, but he still
seemed to many a Hitchcock clone, an inferior one at that. Several critics
noted that *Dressed to Kill* lacked the sly humor of *Psycho*, something
which made Hitchcock's violence easier to accept. In a lengthy review of
the film, Kenneth MacKinnon underscored De Palma's relationship to the
old master Hitchcock:

> The end of one of the key sequences of *Dressed to Kill* suggests a nod to
> the cognoscenti, an in-joke about borrowed garments. As [Kate] leaves
> [the museum], she discards a glove, which is picked up and retained, on
> her departure, by another blonde. The eagerness with which the cast-off
> is reclaimed hints at the self-conscious relation of De Palma to Hitchcock,
> the retrieval and jealous guarding of the latter's effects and "big sequences"
> by the former, the wearing by De Palma of Hitchcock's hand-me-downs.
> More than any other contemporary American director . . . De Palma in-
> vites knowledge of other directors for comprehension of his films. He
> positively demands knowledge of Hitchcock.[52]

The Untouchables

As he moved into his forties, becoming ever more bearlike physically
and with more and more gray in his beard, De Palma could not shake his
image as a technically proficient *Wunderkind* who manipulated images
brilliantly but to little human effect. It apparently slowly dawned on De
Palma that what he needed to do was to work with good writers rather than
directing his own scripts.

During the making of *Scarface*, De Palma spoke of "a new way of
working":

> Here I've got a very strong script, an actor who knows what he wants, and
> a producer who's in on every detail. This is more like a collaboration. It's
> a discipline after my former ways of working. You can't keep repeating
> yourself. You can, but suddenly you're out of the business. Spielberg
> learned this after *1941*. He indulged himself, let it all out, and flopped.
> Then he made a very smart move. He let Lucas rein him in. But other

directors of my generation — Altman, Bogdanovich, Friedkin, Coppola, Scorsese — haven't learned it.... Look how [*The King of Comedy*] is doing. With all the talent, Scorsese is in danger of ending up like Altman — not making movies.[53]

"I'm good with story ideas and visual ideas," De Palma says, adding, "but I'm not good at writing characters. There are 8,000 quotes of me saying 'Form is content.' Well, it's true. Form *is* content. But other stuff is content, too."[54]

For *The Untouchables*, De Palma had a chance to work with one of the finest playwrights around, David Mamet. After Mamet had won a Pulitzer prize for his Broadway play *Glengarry Glen Ross*, producer Art Linson took him to dinner and suggested he tackle remaking the successful TV series. Mamet, who is from Ness and Capone's Chicago, decided to take on the challenge of writing a script that wasn't a parody but rather in Linson's words, "a big-scale movie about mythical American heroes."[55]

Because David Mamet's first draft was little more than an outline, Dawn Steel, president of production at Paramount, wanted De Palma to flesh it out. "In the past," Steel said, "Brian hasn't chosen the material that he was worthy of. He was making homages to Alfred Hitchcock. This one is a homage to Brian De Palma — he felt it instead of directing it. With this picture he became a mensch."[56] De Palma agrees with that assessment: "David forces you to get out of your own cliches and whatever you're obsessed with and work in someone else's nightmare for a while."[57]

Producer Linson described why De Palma was his first choice to direct the film:

> I wanted De Palma because he makes things look important and at the same time he's great with action. For the first time, he's been given a screenplay that has a lot of heart and sentiment. It might be the first De Palma movie where audiences cry at the end. He's always amazed you, he's always scared the shit out of you, he's always pummeled you and he's always made you feel that he's a brilliant filmmaker — but you didn't always love the movies or the characters. I know women who walked out of *Scarface* and wouldn't see *Body Double* who go up to him afterward and say, "Oh, Brian" — and this is a pretty violent movie. But it doesn't seem violent because you love the characters so much.[58]

When De Palma was shown Mamet's third draft, he was immediately interested. "What was different for me about *The Untouchables* was that I found myself caring a lot more about the characters," De Palma said when he was asked why he had forsaken his customary thrillers. "With a suspense movie, the point had been just to shock people." Besides, De Palma added, "I never saw it as a gangster movie. I saw it more like a *Magnificent Seven*."[59] De Palma explained this reading: "It's like a John Ford Western. A good guy is on a mission and gets help. At the end he walks off into the sunset. It's a simple story told in a classical way."[60] Yet, despite the good-guys-vs.-bad-guys theme, De Palma faced a problem: "These were real people. You want to see Capone killed, and yet you just can't have Ness shoot Capone."[61]

Originally budgeted at $17 million, the film eventually cost $24 million. In Mamet's script, Ness (Kevin Costner) and Stone (Andy Garcia) halt the train (authentically vintage, of course) taking away Capone's bookkeeper, and in a shoot-out that kills several of Capone's men take him prisoner. The only problem for De Palma and Linson was that the scene would cost nearly $250,000; the money men balked at that kind of added expense, and it was up to De Palma to devise a cheaper alternative. "It was Brian at his best," Linson recalled. "He just sort of said: 'OK, guys, we've run out of money. So give me a staircase, a clock, and a baby carriage.'"[62]

"You try to get all your story and character elements merged in a physical action section of the movie," De Palma says of his bravura Union Station sequence. "You develop your characters, you develop your story, then suddenly you bring it into a total cinematic confrontation."[63]

De Palma explains the thematic idea behind the sequence:

> *The Untouchables* is essentially about how the innocents get slaughtered in the conflict of the gangsters. Eliott Ness has to get the guy and protect the innocent simultaneously. And suddenly, somehow, *Potemkin* popped into my head. Of course, the image of a baby carriage bouncing down those steps in the midst of a crossfire is an image that's very strong. Ordinarily, I storyboard everything, but this time I didn't have a chance. The most important thing was location. We needed a set of steps. . . . We finally came up with the train station. And when I looked at it . . . I had all of it in my head. I could see the baby carriage going up and down in the crossfire. I could see sailors passing through.[64]

As Jesse Kornbluth reports, "De Palma had no time to plan this sequence in advance. Or to screen *Battleship Potemkin*, which he hadn't seen in 30 years. Indeed, he was so busy by then that he wasn't even able to write the scene. In the final script, it's practically a footnote: 'Ness and Stone go into action. The action will take place on the steps, to be outlined later.' Not surprisingly this directorial tour de force became a Hollywood legend even as it was happening. 'Spielberg told me the stuff was great,' De Palma notes."[65]

For the Italian restaurant scene where the Untouchables form their close bond, cinematographer Stephen H. Burum, ASC, wanted to dissolve from position to position, slowly moving closer, giving the impression that they've been there for a long period of time. "Brian said it's a good idea," Burum recalled, "but he'd like to circle around them. I realized, by knowing his other pictures, and working with him before, that this is one of his visual symbols. It represents love and camaraderie. He's done this in *Carrie*

Kevin Costner as Eliott Ness in The Untouchables. *De Palma's staging of a climactic shootout on the railroad station's steps was a technical tour de force homage to the Odessa Steps sequence in Eisenstein's* Battleship Potemkin.

and *Obsession* and in *Body Double*. It's one of his visual signatures."[66]

The Untouchables marked the first time De Palma and DeNiro had worked together since their counterculture films of the sixties and early seventies. This time around, DeNiro was a major star who received $1.5 million for 18 days of work. Just as he had for Scorsese and *Raging Bull*, DeNiro transformed himself physically for the role of Al Capone, gaining 25 pounds in five weeks. DeNiro still said, "I wish I could have been heavier." Although DeNiro had "fun" playing Capone, he admitted that "Gaining the weight was very hard, very, very depressing. It's the last time I'll ever do that."[67]

With *The Untouchables*, De Palma finally got rid of the ghost of Alfred Hitchcock, a specter haunting even a film as recent as *Body Double* (1984) with its 360-degree *Vertigo* kissing shot. In *The Untouchables*, De Palma makes the shot his own and uses it in context: his circling around the four Untouchables stops short of a full revolution — two of them will be killed before the film's end, breaking their circle of friendship.

The Untouchables is one of De Palma's more emotionally satisfying films; now the violence happens to characters the audience had been given reasons to care about. It raises disturbing questions about good and evil, and how far a society should go in turning the violent methods of criminals

De Palma (center) directs Robert DeNiro as gangster Al Capone in The Untouchables. *DeNiro gained 25 pounds for the extended cameo role.*

back on them. His trademark visual pyrotechnics are now harnessed to a script and to situations that are enhanced by them, not undercut by their superiority to the often underdeveloped characters and story lines. While the baby-carriage sequence is a homage to Eisenstein's Odessa Steps montage, De Palma has taken nothing from the original but the visual concept of the carriage and the steps. In every way, his brilliantly constructed sequence justifies itself: in the plot, Ness' and Stone's characters, and the film's central theme of innocents having to pay for our allowing the law to be broken with impunity by immoral gangsters and sociopaths.

Casualties of War

The real-life events of *Casualties of War* were first reported by Daniel Lang, a war correspondent. His account of the story first appeared in the October 18, 1969, *New Yorker* and later was a 123-page book. The events depicted in his magazine article took place in October 1966. A five-man squad of soldiers from the Army's First Air Cavalry Division were sent on a reconnaissance patrol in an area with high levels of Vietcong activity. On the day they left, the sergeant in charge kidnapped a teenage Vietnamese girl from a friendly village and took her with them. She was brutally and repeatedly raped by the American soldiers. When they became concerned that she might report them, the soldiers killed her.

Lang's piece made a strong impression on De Palma. "But there was no way for me to get control of it then," De Palma says. "A couple of screenplays were written, but ... it kind of vanished." Ten years later, Vietnam veteran and playwright David Rabe (*Streamers*) told De Palma he was interested in writing the script for a film based on Lang's tale, but De Palma still lacked the clout he needed to get such a controversial project approved.[68]

It was the success of *The Untouchables* in 1987 which opened a window of opportunity for De Palma's desire to make *Casualties of War*. Paramount, which produced *The Untouchables*, was cajoled into purchasing the rights to Lang's article and hiring Rabe to write the script. De Palma was set to begin filming in Thailand when Paramount suddenly got cold feet and pulled out. Later, all De Palma would say was "All Vietnam films are difficult to get made."[69]

Dawn Steel, the president of production at Paramount who'd helped to choose De Palma to direct *The Untouchables* (and seen her judgment vindicated by that film's hefty box-office returns), had ridden her success to the top position at Columbia. As her first act as president of Columbia, Steel greenlighted *Casualties*.

De Palma saw the film as a chance to explore America's Vietnam experiences in ways other films about the war had not pursued:

> It expresses the Vietnam dilemma in a particularly dramatic and terse form. The whole experience of our involvement there is in this kind of mini-tragedy. It showed that we were over there basically fighting ourselves instead of the enemy, that to the boys of that age the whole world of this strange land must have been like being on a different planet where values can get turned upside down. It shows what happens when there seems to be no moral compass at all, the whole kind of irrationality that became the Vietnam War. Most Vietnam movies are documentary in an episodic way, hallucinogenic or surrealistic; you know, "The horror, the horror." It's a story that still brings all the war issues to bear, and the fact that it's real makes it all the more shocking.[70]

De Palma is the first to admit he is not a Vietnam War veteran. "I think I was lucky I didn't go to Vietnam," De Palma confessed. "Maybe it would have given me an understanding of some things I only understand secondhand. But I think you'd be so horribly scarred by it. I mean, the people I know who have been there, like David Rabe, there's something that's behind their eyes that isn't behind mine."[71]

Although Rabe adheres closely to Lang's book, the fact that he was writing a movie script induced him to create a series of incidents, like Brownie's death in a "friendly" village, to give the soldiers more convincing reasons for acting as they did. Presumably, Rabe and De Palma felt this "preparation" was the best they could do to give people who'd never been there a sense of the rage and anguish they felt — rage and anguish, which in this case led to an atrocity.

Yet Rabe gives Eriksson (Michael J. Fox) a speech in which this rage and sense of vulnerability are attacked as a license to throw away moral principles:

> I mean, just because each one of us might at any second be blown away, everyone's acting like we can do anything, man, and it don't matter what we done — but I'm thinkin' maybe it's the other way around, maybe the main thing is just the opposite. Because we might be dead in the next split second, maybe we gotta be extra careful what we do — because maybe it matters more — Jesus, maybe it matters more than we even know.

In the real case, unlike the impression given by the film, none of the convicted soldiers served longer than five years, but Rabe and De Palma decided not to address that issue. "I felt that the reduced sentences was [sic] one more ironic turn that the movie didn't need," De Palma told Michael Norman. "I felt, emotionally speaking, there should be some peace on earth for the character Eriksson and that justice was done. In fact, they did go to prison; if we left in how fast they got out, that point would have left the movie dramatically stalled."[72]

Casualties of War "epitomizes the Vietnam experience," De Palma argues. "To me, the Vietnam experience is the sore that will never heal. So many things happened to these kids, and marred their lives forever, and there's no rational way to explain it."[73] The film's weakest link, then, especially in light of De Palma's words, is the pat ending, which allows Eriksson to pretend that he has put the nightmare of Vietnam and the rape and murder behind him. The real Eriksson is still in hiding somewhere in the Midwest, afraid of the retribution of the men he caused to be sent to prison.

The killing of the girl, Oanh (Thuy Thu Le), is so harrowing, so compelling, that the viewer is stunned — a testimony to De Palma's ability to manipulate images and the power of the film's visualization of the inhumanity of war. After being stabbed, Oanh rises, a bloody specter, pleading, her hands outstretched for mercy. Pauline Kael recounts Lang's version of the soldiers' testimony, in which they described the girl's refusal to accept death. Lang called her "a wounded apparition."[74] Finally, in a scene of unbearable pain and brutality, the soldiers kill her with automatic weapons. She falls from the railroad trestle and into our consciences — both victim and myth.

De Palma's powerful film was, predictably, denounced by several

Vietnam veterans groups. "There are a lot of stories about Vietnam," De Palma said. "To take issue with this one seems unfair." De Palma also said he had received "many letters from Vietnam veterans saying [*Casualties*] is incredibly accurate."[75]

Ultimately, the title of this powerful and affecting film rings true by suggesting that all the soldiers and civilians in the film — and maybe those of us back home — are "casualties" of the war. It has scarred America for more than 20 years, and its effects are still being felt.

De Palma, having made two fine films in a row, is hungry for more and aware now that the camera is not everything. "What a camera does is essential to being a filmmaker. But when you do it all — when you have a great script, great actors, and a director who has an incredible visual sophistication — that's when you're going to make a truly great movie. I'm at the point in my career where I want to push as far as I can."[76]

Chapter 5
Steven Spielberg

The thing that I'm just scared to death of is that someday I'm gonna wake
up and bore somebody with a film. — Steven Spielberg[1]

Steven Spielberg was born December 18, 1947, in Cincinnati, the first
child of Arnold and Leah Posner Spielberg. Spielberg didn't grow up in
Ohio, however, as his family made the first of several moves to accommodate Arnold's career as an electrical engineer. Before settling in Phoenix,
Arizona, the Spielbergs lived in New Jersey.[2]

Spielberg soon had three younger sisters to share his parents'
affections — and for him to torment in ingenious ways. Besides locking them
in the closet and throwing in things they were afraid of, he would sneak
under their window when they were in bed and whisper, "I'm the moon!"
Spielberg was good at thinking up ways to scare his sisters because he was
so full of childhood fears and phobias himself. "My biggest fear was a clown
doll," he later recalled. "Also the tree I could see outside my room. Also
anything that might be under the bed or in the closet. Also *Dragnet* on TV."
As Richard Corliss noted, "Those boyhood fears form the spine of the
Poltergeist plot."[3]

The 10-year-old Spielberg also matched wits with his parents over
watching television. Forbidden to watch, he would sneak into the TV room
while the babysitter was there and stay up late watching old movies. Aware
of his tricks, his parents attempted countermeasures:

> So they would put a blanket over the screen and arrange plants and things
> on top with precise measurement. Sometimes my father would attach
> hairs in exact positions so he could tell if I had lifted up the dust ruffle over
> the RCA nineteen-inch screen and snuck a peek at *The Honeymooners* or
> *Dragnet*. . . . I always found the hair, memorized exactly where it was and
> rearranged before they came home.[4]

Although he was to make up for it with a vengeance when he was
older, Spielberg did not see as many films as a child as did the other young
lions. And what he did see was rather proscribed:

> I remember the first film I ever saw was *The Greatest Show on Earth* by

C. B. De Mille, and everything after that happened to be a Disney cartoon or a Disney adventure. Television to me was Imogene Coca, Sid Caesar, Soupy Sales, and *The Honeymooners*. In Phoenix, Arizona, television never really carried very good movies. They kept showing *The Atomic Kid* with Mickey Rooney four times a week.[5]

The director of *Jaws* and *Raiders of the Lost Ark* remembers his first moviegoing experience: "My father said, 'It's going to be bigger than you, but that's all right. The people in it are going to be up on a screen and they can't get out at you.' But there they were up on that screen *and they were getting out at me*. I guess ever since then I've wanted to involve the audience as much as I can so they no longer think they're sitting in an audience."[6]

"Steven makes his movies sitting front-row center with popcorn," says *E.T.* screenwriter Melissa Mathison. "He *is* the audience." One of Spielberg's favorite movies is Disney's *Fantasia*. "I take people who have never seen it," Spielberg says, "only to reexperience it through their eyes."[7] Spielberg has been noted for his references to Disney films and characters in his work — "When You Wish Upon a Star" at the end of *Close Encounters of the Third Kind, the Special Edition*, scenes from *Dumbo* in *1941*, his and others' characterization of himself as Peter Pan — and it's easy to link those homages to the movies his parents would allow him to watch. Totally middle class, Spielberg was also influenced by the Disney films' strong moral centers, their lessons about good and evil — and the childhood terrors they plumbed, like the parent-child separations in *Dumbo*, *Pinocchio*, and *Bambi*.

Noting his interest in the family films his father made, the Spielbergs got their son an inexpensive Kodak movie camera of his very own, and soon he was engrossed in writing scripts, doing primitive storyboarding, and shooting his own films. Any family outing became fair game for Spielberg's moviemaking mania, and he usually turned mundane trips into exciting melodramas. As he said later, "I never thought life was good enough, so I had to embellish it."[8]

Spielberg's home movies were an escape from peer rejection. He was no good at athletics, and the other boys in his physical education class called him "the retard" and picked him last for any group activity. When he had to dissect a frog in a junior high biology class, he and a few others ran outside to throw up — "and the others were all girls," he recalls.[9] "Some kids get involved in a Little League team or in music, in band — or watching TV. I was always drowning in little home movies. That's all I did when I was growing up. That was my escape."[10]

"I hated school," Spielberg confesses:

From age 12 or 13 I knew I wanted to be a movie director, and I didn't think that science or math or foreign languages were going to help me turn out the little 8mm sagas I was making to avoid homework. . . . My mom

> let me off school at least once a week. I would fake being sick on Mondays
> so I could cut the movies I'd shot over the weekend. I'd put the ther-
> mometer up to the light bulb — young Elliot does the same thing in *E. T.* —
> and call her in and moan and groan.[11]

Spielberg had other reasons for staying home from school. He was a
favorite target for bullies and mean-spirited football jocks who relished
pounding on him. Spielberg recalled how he used his filmmaking to his
advantage:

> When I was about 13, one local bully gave me nothing but grief all year
> long. He would knock me down on the grass, or hold my head in the dirt
> and give me bloody noses . . . in phys. ed. He was my nemesis; I dreamed
> about him. Then I figured, if you can't beat him, try to get him to join you.
> So I said to him, "I'm making this movie about fighting the Nazis and I
> want you to play this war hero." At first he laughed in my face, but later
> he said yes. He was this big 14-year-old who looked like John Wayne. I
> made him the squad leader in the film, with helmet, fatigues, and
> backpack. After that he became my best friend.[12]

If he was thought of as a nerd or a wimp, Spielberg insists he wasn't
really considered "weird":

> But I was considered different by the neighbors who saw me making
> movies on the weekends with twelve- and thirteen-year-old kids dressed
> up as adults with fake mustaches and beards, army uniforms, and
> sometimes monster suits. And I think that probably several of my friends
> were warned about playing with . . . somebody who makes movies in
> eight millimeters at twelve years old. I had a good time growing up. I can't
> complain about my childhood.[13]

Spielberg's talent for making movies helped him in other ways. He
became a Boy Scout, and his skills won him a photography badge and
ultimately helped him attain the rank of Eagle Scout at 13. At Scout camp,
Spielberg unleashed another of his talents. "I've always enjoyed telling
stories — I was a great storyteller in Boy Scouts; I used to sit around the
campfire and scare forty Scouts to death with ghost stories."[14]

Spielberg came by his storytelling ability naturally. In addition to
helping his son build sets for his 8mm movies, Arnold Spielberg spun
magical stories. "At night I'd tell the kids cliffhanger tales about characters
like Joanie Frothy Flakes and Lenny Ludhead. I see pieces of me in Steven.
I see the storyteller."[15]

The stories, at least his father's,[15] ended when the Spielberg family was
divided by divorce:

> My parents got a divorce when I was 14, 15. The whole thing about
> separation is something that runs very deep in anyone exposed to
> divorce. . . . The breaking up of the mother and father is extremely
> traumatic from 4 up. All of us are still suffering the repercussions of a
> divorce that had to happen.[16]

Later, Spielberg would use his feelings about the divorce to infuse the Elliot-E.T. relationship with special poignancy.

Spielberg, like Coppola, was also interested in sound. His 8mm films all made use of recorded music. Spielberg explains:

> Well, I've been collecting sound tracks since I was about nine years old. My first sound track album was . . . *Destination Moon*. I've been collecting sound tracks ever since I can remember . . . and I used to make my 8mm home movies when I was a kid by taking the sound track from some score like *The Great Escape* or *Spellbound* and inventing a movie *to the music*.[17]

When he listened to the sound tracks from *The Reivers* and *The Cowboys*, Spielberg discovered a composer he called a "modern relic from the lost era of film symphonies." He met the composer, John Williams, and hired him to write the music for his first feature film, *The Sugarland Express*. Williams wrote the attention-grabbing music for *Jaws* and *Close Encounters* and was recommended to Spielberg's friend George Lucas — for whom he wrote the music for the *Star Wars* trilogy. Williams also wrote the heroic music for *Superman*. Spielberg's knowledge and appreciation for the scores of Hollywood classics like *The Sea Hawk*, it can be argued, helped to usher in a new "old" era of bravura film scoring.

Spielberg's Monday-morning hooky playing caught up to him when his poor grades kept him from attending USC's film school. Instead, he attended California State University at Long Beach, majoring in English, and consciously set out to make himself movie literate. As Pye and Myles note,

> He watched every film on late night television, memorizing names and faces, recalling shots or credits at will. He became a scholar of film. . . . He began to work out which films he most admired . . . [like] John Ford's *The Searchers* . . . [and] Robert Wise's thriller . . . *The Haunting*. He had made himself into a graduate of the school of Hollywood.[18]

Spielberg got more from the classics. He told a *New York Times* writer that Frank Capra films like *Meet John Doe*, *A Pocketful of Miracles*, and *It's a Wonderful Life* taught him valuable lessons about characterization and storytelling.[19]

While he is a classic stylist, an auteur in the sense of his films being as visually and thematically identifiable as John Ford's films, Spielberg's film studies made him admire the journeymen directors who toiled in the Hollywood factories:

> I admire directors like Michael Curtiz and Victor Fleming, who are the unsung heroes and the workhorses of the '30s and '40s. They were upstaged by the great filmmakers like Hitchcock and Capra and Sturges, who had their own personal signatures. These directors didn't have signatures, they were chameleons. They could adapt to any story, in any period, with any premise.[20]

When he wasn't in class, Spielberg was sneaking onto the Universal lot to watch them make films, even crashing a closed Hitchcock set. When knocking on studio doors failed to open them wide enough for him to stick his foot inside, Spielberg decided to forget about the "esoteric" 16mm films he'd been making and shoot a short 35mm film to prove his mettle:

> *Amblin'* was an attack of crass commercialism. I wanted to shoot something that could prove to people who finance movies that I could certainly look like a professional moviemaker. *Amblin'* was a conscious effort to break into the business and become successful by proving to people I could move a camera and compose nicely and deal with lighting and performances.[21]

"When I look back at the film," Spielberg confessed, "I can easily say, 'No wonder I didn't go to Vietnam or I wasn't protesting when all my friends were carrying signs and getting clubbed in Century City.' I was off making movies, and *Amblin'* is the slick byproduct of a kid immersed up to his nose in film."[22]

"I've never been robbed or in a fistfight. I never saw a dead body," said Spielberg. "Until I went to New York City, I'd never eaten real Italian food. Walt Disney was my parental conscience. And my stepparent was the TV set."[23] "I have always felt like Peter Pan. I still feel like Peter Pan. It has been very hard for me to grow up."[24]

"I think it's easier for me to have a complete conversation from Pac-Man to exobiology with an 11-year-old than it is to sit down with an adult and discuss Nietzsche and the Falklands. Why? I guess because I'm probably socially irresponsible and way down deep I don't want to look the world in the eye. Actually, I don't mind looking the world in the eye, as long as there's a movie camera between us."[25]

Duel

Duel was a 1971 made-for-TV movie that gathered such raves and attention that it was later released to movie theaters in a lengthened version. The story is deceptively simple. A tired businessman gets into an inexplicable highway duel-to-the-death with the unseen driver of an evil-looking tractor-trailer truck. To survive, he must call upon resources he has not had to resort to before. As Spielberg said, "The hero of *Duel* is typical of that lower middle-class American who's been insulated by suburban modernization. A man like that never expects to be challenged by anything more than his television set breaking down and having to call the repair man."[26]

Tom Allen compares Spielberg's technical sophistication to one of the young lion's role models: "With less resonance and more immediacy, [the complex editing design] is as intricate as the storyboard for the runaway car in Hitchcock's *Family Plot* as reproduced in Donald Spoto's *The Art of Alfred Hitchcock.*"[27]

Dennis Weaver was quickly, and perfectly, cast as the hero. Finding the villain, the right truck, was just as important, as Spielberg told Judith Crist:

> This was the smallest truck of all the semis on the back lot — the smallest one, but the only one that had a great snout. I thought that with some remodeling we could really get it to look human. I [added] two [hydraulic] tanks to both sides of the doors. . . . They were like the ears of the truck. Then I put dead bugs all over the windshield so you'd have a tougher time seeing the driver.[28]

Spielberg and the art director succeeded in giving the truck an evil, threatening persona. With its engine-hood snout, its headlight eyes, and its massive physicality, the truck resembled a prehistoric creature in search of prey. Spielberg used all the classic Hollywood tricks to suggest the truck's menace: wide-angle shots, low-angle shots just above the surface of the road, point-of-view shots, heightened sound effects, and precision, fast-paced editing.

"Carefully storyboarded, almost to the point of animation, the film reflects the influence of Chuck Jones' Road Runner cartoon," observed Donald Mott and Cheryl Saunders. "Just as in the cartoon, when David thinks he has outrun the truck, it appears again for another attack."[29]

The film ends with Weaver tricking the truck driver into driving over a cliff. The final image we're left with is the survivor's animalistic celebration of victory. He has won the duel.

The Sugarland Express

After spending ten weeks in preproduction on a Burt Reynolds film called *White Lightning,* Spielberg realized he wanted to do something more memorable for his first theatrical film. "I didn't want to start my career as a hard-hat, journeyman director. I wanted to do something that was a little more personal." That something was *The Sugarland Express.*[30]

Spielberg's choice was an audacious one: to make a film about a pair of lower-class losers who kidnap a Texas highway patrolman to get their little boy back from a foster home is certainly not playing it safely. And much the same happened to Spielberg that happened to Lucas (*THX 1138*) and Coppola (*You're a Big Boy Now*) for not playing safely with their first films. *The Sugarland Express* drew cheers from critics but only a ho-hum response from the popular audience. It was a lesson none of the three men forgot, Spielberg and Lucas especially.

The Sugarland Express *was Steven Spielberg's first theatrical film. From left to right: William Atherton, Goldie Hawn, and Michael Sacks.*

USC film-school graduates Hal Barwood and Matthew Robbins wrote the screenplay from Spielberg's story. Spielberg's major postmodern contribution to the film is his insertion of a *Road Runner* cartoon into the story. While on the run, Clovis (William Atherton) and Lou Jean (Goldie Hawn) can see the screen of a nearby drive-in theater showing the cartoon. At first, Clovis provides the sound effects for Lou Jean, but slowly he senses a parallel between the animated chase and their own.

In the world of the road runner and the coyote, the coyote, while doomed to failure time and time again, is never really hurt. No matter how many times he falls to the bottom of the canyon, he's back chasing the road runner in the next scene. But for just a moment, Spielberg juxtaposes Clovis' pensive face with yet another of the coyote's falls to the canyon floor — this time with a loud WHOMP! Spielberg's point is not subtle: The coyote prefigures Clovis' fate at the end of the picture. And Clovis, when he lets himself think straight, knows it. He also knows that unlike the coyote, he is not a cartoon figure and will not bounce back unhurt for the next "scene."

"I'm a big fan of Chuck Jones, who did those [*Road Runner*] cartoons, and I've been a big fan of the Warner Bros. cartoons as long as I can remember seeing them," Spielberg explained. "In fact, Chuck's the visual consultant on *1941*. I see a lot of tragedy in cartoons. I see a great deal of pathos in the Road Runner and Coyote pursuit."[31]

The Sugarland Express is an extremely well-made first film (if you discount *Duel* and Spielberg's other TV work when you say first). Predictably, the scenes of dozens of police cruisers flowing across the landscape are well handled, given Spielberg's visual sophistication (although a nighttime confrontation–near collision between the principals' police car and two Louisiana State Police cruisers is muddled and confusing).

Spielberg gets good performances from Ben Johnson, William Atherton, and, especially, from William Sacks. The only disappointment is Goldie Hawn's stereotypical "white trash" Lou Jean. Her "star" casting, meant to be a plus, was probably a drawback. In 1974, audiences were not ready to see Goldie Hawn in such a role because their horizon of expectations was such that they probably performed the following mental calculation: "Goldie Hawn means comedy." So no matter how good she might have been in the part, she was, in this sense, "miscast."

Spielberg recognized this problem, one of "stars" versus "actors," when he cast Richard Dreyfuss, Robert Shaw, and Roy Scheider in *Jaws* a year later instead of Burt Reynolds, Lee Marvin, and Robert Redford. "For certain special types of movies, where half the struggle is verisimilitude, if Burt Reynolds had played Richard Dreyfuss' part, there would have been too much imagery of Burt in other movies, with fast cars, attractive women, and blazing action."[32]

Jaws

When Spielberg was first offered *Jaws*, he hesitated, fearing that the great white shark would be compared to the truck in *Duel*. His well-developed popular-story sense also identified another problem with the book and the original script:

> When I came on the project I asked Dick [Zanuck] and David [Brown] if they would grant me two wishes, as actual conditions for my doing the film. One was that I didn't want to show the shark until much later in the movie. The book introduces the shark in the first few pages . . . in detail. I thought Jaws would be more menacing as an invisible idea. Second, I wanted to lose the love triangle between the ichthyologist and the then-cuckolded husband and his wife.[33]

By showing the shark as little as possible at the beginning, Spielberg put his trust in the audience's ability to scare itself:

> I think the collective audience has a better, broader imagination than I do. They fill in the spaces between the lines. They saw a much more horrific shark in their heads when I suggested an occurrence below the surface than I provided with the rubber shark when my commercial sensibilities told me I had to make it visible.[34]

Spielberg was also right to see that since the story concerned primal fears and emotions, the love triangle was detrimental to the high-velocity adventure he planned. Whether or not one thinks of *Jaws* as "art," few can deny its visceral power to reach us on a basic level, to frighten us. In the film, the shark is described as a coldly efficient "eating machine." That's an apt description of the film: a coldly efficient fright machine. The shark is posited as an unthinking force of nature—it has no meaning; it just *is*. Therefore, to try to inject "meaning" into the film is like trying to assign a meaning to the physical sensations provided by a ride on a roller coaster. The experience, it can be argued, is the meaning, the whole purpose of the enterprise.

Spielberg believes in his audiences, wants to give them the best time he can, even things that seem fine as they are.

> And after this extraordinary preview in Dallas of *Jaws*, I still didn't feel I had a big enough reaction in the second act of the movie, so I designed the head coming out of the hole in the boat, which I shot in a friend's swimming pool. And that became the big scream of the movie. I felt the movie needed an explosive surprise at that point.[35]

With a brilliant advertising campaign (the poster showed the shark rising to attack the girl on the surface), the film became a popular-culture sensation. The shark was a perfect metaphor for just about anything you wanted to use it for—inflation, political campaigns, the OPEC cartel, big business, big government. Pye and Myles note that after seeing the plethora of cartoons parodying the poster, Universal took pains to remind people that *Jaws* "is a movie, too."[36]

One film writer angrily snapped at the critical support *Jaws* received, saying he could understand the popular success of the film, "a predictable horror picture without a trace of wit or imagination or visual beauty," but he failed to see why otherwise "intelligent reviewers like Richard Schickel, Gary Arnold, and Frank Rich—have acclaimed the film as a classic suspense melodrama. If critics can fall for such a crudely calculated, manipulative scare show, then there really is no chance to buck high-powered advertising."[37]

When this critic derides others for overlooking the film's "glaring flaws," he's saying, "Why doesn't *your* opinion jibe with *mine*, the *correct* one, rather than coming down on the side of the lumpen proletariat?" Even so, I'm sure the critics didn't really call *Jaws* a "great film" (whatever that means), as much as they recognized it as an example of "great filmmaking."

Jaws was a monster hit in more ways than one. Here, Spielberg playfully poses inside the mechanical shark's jaws.

Clearly, the film tapped into some mass conscious and unconscious that could not have been predicted before its release. If the film had offered nothing more than the schlock scares of a B horror film, it would not have been the commercial—and critical—success it proved to be. Spielberg, once the little boy who was afraid of what might be lurking in his closet or under his bed, got a whole nation wondering what might be lurking just beneath the surface of the sea. It would be appropriate, if unnecessary, to ascribe to *Jaws* a full litany of Freudian psychological meanings, especially castration fears.

"Director Steven Spielberg took a routine fish-bites-man story and transformed it into a show business phenomenon," wrote Frank Rich. "*Jaws*, a merciless attack on the audience's nerves, quickly established its creator as the reigning boy genius of American cinema and went on to pile up the largest box office take in the history of the movies."[38]

Standing ankle-deep in water, Spielberg (center, glasses) ponders the rigors of location shooting on the set of Jaws.

Close Encounters of the Third Kind

When he was 16, Spielberg made a 140-minute film called *Firelight* about an alien invasion. This early effort, which cost $500, was shown at a Phoenix theater and made $600 — a $100 profit. The idea for a film dealing with UFOs remained in Spielberg's mind. *Close Encounters of the Third*

Kind (1977), the version he made over a decade later, was quite different from his original concept, but it too was profitable.

Spielberg's first attempt at a story for his UFO movie was called *Watch the Skies*, taken from the newspaperman's warning at the end of Howard Hawks' *The Thing (From Another World)* (1951). Initially, Spielberg's aliens, like Hawks' "intelligent carrot," were hostile. Michael and Julia Phillips, *Close Encounters'* producers, hired Paul Schrader (*Taxi Driver*) to write a script. Although he contributed its memorable title to the film, Schrader found little about Spielberg's story he felt he could do anything with. "I didn't want the hero to be a *putz*," said Schrader. "But all I could see was this schmuck taking off in a spaceship to set up a chain of McDonald's in outer space."[39]

Spielberg, for his part, didn't like Schrader's script. As Tony Crawley noted, "In a word, Spielberg *loathed* it. . . . He felt the script was a typically Calvinist tract from Schrader, [had] little to do with UFOs, *nothing* to do with Spielbergian UFOs."[40]

Spielberg decided to write the script himself, and later recalled some of his many influences:

> When I began *Close Encounters* . . . I had four things in mind. One of my favorite movies is *Fantasia*, and I had the mountain from the "Night on Bald Mountain" sequence fixed in my mind — along with the song "When You Wish Upon a Star" as sung by Cliff Edwards [the voice of Jiminy Cricket]. I pretty much hung my story on the mood the song created, the way it affected me emotionally. The mountain became the symbolic end zone of the movie.[41]

Spielberg had more than *Fantasia* (1940) and *Pinocchio* (1940) in mind, however. Like George Lucas' films, Spielberg's *Close Encounters* is a virtual compendium of movie history — a postmodern *Familiar Quotations* of film and TV. The besieging of the Guiler house by a UFO, especially when the aliens seem ready to force their way in via the chimney or any means they can, recalls not only Alfred Hitchcock's *The Birds* (1963) but also "The Invaders," an episode on the original Rod Serling *Twilight Zone* which starred Agnes Moorehead as an old woman menaced by tiny space invaders.

Roy Neary's (Richard Dreyfuss) fruitless attempts to convince his disbelieving family and the authorities that he really saw UFOs recalls William Cameron Menzies' *Invaders from Mars* (1953). Neary and several police cars chasing a bevy of UFOs down Indiana highways is yet another Spielbergian tribute to Chuck Jones' *Road Runner* cartoons. Pye and Myles suggest that when little Barry (Cary Guffey) runs away following the spaceships, it is through an artificial woods that looks suspiciously like the woods in Walt Disney's *Bambi*.[42]

At one point in the film, several larger (adult?) spacecraft are trailed by a Tinker Bellish red ball of light which Jack Kroll calls "a classic Disney device—a little red UFO that comes skittering along after the bigger ships is the old Disney gag of the last little dwarf or chipmunk stumbling after his dignified elders."[43]

Frank Rich noted that "Roy Neary (Dreyfuss) is a . . . kind of man-in-the-middle played by Cary Grant and James Stewart in films like *North by Northwest* and *Vertigo*."[44] Hitchcock's *North by Northwest* (1959) is further referenced by Neary and Jillian's (Melinda Dillon) climb up the face of the Devil's Tower (which parallels the famous Mount Rushmore finale) and by the army helicopters which try to gas them (just as the crop duster menaces Cary Grant).

Spielberg chose Richard Dreyfuss to play the crucial role of Roy Neary in *Close Encounters* because "he is a lot like Everyman. . . . Richard's easier to identify with than, let's say, Robert Redford. Most of us are like Richard Dreyfuss. Few of us are like Bob Redford or Steve McQueen. I've always believed in the movies I've made, my central protagonist has always been—and probably always will be—Mr. Everyday Regular Fella."[45]

In addition to being "a lot like Everyman," Dreyfuss is a lot like . . . Steven Spielberg. Neary is much more interested in the toys in the "family room" than are the kids, and the train set that covers much of the room is probably his rather than his TV-narcotized children's. Just as Spielberg was able to outwit his parents and get to see forbidden TV shows, Dreyfuss' Neary outwits the civilian authorities and the army to answer the aliens' subliminal summons.

If *Close Encounters* shares traits with many SF films of the fifties, one thing it does not have in common with most of them is their paranoid view of the alien visitor(s). Even before the invention of film, H. G. Wells' novel *The War of the Worlds* (1898) posited hostile aliens intent upon conquering us. And in the classic *The Day the Earth Stood Still* (1951), a man runs down the street after the saucer has landed shouting, "They're here. They've landed on the [Washington, D.C.] Mall!" Whoever *they* are, surely they mean us no good. In *Close Encounters*, in contrast, Spielberg takes great care to show us the alien's face—its humanlike smile—at the end. Spielberg's message, unlike the anonymous fifties man-in-the-street's, is "They're here. They're here . . . and they *like* us."

This is a powerful and seductive message for audiences in a troubled era. Stanley Kauffmann described the effect *Close Encounters* had on the opening night's audience—and him:

> To be . . . at the first public showing, to hear the exclamations and applause all during the film, was to see the audience's self-ordained god dispensing miracles of reassurance. Even though nobody really knows whether there's any life out in space, during [the finale] . . . our technology made us masters of unimaginable cosmic mystery. A black man, walking

The tense opening sequence in Spielberg's Close Encounters of the Third Kind. *(Courtesy of Steve and Nancy Gould.)*

ahead of me after the picture, said to his companion, "I feel *good*, man, I feel *good*." So, certainly, did I.[46]

Spielberg had another goal besides making his audiences feel good. He wanted them to *believe* in his story:

> On *Close Encounters*, I had a very important decision to make: whether or not to use the Walt Disney song, "When You Wish Upon a Star" at the end of the movie.... And the only way I could tell was to have two different previews, on two different nights; one night with the song, one night without it.... I made a determination that the audience wanted to be transported into another world along with Richard Dreyfuss [rather than] be told the film was a fantasy.... And I didn't want *Close Encounters* to end just as a dream.[47]

Later, when he cut some scenes, added new ones, and released the result as *Close Encounters of the Third Kind: The Special Edition*, Spielberg restored "When You Wish Upon a Star" to the film's closing credits.

Spielberg is mocked, often cruelly, for his bourgeois, suburban, life-is-sweet, I'm-okay-you're-okay role as "Director Feelgood," for his Capra-corny stories and resolutions, but he senses, with postmodern certainty, what his audience wants. They want, like him, to believe that there is good in the universe. They want to believe that affection, love, hope, and caring still count for something in life. They want to believe that if you wish upon a star, your dreams really do come true.

Interviewed about Spielberg on ABC TV's *20/20*, Richard Dreyfuss said:

> Look how nice his films are.... I mean, just, they're nice. They're about love, they're about wonder, they're about good things.... And "When You Wish Upon a Star" is Steve, it's him sitting around with Jiminy Cricket going, "Let's tell a story."[48]

When his kids vote for *Crazy Golf* instead of a "dumb cartoon," Everyman Roy Neary speaks for much of any audience: "I grew up on *Pinocchio* ... furry animals ... magic, and a lot of fun." Because he believes, truly *believes*, and because he retains his childlike wonder and hope, Roy Neary is allowed to escape his prison of domestic and occupational responsibilities and fly away with Tinker Bell and Peter Pan to Never Never Land and live happily forever after.

E.T. The Extra-Terrestrial

> *E.T.* is a personal film because it's about people and personalities and relationships that I have some experience in. My childhood is still fresh in my memory. I'm sure when I'm seventy and eighty, my childhood will be even fresher in my memory then.[49]

At one point, working on *Raiders*, Spielberg was very lonely:

> I remember wishing one night that I had a friend. It was like, when you were a kid and had grown out of dolls or teddy bears or Winnie the Pooh, you just wanted a little voice in your mind to talk to. I began concocting this imaginary creature [and] thought, what if I were ten years old again — where I've sort of been for thirty-four years anyway — and what if he needed me as much as I needed him? Wouldn't that be a great love story?[50]

"To me, Elliot was always the Nowhere Man from the Beatles song," Spielberg said. "I was drawing on my own feelings when I was a little kid and I didn't have that many friends and had to resort to making movies to become quasi-popular and to find a reason for living after school hours."[51]

"I always thought of the adult world as being symbolized by tall people who cast giant shadows," Spielberg told an interviewer. "People who don't think like kids, but think like professionals. That's dangerous — they might understand E.T. biologically and scientifically, but they'd never understand that he had a heart."[52]

Spielberg opted to tell the story from a kid's point of view, shooting from lower camera setups and using lots of low camera angles. He explained why the teacher at Elliot's school (played by an unseen and uncredited Harrison Ford) and the policeman who comes to Elliot's home are seen only from the waist down:

> I was kind of influenced by the old MGM cartoons of Tom & Jerry — you'd never see any people, you see therapeutic shoes, and skirts, and a hand would reach down and grab the cat. Or someone would come into the shop and swat the cat — and a foot would kick the cat out the door into the snow. That's something I grew up with, adults being taken seriously from the waist down.[53]

Because *E.T.* was the "small film" he kept promising to make, Spielberg decided to "wing" it and eschew storyboards:

> Winging *E.T.* made it a very spontaneous, vital movie. I realized I didn't need the drawings for a small movie like *E.T.* I would never wing *Raiders II*, but I could improvise a more personal picture like *E.T.* . . . more about people and relationships.[54]

Elliot's messy room in *E.T.* was inspired by Spielberg's youthful disaster area. "My bedroom was like all the rooms of all the kids in all the movies I've been a part of. It was a compost heap of everything I never put away. . . . These days, I can really mess up a place in about twelve hours. When I was a kid, I was a little bit faster: it took about thirty minutes."[55]

In *Poltergeist* (also 1982), the closet became a source of terror and fear, reflecting Spielberg's childhood fear of what might be lurking inside. In *E.T.*, Elliot's closet — filled with mounds of clothes, cheerful stuffed animals, and toys — becomes E.T.'s temporary home, the small rose-colored window suggesting the visitor's benevolent nature.

Robert Philip Kolker examines two sequences in the film that demonstrate Spielberg's filmmaking talents and his film's intertextuality:

> Elliot is in school and E.T. is at home, drinking beer. As the creature gets drunk and falls down, so does Elliot. E.T. then watches *The Quiet Man* on television. John Wayne pulls Maureen O'Hara to him and kisses her. The action is matched and cut to Elliot at school who echoes John Wayne's movements with a classmate. The cutting . . . interconnect[s] fictional spaces . . . linking all movie images together. If ever any reflexive openings occur in the sentimental gaze of *E.T.*, they are at points like these, when the film admits its relationship to other film romance, other film fictions. (The process is continued . . . when the children and their alien playmate, costumed for Halloween, walk down the street. E.T. is drawn to a child dressed as Yoda — two movie fictions recognizing one another.) Such self-conscious gestures are . . . never distancing; they continue to propel the viewer into the fiction. The spaces of recognition (of filmic allusions, of editing style) heighten the viewer's affection for the images and their affective pull.[56]

Richard T. Jameson also notes Spielberg's postmodern awareness:

> If movie classicism, the purest manifestation of a pop-cultural medium,
> validates *E.T.*, *E.T.* also returns the favor. . . . E.T. tinkers with a learning
> toy and a TV remote control while also perusing a Buck Rogers strip in
> the comix. Buck has built himself a Rube Goldberg gizmo to 'phone home'
> from a hostile planet. . . . Meanwhile, a TV commercial urges Bell
> Telephone customers to reach out and touch someone.[57]

"The director gets the angles that can render the mundane monumental
without disfiguring or falsifying it," Jameson writes. "He gets the kind of
'shots' one frames to valorize one's childhood (and adult?) itinerary."[58]

At one point, one of Elliot's buddies asks why E.T. can't just "beam up"
à la *Star Trek.* The reply is "This is reality, Greg." Elliot shows E.T. his *Star
Wars* figurines and a shark — Spielberg's salute to *Jaws.* Pop culture
manifests itself in other ways: E.T. drinks Coors beer and eats Pez candy
and Reese's Pieces, and Elliot first discovers the little alien's presence while
taking delivery of a pizza. E.T., hiding in the closet, mimics one of the
stuffed animals, just another cute-grotesque face in a row of them. Later,
E.T. hears the mother reading *Peter Pan* to little Gertie (Drew Barrymore).
Viewers recognize themselves in Spielberg's knowing re-creations of
American life and pop culture and his wholesome mise-en-scène.

Besides *The Quiet Man* (1952) and Lucas' *Star Wars* trilogy, *E.T.*
references *Tom and Jerry* cartoons and SF movies like 1955's *This Island
Earth* (both seen on TV), *The Wizard of Oz* (John Williams' witty musical nod toward the Miss Gulch motif from that film), and Walt Disney's
1953 animated version of *Peter Pan* (as Elliot and his friends fly over the
heads of the adult authorities and off to their rendezvous with E.T.'s mother
ship).

E.T. "will be described as a cunning variation on the 'odd love story,'
or the 'boy and his dog story,'" wrote Charles Michener, presumably thinking of George Stevens' *Shane* (1953 — "Come back, E.T., come back!")
or Disney's *Old Yeller* (1957, except that E.T. lives in the end). Michener also compares *E.T.* to Bryan Forbes' *Whistle Down the Wind* (1961),
The Day the Earth Stood Still, "and all those movies about children
who keep an alien creature hidden from adults who 'wouldn't understand.'"[59]

"I thought I was making this personal statement about the effects of
divorce on children," said Spielberg. "Which is, to me, what *E.T.* was really
about. And other times I thought I was making a kiddie show that would
be unreleasable in motion-picture theaters and would have to be released
on Saturday-morning television next to *He-Man* and *Transformers.* But
E.T. helped me with *The Color Purple.* If I hadn't made *E.T.*, I wouldn't
have had the confidence to make *Color Purple.*"[60]

Raiders of the Lost Ark

Arguably, it is Steven Spielberg's collaboration with friend George Lucas on the Indiana Jones films, *Raiders of the Lost Ark* (1981), *Indiana Jones and the Temple of Doom* (1984), and *Indiana Jones and the Last Crusade* (1989) that most clearly reveals both filmmakers' postmodernist preoccupation with recycling the cinematic inventions of earlier moviemakers. I will deal with *Last Crusade* separately, since it represents a break with the spirit of the second film and is more attuned to Spielberg's later works than the empty pyrotechnics of *Doom*.

"Marty [Scorsese] would have to be the best *filmmaker* of our generation," Spielberg told an interviewer, "[but] George Lucas is the best *moviemaker*. You see, George and I have fun with our films. We don't take them as seriously. And I think that our movies are about things that we think will appeal to other people, not just to ourselves. We think of ourselves first, but in the next breath we're talking about the audience and what works and what doesn't."[61]

Following the success of Lucas' *Star Wars* and before the release of Spielberg's *Close Encounters of the Third Kind*, the two moviemakers were on a vacation together in Hawaii. When Spielberg mentioned to Lucas that someday he'd like to make a "James Bond-esque" movie, Lucas said, "I've got something better than James Bond" and told him about an adventure film he'd been thinking about for years, something that would pull together all the serials and action-packed B movies he'd loved as a child.[62]

Spielberg recalled the incident this way: "[George] told me about Archaeologist/Adventurer Indiana Jones and his heroic 'raid' to save the Ark of the Covenant.... I quickly became George's first preview audience."[63] It was a movie both men wanted to see, and the only way to achieve that goal was to make it themselves.

Spielberg had long wanted to do something that harkened back to the serials of his postmodern-generation childhood:

> I had grown up with serials. There was a revival theater near my house in Phoenix, Arizona ... and on Saturdays they would show a double feature and sandwich in between 10 cartoons, previews of coming attractions from 20 years past, and usually two serials. Every Saturday I would go there and ... see these old revival movies and ... serials: *Tailspin Tommy*, and *Masked Marvel*, *Spy Smasher*, *Don Winslow of the Navy*, *Commander Cody* — and I always wondered why Hollywood hadn't done anything to revive the *genre* of the outdoor adventure; of narrow misses and close calls.[64]

Spielberg and Lucas' concept was simple: Take everything — *everything* — that was exciting about those old serials and programmers and stuff it into one movie, give it an eighties gloss, and let one of filmdom's most technologically proficient directors loose to direct the whole smorgasbord. Chastised by critics for his profligacy in shooting *1941* (1979), Spielberg allowed the tightfisted Lucas to ride herd on him and curb his instinct to reshoot a scene until he thought it was "perfect." Thus, even though *Raiders* had a much longer shooting schedule than any of the cheapies it emulated, it still retained enough rough edges to remain true to the form.

But not *too* true to the form. Both Spielberg and Lucas realized that their memories of the films and serials that had thrilled them as children were not accurate — the originals didn't hold up on re-viewing. As Spielberg told Todd McCarthy, "When George and I first began talking about this project, we sat in a screening room at Universal and saw *Don Winslow in the Navy* — all fifteen episodes — and we were bored out of our minds." After Spielberg and Lucas got over their depression, they said, "Well, we'll make an *original movie, like nobody's ever seen before*. And we won't really base it on the serials, but we certainly will tip our hats in that direction, because that's where the inspiration first struck. *It won't be anything like the serials of the fifties.*"[65] (Emphasis added.)

Certainly Spielberg's protestation that he and Lucas took only a fleeting, initial inspiration from earlier films is self-serving and flat-out misleading. David Ansen complained about "Hollywood's increasing tendency to cannibalize itself" and said that "*Raiders of the Lost Ark* . . . is a virtual encyclopedia of old movie devices."[66]

The movie begins with a visual joke that recalls a similar moment in the 1945 Crosby-Hope *The Road to Utopia* where the comedy duo see the Paramount mountain logo in the distance (Veronica Geng has noted that *Spielberg* means "Playmountain").[67] In *Raiders*, the Paramount logo dissolves to a shot of a mountain remarkably like the logo. The action begins with archaeologist-hero Indiana Jones seeking a golden idol even better protected than the all-seeing eye that Sabu steals in 1940's *The Thief of Bagdad*. The first shot we see of Indiana Jones is of the seat of his baggy pants — à la Mifune's raggedy-man Samurai adventurer in Kurosawa's *Yojimbo*. When the camera pans up to Indy's face, however, we can see that from his days-old stubble of beard to the hat he wears, he is more evocative of Humphrey Bogart's Fred C. Dobbs, the scruffy goldminer in *The Treasure of the Sierra Madre* (1948). "My image of Harrison [Ford] was always Fred C. Dobbs," said Spielberg. "Five o'clock shadow and the kind of grumpy and grizzled view of everything."[68]

As Indy quests for the Ark of the Covenant, we trace his progress by means of an arrow moving across a map — a hoary device much used in thirties and forties films. Indy links up with Marion Ravenwood, a woman who strongly recalls the tough-tender heroine of many a Howard Hawks film — the "Hawksian Woman," able to dish it out as well as take it. "I

Indy's hat and look were inspired in part by Humphrey Bogart's scruffy Fred C. Dobbs in The Treasure of the Sierra Madre *(1948).*

screened a lot of movies for Karen [Allen] before we went to London," Spielberg said. "I showed her . . . *Red River* — I showed her movies in which women were really perky, like spitfires, and I said, 'This is the way I hope you'll be.'"[69]

Indy reenters Marion's life in a shot that recalls the film noirish look of so many forties films: his long shadow falls on the wall and her before he is seen. Just as the secondary villain of the piece, Toht, the sadistic Nazi agent, recalls Peter Lorre, the Nazi soldiers bear a remarkable resemblance to the cardboard-cutout one-dimensional storm troopers of World War II Hollywood films like *Hitler's Children* (1943). These scenes are double-edged: older filmgoers recall the B-movie clichés with fondness, and younger audiences thrill to the novelty (for them) of the old devices.

Raiders' thrilling set piece, Indy's transfer to the truck transporting the Ark and his ensuing battle to wrest control of the vehicle from its Nazi driver, is the action highlight of the film. Like so much else in *Raiders*, however, it is a homage to earlier films, not an original concept. As David Ansen wrote, "The inspiration for *Raiders of the Lost Ark* — an old movie poster of a Zorro-like hero jumping from a horse to a truck — came to

George Lucas before he made *Star Wars*."[70] Actually, the hero making the perilous transfer isn't just "Zorro-like" — he *is* Zorro. The scene is from Republic's 1937 serial *Zorro Rides Again*. To anyone familiar with the scene in *Raiders*, seeing the photograph showing the action in the original film is all that is necessary to convince one that that is where Spielberg and Lucas got the inspiration for their version. The truck used in *Raiders* even looks like the one in *Zorro*. The truck-chase sequence is reminiscent of *Stagecoach* (1939) for the chase alone, but it also contains an exciting and exhilarating under-the-truck salute to Yakima Canutt's famous under-the-stagecoach stunt.

Raiders' final image, a matte shot showing the crated-up Ark of the Covenant being stored among a plenitude of similar wooden crates, recalls the vast warehouse in Welles' *Citizen Kane* (1941) containing Charles Foster Kane's possessions.

Even Spielberg's recollections of the rigors of the location shooting — filming in 130-degree heat — make reference to another filmmaker, one of his idols:

> I kept thinking of David Lean, and I think what kept us going was the thought that Lean, at 60, had done this every day for a year. David Lean was our criterion for survival. At least we had hotels in Nefta and Gafsa with air conditioning. David Lean slept in tents during the making of *Lawrence of Arabia*.[71]

Indiana Jones and the Temple of Doom

"I had separation pangs," Spielberg said when he contemplated another director taking on *Indiana Jones and the Temple of Doom*. "I knew if I didn't direct, somebody else would. I got a little bit jealous, I got a little bit frustrated, and I signed on for one more."[72]

Not to be outdone, *Temple of Doom*, *Raiders'* 1984 "prequel," contains as many references to serials and earlier films as its predecessor — as well as the inevitable salute to *Star Wars* (the film's initial sequence takes place in the Club Obi Wan). A huge gong is struck at the beginning of the floor-show, reminiscent of the gong struck at the opening of J. Arthur Rank films and George Stevens' 1939 adventure classic, *Gunga Din*.

After Indy escapes from a melee at the Club Obi Wan, he flees Shanghai in a plane flown by mysterious oriental pilots, a plot twist recalling a similar one in *Lost Horizon* (1937). As in *Horizon*, the passengers awake to find they've been flying in the wrong direction, high over the mountains of Tibet. Lucas and Spielberg now begin mining the history of movies and serials in earnest. Returning to *Gunga Din* they exhume the murderous cult of Thuggee — stranglers who do in their victims with a short

Harrison Ford as the fedora-wearing Indiana Jones. (Courtesy Steve and Nancy Gould.)

length of cord. Also from *Gunga Din* (and many a serial and B movie) comes the rope bridge high over a gorge containing man-eating crocodiles.

Having turned to *The Wizard of Oz* for inspiration for many of his films, Spielberg goes back to the well once again. The guards who stand watch over the underground mining operation look suspiciously like the guards at the Wicked Witch's castle (which itself is suggestive of *Temple of Doom*'s Pankot Palace; both, of course, are matte paintings). The escape in the mining car recalls both *Rollercoaster* and Buster Keaton's *The General*.

As in the 1942 serial *The Perils of Nyoka*, Indy faces impalement upon spikes emerging from the floor and ceiling. And just as the horseback-to-truck transfer in *Raiders* is a virtual shot-for-shot lift from *Zorro Rides Again*, *Temple of Doom*'s scene in which Indy, Willie, and Short Round outrace a torrent of water through a mine shaft is stunningly similar to just such a scene in *Manhunt of Mystery Island*, a 1945 Republic serial. *Temple*'s shot of the water exploding out of an opening in the cliffside is identical to the same shot in the serial.

Unfortunately, Lucas and Spielberg not only copy the action sequences of thirties and forties films but also (presumably unconsciously) copy their implicit racism. The white male hero must once again save the poor good colored people from the evil colored people. As Harlan Jacobson noted, "The problem is not that villainous Asians, or Marlboro men, or dumb broads shouldn't show up in a movie (a kind of cultural fascism results from that line of thought), but the ones who show up here lack any shading or dimension, and so their atavism is all that one notices."[73]

Spielberg and Lucas, resurrecting the old stereotypes along with the thrills and adventure, seem not to notice them or to believe that they're part and parcel of the package. And that is one of the problems postmodernist filmmakers face: In uncritically recycling the old films, they are often unaware of troubling political or sociological elements that may come with the old story lines; their inability to discriminate is directly related to the lions' ideological naivete.

The Color Purple

The Color Purple (1985), was based on Alice Walker's novel, a story set in the Deep South. Told through the letters that Celie, a black woman, writes to God and to her sister Nettie, Color Purple was both an unlikely film for Spielberg to make and a bold attempt by a caged young lion to break free of his self-imposed limits.

As he confessed to one interviewer,

> I was more afraid of myself. I was afraid of discovering my limitations. I was afraid of discovering a wall that said: Go no further! This is as far as you can go in life! Stay in the area that you do best and do not wander! Go back! Warning! BEWARE! DO NOT CROSS THIS LINE! ELECTRIFIED FENCE! HIGH-VOLTAGE! CONTAMINATED! BIOLOGICALLY DANGEROUS! All that sort of stuff. That's what I was afraid of.[74]

Spielberg used his minority status as a Jew growing up in Phoenix to connect emotionally to the material. He felt that was enough because, as he said, "I never looked at Color Purple as just a black movie. I looked at it as a story for everybody."[75]

Spielberg tried hard to escape his past in Color Purple, once again going without storyboards, as he did on E.T. While the film was a modest financial success, it didn't fare as well with the critics. Most commended Spielberg for attempting to break new career ground, but many also observed that Spielberg's personal vision, so benign, so suburban, was too circumscribed for Walker's story of degradation and triumph. Spielberg had no problems with the story's glowing, brightly lit moments, but his palette contained few truly dark colors.

Richard Corliss commented, "Spielberg has chosen to elegize the story

Cary Grant, Victor McLaglen, and Douglas Fairbanks, Jr., in 1939's Gunga Din, *one of the many classic Hollywood films to influence Lucas and Spielberg's* Indiana Jones and the Temple of Doom.

by romanticizing it, swathing the characters in Norman Rockwell attitudes, a meddlesome symphonic score and a golden fairy dust that shines through the windows like God's blessing."[76]

Robert Kolker notes John Ford's continued gravitational pull on Spielberg's work:

> The influence of John Ford on the film is consuming, a force that helps pull it in toward convention and the conservative reclamation of its liberal

Whoopi Goldberg listens intently as Spielberg explains what he wants from her in a scene for The Color Purple, *the director's first attempt to "grow up."*

project. Of course, Ford's presence hovers over most of Spielberg's work. Both filmmakers are preoccupied with families and security, with threats to domestic . . . order and its reestablishment.[77]

Variety's "Jagr." observed that "Spielberg leans heavily on all the key emotional scenes so that the audience knows what to feel and what's coming. Spielberg has smoothed out most of the rough edges, giving the film a rather limited emotional range   The emotional notes are familiar, sometimes they ring true, more often they seem manipulated and overstated."[78]

Seeing the film reveals that while Spielberg was able to downplay his usual childhood fantasy elements and cinematic dexterity, he was unable, or unwilling, to cut himself totally loose from either preoccupation. The fantasy elements in a story about black life, set in a classically Hollywood Deep South (the location of such similar films as *Cabin in the Sky* and *The Green Pastures*), are less obvious than in a story about the healing intervention of a little green man from outer space into the life of a lonely child, but they are both soothing, redemptive fantasies nonetheless.

While Spielberg refused comment on most of the criticism directed at his direction and at the film, he rejected the charges that he presented a whitewashed picture of the time or the people:

> I knew I had a responsibility to *The Color Purple*, and yet I didn't want to make the kind of movie from the novel that some people wanted me to. Because that's not who I am. Some people wanted the movie to be about the tumbledown, ramshackle Deep South. But Alice Walker's grandparents were well-off, they were successful, and we based Celie and Mister's house on pictures Alice showed us. We took criticism on *The Color Purple* for the art direction from people who weren't aware that her grandparents were wealthy by the standards of the day. I think some people had a kind of *Uncle Tom's Cabin* view of what the picture should be, which is wrong. And, ironically, it pointed out their own inclination for racial stereotyping, which is what some of the same people said *we* were guilty of.[79]

Empire of the Sun

With the "failure" of *The Color Purple* (at least in terms of smashing reviews or Academy awards), pundits and naysayers were wondering if Spielberg really could make the sort of "serious" films he professed to want to make. And having just turned 40 ("It ain't been so easy," he acknowledged), Spielberg confronted what he wanted to do with the rest of his professional life. Financially secure, he decided that it was time for him to satisfy himself first (although I see little evidence that this has been a real problem for the young lion):

> I suddenly realized that, "God, maybe I should please a part of me I haven't pleased before — that *Empire* has just started to please, which is a side that doesn't necessarily think of the audience with every thought and breath, but thinks about what I need to be satisfied."[80]

When David Lean asked Spielberg to help him acquire the rights to J. G. Ballard's autobiographical novel and to serve as his producer, Spielberg read the book — and was hooked. "From the moment I read the novel, I secretly wanted to do it myself," he said. "I had never read anything with an adult setting — even *Oliver Twist* — where a child saw things through a man's eyes as opposed to a man discovering things through the child in him. This was just the reverse of what I felt — leading up to *Empire* — was my credo."[81]

Empire (1987) was both an opportunity and a trap. Although it was clearly his most ambitious project to date, it bore a surface resemblance to many of his earlier works. It also incorporated his signature narrative spine: A child, usually a boy, is separated from his parents, undergoes a series of alternately exhilarating and frightening adventures, and is finally returned to them in a cathartic reunion. It is to Spielberg's credit that he

In Empire of the Sun *Spielberg attempted to mix spectacle and story, à la his idol, British director David Lean.*

succeeded in making a film about a child's fear of separation and loss that relies not on science fiction or horror but the innocent split-second choice of a boy unaware of real-life consequences: When Jim (Christian Bale) releases his mother's hand to retrieve a favorite toy airplane, a crowd pulls them apart, separating Jim from his family for the duration of World War II. When Jim faces real suffering and death in a Japanese concentration camp, his experiences are intensely horrific, light-years beyond those suffered by other Spielberg protagonists.

"Spielberg heroes often step into other worlds — the hero of *Close Encounters* entering the mother ship, E.T. emerging on Earth," David Ansen noted. "But here his young hero enters the underworld, where his proper upbringing fails to apply. This is the first Spielberg adventure set in hell. The only way for Jim to survive is to cast childhood brutally aside."[82] It is as if little Barry Guiler had not only been kidnapped by the aliens in *Close Encounters* but also been held prisoner for years and subjected to a life of deprivation and constant fear.

Spielberg has lost none of his visionary intensity in *Empire*. His images are striking, so striking that they risk overwhelming the narrative with their incredible beauty. One scene is especially unforgettable: Jim standing in awe of a Japanese fighter plane, the night sky filled with a golden shower of sparks as he reaches out to caress it. The problem with such moments is that they undercut the story's emotional impact while we marvel at Spielberg's ability to stun us with his virtuosity.

While *Empire* was a big-budget bust at the box office, it amassed a host of critical kudos:

"*Empire of the Sun* is a grand adventure movie," gushed Vincent Canby. "It's also the best film ever made about childhood by a director born and bred in this country, where movie makers tend to take a safely revisionist view of childhood, one that's limited by expectations of what audiences want to believe about themselves."[83]

Raved Molly Haskell: "This is a tremendous breakthrough for Spielberg, and the smart money is on it as *the* enduring masterpiece of '87 [rather than Bertolucci's *The Last Emperor*]."[84]

"Spielberg . . . again proves he is our top picturemaker," said Richard Corliss. "He has energized each frame with an allusive legerdemain and an intelligent density of images and emotions. He has met the demands of the epic form with a mature spirit and wizardly technique. Spielberg has dreamed of flying before, and this time he earns his wings."[85]

Indiana Jones and the Last Crusade

"George and I shook hands when the Indy films began," Steven Spielberg recalled. "We agreed that, if the first one worked, we would do three."[86] Spielberg was disappointed with what they had wrought in *Indiana Jones and the Temple of Doom*, however, and was less than eager to make the third in the series.

"I wasn't happy with the second film at all," Spielberg confessed to Nancy Griffin. "It was too dark, too subterranean, and much too horrific. I thought it out-poltered *Poltergeist*. There's not an ounce of my own personal feeling in *Temple of Doom*." Indeed, Spielberg said he could be cajoled into making the third film only if besides living up to his agreement with George Lucas, it satisfied two reasons: a better script could be written than several versions he had seen, and this go-round would offer him the opportunity "to apologize for the second one. I wanted to make a movie I could stand naked on top of."[87]

"It wasn't until we maneuvered into the Grail myth, this father-son thing, that it became exciting to everybody," George Lucas said. "The real issue in the Grail legends is finding inner happiness, eternal satisfaction. The film is about a father and a son finding one another, rather than going after some specific thing. They find the Grail in each other."[88]

Spielberg and Lucas also decided to bring back the Nazis as the villains after being pilloried for their Third-World villains and victims in *Temple of Doom*. "We tried to make a film with other villains and we got attacked

George Lucas (wearing THX shirt) and Steven Spielberg (seated) ponder what to do next on the set of Indiana Jones and the Last Crusade, *their third collaboration in the popular series. (Courtesy of Steve and Nancy Gould.)*

from every which side," George Lucas said. "It's a very interesting problem that's come up. There are so many special interest groups now that no matter what you make a film about someone is going to be offended."[89] Presumably, the Nazis have no pressure group or public defenders.

Last Crusade's (1989) real coup, casting Sean Connery as Indiana Jones' professor father, was Spielberg's idea — one Lucas resisted until he saw the tough Victorian schoolmaster Connery became. "When Sean and Harrison arrived on the set," Spielberg told Richard Corliss, "everyone got quiet and respectful. The two are like royalty — not the royalty you fear because they can tax you, but the royalty you love because they will make your lives better."[90] And of course the series began with Spielberg and Lucas' desire to make a "James Bond-esque" adventure. How better to end than with James Bond himself?

As Pauline Kael observed, "He rags the two-fisted Indy as if he were still a kid, and uses paternal authority to outrank him — even to the point of slapping him in the face for using 'Jesus Christ' as a swear word. Professor Henry Jones, Sr., is the only man alive who isn't in awe of Indiana Jones."[91]

If *Last Crusade* continues its two predecessors' tradition of looting old movies, the film's opening both mocks that tendency and flaunts it. We see the young Indy (River Phoenix) in Monument Valley (hello, John Ford) dueling with a band of looters for a jeweled cross which he haughtily

Left to right: Spielberg with Harrison Ford and Sean Connery. Connery's portrayal of Henry Jones, Indiana's father, added a warmth and psychological depth to In-diana Jones and the Last Crusade that was missing from the two earlier films. (Courtesy of Steve and Nancy Gould.)

declares "belongs in a museum." Besides showing how Indy got his scar, his whip, his hat, his nickname, and his profession, the self-reflexive sequence directs us to recall the first film—and Indiana Jones' introduction to au-diences as an audacious looter.

Just as they developed visual sophistication from watching so many old movies, Spielberg and Lucas now expect it—and get it—from their au-diences. As Douglas Slocumbe, the director of photography for all three of Indy's adventures, says:

> A long time ago, you had to leave something on the screen for a good bit for people to grasp it. Now, with the visual experience of moviegoers, an image can actually have an impact in quite literally a few frames. It's amazing what the retina and the mind will accept and retain after just a few frames. Also, the continuity can make great jumps, with no need for comings and goings, without losing the audience.[92]

Although vowing that *Last Crusade* is his last Indy excursion, Spielberg says, "I've learned more about movie craft from making the In-diana Jones films than I did from *E.T.* or *Jaws*. And now I feel as if I've graduated from the college of Cliffhanger U. I ought to have paid tuition."[93] He adds, "It feels like the end of an era, and the end of a quest."[94]

Farewell to Peter Pan?

Stanley Kauffmann says of Spielberg, "He is right in the heart of an American generation that grew up with revised attitudes toward film and electronic media, with those media as refuge, as structures of self and fantasy before they even got to the function of communication. If Spielberg is what's called a post-literate, he has the strengths as well as the defects of post-literacy."[95]

In 1985, David Lean had this to say about his youthful admirer:

> He has this extraordinary size of vision, a sweep that illuminates his films. But then Steven is the way the movies used to be. He just loves making films. He is entertaining his teenage self—and what is wrong with that? I see Steven as a younger brother. I suppose I see myself in him.[96]

Once at the leading edge of the young lions in movie knowledge, Spielberg says:

> The generation now coming up was raised even more on movies than I was. All of my friends who are just beginning to make movies are incredibly well informed. They are almost film historians. They can talk circles around me about who did what.[97]

Spielberg now wants to make movies that are more mature, less readily identifiable as "a Steven Spielberg film." As he told one interviewer, "*E.T.*, *The Color Purple*, *Empire of the Sun*, and *Close Encounters*—I made those movies without having to think. It was like playing the piano with your eyes closed."[98]

Spielberg has the skills and the intelligence to grow, to make more and varied films. The question is why does he feel he should? Increasingly, he seems more and more infected by "Woody Allen's disease." He has nagging self-doubts about the superior popular entertainments he makes because they're not the sort of pictures Ingmar Bergman makes. Vincent Canby addresses this issue:

> The movies of Steven Spielberg . . . are designed for today's kid/adult audiences, but they are so full of wit and intelligence and even genuine feeling that they embrace others. It's Mr. Spielberg's unfortunate obsession to want to make "serious" movies like *The Color Purple*, without being aware that his adventure epic *Empire of the Sun* is as serious a film as any serious Hollywood director could hope to make.[99]

Pauline Kael, not always a fan of the "old" Spielberg, nonetheless prefers that model to the "new and improved" director, as she made clear in her review of *Last Crusade*:

> He must have begun to distrust his instincts—to think he was doing the wrong thing. Directors who made big commercial hits used to feel

guiltless, but Spielberg is too anxious, too well intentioned; he thinks it isn't good enough to give the audience pleasure. Trying to give it what he feels he owes it (wisdom), he softens and sentimentalizes the action. And, of course, he is being congratulated for his new, grownup approach. . . . Spielberg, who was perhaps the greatest of all pure, escapist movie directors, is being acclaimed for turning into a spiritual wimp.[100]

"Why all the pressure on Steven Spielberg to become a 'serious' director?" wrote one fan in the Letters column of *Premiere*, a film magazine. "Spielberg already is a great director — a legend in his own time — and he has nothing to prove. Let's hope that Spielberg doesn't turn his back on his ardent and loyal supporters just to attain more professional acceptance."[101]

Perhaps Spielberg should remember a statement he made in 1978: "I think that a lot of the people I'm meeting today are more concerned with getting people into the theater and hearing them laugh and scream and clap. Then, once in a while, they'll go out and make *The Red Desert*."[102]

But what about being Peter Pan? "Peter Pan didn't have courage," Spielberg now says. "I'm trying to grow up."[103]

Chapter 6
Martin Scorsese

Martin Scorsese was born in Flushing, New York, on November 17, 1942, the son of lower-middle-class Italian-American parents (his father, Charles, was a clothes presser). After his parents moved to Elizabeth Street, Scorsese grew up in the streets of New York's Little Italy. A sickly youth who suffered from asthma, pleurisy, and other ailments, Scorsese's poor physical condition barred him from playing stickball and city sports, isolating him from much real contact with other kids his age. He attended movies with his father as devotedly as he attended Sunday mass, and it's not hard to understand the appeal and the escape films represented for him — their almost religious significance in his early life.

"I just have a feeling," Scorsese said, "of how I loved films so much when I saw them as a child and growing, and how much they influenced me and my growing."[1]

Scorsese has spoken fondly of John Boulting's 1951 British film *The Magic Box* about cinema's early days:

> I saw it as a child. It was *the* film that taught me a lot about the magic of movies. (Specifically, it taught me how to do flip books.) The scene where Robert Donat shows Laurence Olivier his film is a scene that says everything about movies; it opened the whole magical quality of filmmaking. The magical and the mad: a man who would continue to try and try — at the expense of his family, his career, everything. The obsession of it! It makes you want to sign up. When you're eight years old, it makes you want to be a filmmaker.[2]

It was a small leap from watching films to wanting to capture their magic for himself. Significantly, he made "movies" long before he ever made "films." "The first thing I ever did was work with comic frames, not strips, because I couldn't flip them," Scorsese told Marjorie Rosen. "I put them through a piece of cardboard from which I'd cut a hole for the screen. I'd slip the pictures through individually. I did that from the time I was eight until I was thirteen. I colored them all in. It was a big production."[3]

Scorsese's youthful efforts continued, and he soon graduated to more ambitious projects:

At twelve, I did the costumes from *Quo Vadis*; I drew the pictures from the screen. And sometimes I'd copy the small pictures, B-pictures, which were small screen, which I'd transfer to a 3x4 box; I'd draw them in black and white, in ebony pencil, and sometimes I'd color them in sepia. Occasionally I'd copy a television show like *Danger*. . . . And I'd have credits such as "Hecht and Lancaster Presents. . . ." Sometimes I'd even do 3-D; every once in a while I'd paste a gun coming out of the frame, especially with the low-budget sepia-tone Westerns.[4]

Scorsese dropped his 3–D productions almost as quickly as Hollywood did when his parents thought he was cutting out paper dolls.

"I went to a preparatory seminary during my high school years in the late fifties, my *American Graffiti* years. And I became more interested in drawing pictures, and in film," Scorsese said. "I used to like a lot of spectacles, and I think that eventually I'm going to do one, one that has an added kind of humanity that would be accessible to people today."[5]

After attending Cathedral College for one year, the seminary for the New York Archdiocese, Scorsese transferred to Cardinal Hayes High School in the Bronx. When Fordham University denied him admittance because of his grades, he gave up the idea of becoming "an ordinary parish priest" and went to New York University (NYU). He soon changed his major from English literature to film communications and graduated with a B.S. in 1964; in 1966 he received his M.A. in the same field.

Film school was not an altogether satisfying experience for Scorsese:

They told us in film school that we had to like only Bergman. Now Bergman's good, but he isn't the only one. I discovered that I had liked most of the films those auteurist guys were talking about. I found . . . that you didn't have to reject totally the films you liked as a child. For three years I hadn't looked at American movies. I found that very damaging. *I had to catch up on TV.*[6] [Emphasis added.]

Scorsese stayed at NYU as an instructor, teaching a heavy load of production and film-theory courses. Filmmaker Allan Arkush was a junior at NYU film school in 1969 when he encountered Martin Scorsese. He and the other film students demanded that several courses be reserved solely for the film-school students rather than being open to the rest of the undergraduates. One of the first of the exclusive courses was Scorsese's American Movies. As Arkush remembered, "Those Tuesday afternoon classes changed my view of movies forever":

When it came to teaching film history, I have never seen his equal. Before every film, he'd pace in front of the class with Andrew Sarris' *The American Cinema* in one hand. He'd read off paragraphs or lists of pictures by a director. Then he'd act out scenes or shots from a movie and connect all the director's movies with an analysis of theme and style. It was unlike any other film history course I'd ever taken because it was being taught by a filmmaker, not a literature professor. Marty made me understand why as a child I had loved *Rio Bravo* and *The Horse Soldiers* and taught me how to love them all over again.[7]

Scorsese made a number of films while he was at NYU, notably *It's Not Just You, Murray!* and *Who's That Knocking at My Door?* (Originally titled *I Call First*). Heavily influenced by the French *Nouvelle Vague* (New Wave), both films are chockablock with self-conscious homages to French and American films.

Scorsese once admitted that there are many Truffaut shots that "I will never get out of my system. There's a shot in *Shoot the Piano Player* . . . [where] he cuts three times, coming closer each time. That shot's in every picture I make, and I don't know why."[8]

Scorsese has said of *Murray*:

> The film itself is a sort of . . . homage. . . . That is, film references were drawn from the structure of certain types of films, like *The Roaring Twenties* by Raoul Walsh. And the style is very important. *Murray* recalls the Warner Bros. films of the late thirties, early forties. . . . But within that structure I used actual stories about the neighborhood . . . intermixed with . . . the gangster filmmaking tradition [and] a touch of Fellini, whom I was very much influenced by at that time.[9]

In *It's Not Just You, Murray!* Scorsese abruptly cuts from a hospital scene to one which has Murray dancing in a big Busby Berkeley–style musical production. Another sequence begins with Murray talking to his boss but cuts to one where Murray and several other characters are dressed as circus clowns in a Felliniesque moment.

In *Who's That Knocking at My Door?* Scorsese's movie-crazy protagonist J.R. (Harvey Keitel) sees himself as a John Wayne hero and spends a long time discussing John Ford's *The Searchers* with a pretty girl he's trying to pick up (Zina Bethune). She insists she's never seen the movie, until suddenly:

> *Girl*: Oh, wait a minute! Was that the picture where Jeffrey Hunter's supposed to be trading Indian rugs, and he winds up trading for an Indian bride, and he doesn't know what to do with her?
> *J.R.*: Right! That's the picture!
> *Girl*: That was a good picture.
> *J.R.*: *Good*? That picture was *great*!

At a party in *Knocking*, when a man blasts a row of liquor bottles with a gun, Scorsese cuts to a photograph of John Wayne with a revolver and montage of stills from *Rio Bravo*, Howard Hawks' 1959 Western, which is almost as much a cult favorite as *The Searchers* (1956).

If *Who's That Knocking at My Door?* wasn't a great film, it nonetheless deserved to be shown commercially. After the film had been on the shelf for several years, a distributor of sexploitation films agreed to release

Martin Scorsese was heavily influenced by the French New Wave, especially direc-tor François Truffaut's 1960 film Shoot the Piano Player, *which contains a shot Scorsese uses "in every picture I make." (Courtesy of Steve and Nancy Gould.)*

Knocking if Scorsese would include a nude scene. Incredulous but willing, Scorsese flew Harvey Keitel to Amsterdam and shot a brief erotic sequence that had nothing to do with the rest of the picture.

After acting as an editor for the documentary *Woodstock,* Scorsese finally got his first real break when schlockmeister Roger Corman hired him to direct *Boxcar Bertha,* ostensibly a sequel to *Bloody Mama.* Scorsese discovered, as had Coppola, that Corman paid poorly, that his films were made on shoestring budgets, but also that they provided quick access to the industry. As long as Scorsese and Corman's other young directors didn't stray too far from the expected genre conventions, he left them alone.

When asked if *Boxcar Bertha* was valuable as a training ground for *Mean Streets,* Scorsese replied:

> Yes, definitely. It was *the* training ground. I couldn't have made this film without having made *Boxcar Bertha,* which I made in 24 days in Arkansas for Roger Corman. Roger taught me a lot.... We used practically the same crew that we used for *Boxcar Bertha.* We used the same ideas, the same fast-paced work, except for a different kind of film.[10]

Following the forgettable *Boxcar Bertha* (1972), Scorsese was having dinner with Jonathan Taplin, the road manager for The Band, who was eager to get into films. Scorsese showed him *Boxcar Bertha*, which Taplin liked, and then the script for a film he'd written years earlier with Mardik Martin, based on the opening of *It's Not Just You, Murray!* Taplin got the money together, and they made the picture — *Mean Streets*.[11]

Mean Streets

Ironically, because *Mean Streets* was made for just $350,000, it was shot in Los Angeles, not in the streets of Little Italy where it is set and where Scorsese grew up.

In *Mean Streets* Scorsese is clearly doing more than paying homage to other films, quoting from them more or less obviously. He is also using our awareness of older films and their images in our memories to comment upon the strange intertextual impact such linkages have on us. "The viewer is urged to observe the film's relation not to 'reality' but to the reality of films and their influence upon each other," Robert Kolker writes. "*Mean Streets* is a film, and by playing upon the various signs of its existence as film, it becomes a documentary not only of the fictive events, but of itself."[12]

At one point Charlie (Harvey Keitel) is lying in bed. Scorsese inserts three quick cuts, each moving us closer to Charlie's head. This is Scorsese's tribute to the triple cut in Truffaut's *Shoot the Piano Player*, the one he tries to use in all his films. Another scene has Charlie and Johnny Boy (Robert DeNiro) attending a 42nd Street showing of Roger Corman's *The Tomb of Ligeia*. When the two leave the theater, Scorsese places Charlie under a poster of *Point Blank*, a violent John Boorman gangster film. Lee Marvin's gun is pointed ominously at Johnny Boy's head, foreshadowing his fate.

Charlie sees *The Searchers* during one of his moviegoing excursions. Scorsese shows a clip from the Ford movie, the fight scene between Jeffrey Hunter and Ken Curtis. It was chosen, according to Stuart Byron, "after John Wayne declined to be seen in an R-rated film."[13]

In his "Guilty Pleasures" article, Scorsese wrote that *Night and the City* (1950, Jules Dassin) "was an important film for me in terms of background for *Mean Streets*. Richard Widmark is a character obsessed . . . panicked, desperate — like Charlie in *Mean Streets*. And he winds up ruined, like Charlie — doom on his face."[14]

In the climactic sequence where Charlie and Johnny Boy are shot (Scorsese played the assassin himself), a scene from Fritz Lang's *The Big Heat* intrudes — it's an image that Charlie's uncle Giovanni is watching on his television set. Allan Arkush said, "Looking back, one of the most

Charlie (Harvey Keitel, right) confronts Johnny Boy (Robert DeNiro) in Scorsese's homage-laden Mean Streets.

interesting aspects of [Scorsese's film] class was the connection between the movies Marty screened and the movies he made. The scene he reran in *The Big Heat* showed up in *Mean Streets* on a TV set."[15]

Scorsese, in addition to playing Shorty, the killer in the car, cast his mother in a small role (the woman on the landing). With a self-reflexive nod to *Boxcar Bertha*, that film's David Carradine plays a drunk who is gunned down by a hood played by his younger brother Robert Carradine.

Alice Doesn't Live Here Anymore

> Well, *Alice* has a great deal to do with homage to other films, too. A great deal. But at the same time, it was really a genuine attempt to try and understand the relationship between men and women.[16]

After making *Boxcar Bertha* for Roger Corman, Scorsese could have found himself unable to escape from the exploitation movie trap. After *Mean Streets* Scorsese was offered more gangster films, but he wanted to avoid that trap too. John Cassavetes, among others, advised him to make small personal films, films he could be proud of. Scorsese may also have

Diane Ladd (left) and Academy Award winner Ellen Burstyn as waitresses in Scorsese's "woman's picture": Alice Doesn't Live Here Anymore.

felt moved to demonstrate that he could make a film which was neither about Italian-Americans nor the Little Italy streets of his childhood.

His response was to make *Alice Doesn't Live Here Anymore* (1974). "This film attracted me, first of all because I respected Ellen Burstyn's talents and wanted to work with her," Scorsese told Marjorie Rosen. "Also because it was a challenge to make a picture about a woman as realistically and honestly as possible, yet a picture that would be fun as well."[17]

The film opens with credits appearing across satin and Alice Faye singing "You'll Never Know Just How Much I Love You," from *Hello, Frisco, Hello* (1943). Standing before an obviously studio-built farmhouse, a young girl — the young Alice — takes over singing the song. A tribute to *The Wizard of Oz* and all those movie-musical sets that stood in, however unconvincingly, for outdoor locales, Scorsese's $90,000 set is bathed by the red glow of the setting sun. Abruptly the viewer is thrust into "now" — Socorro, New Mexico.

"*Alice* is also a comment on old movies, on the women's pictures or 'handkerchief flicks' of the forties, such as Bette Davis' *Deception*," said Scorsese. "That's why we open the credits with script lettering on satin and have a stylized flashback of Alice as a girl. Eventually, at the end, the style of the picture becomes familiar to an old film and refers back to the beginning."[18]

Scorsese's famous opening sequence, both striking and audacious, serves two purposes: it is clearly yet another of his tributes to movies past, but it is also a (slightly heavy-handed) cautionary reminder that the past that we so lovingly evoke as if seen through rose-colored glasses is a fraud, a "never was."

Harvey Keitel made his obligatory appearance, playing Ben, the violent married man Alice has an affair with before settling down with Kris Kristofferson's David. Scorsese appears briefly in one diner scene, and Mardik Martin, the coscripter of *Mean Streets*, is a customer in the club during Alice's audition. Jodie Foster played the tomboyish Audrey and would return as the young hooker in *Taxi Driver*.

About the film's upbeat (for him) ending, Scorsese has said, "When [Alice] and the Kris Kristofferson character finally get together, it's happy, it's upbeat and romantic, but it's also a compromise. They both have problems to deal with, and each meets the other halfway and begins treating that person like a human being."[19]

Scorsese's direction of the actors was typically first rate, and Ellen Burstyn won the Academy Award for Best Actress for her performance.

Taxi Driver

I'm God's lonely man.
— Travis Bickle

After calling *Murder by Contract*, a 1958 film directed by Irving Lerner, "the film that influenced me the most," Scorsese said that "the spirit of *Murder by Contract* has a lot to do with *Taxi Driver*."[20]

Taxi Driver is Martin Scorsese's most controversial film — at least until *The Last Temptation of Christ* in 1988. The film was denounced for its ultraviolence and its journey into a sleazy world of pimps, prostitutes, rapists, assassins, and murderers. It was decried for supposedly suggesting a vigilante-style solution to the ills of the inner city. Whatever else it might be, *Taxi Driver* is a brilliant, unrelenting film; it is all but impossible to forget.

Taxi Driver's remarkable beginning, where a Checker taxi emerges from smoke as steam pours out of manhole covers as from a hellish netherworld and Scorsese dissolves to a close-up of a pair of eyes slowly moving back and forth, is perhaps derived from *The Conformist*, Bernardo Bertolucci's 1971 study of a disturbed young man, or from *In a Lonely Place*, a 1950 Nicholas Ray film.[21]

Taxi Driver's self-reflexivity is maintained in a very early scene where Travis passes a theater showing Tobe Hooper's 1974 cult classic, *The Texas Chain Saw Massacre*. *Massacre* seems to stand out, warning the viewer about the film's bloody climax.

When he filmed the taxi driver's violent outburst at the end, Scorsese followed Samuel Fuller's lead in *Park Row* (1952). Fuller's film contained a long tracking shot that began in an office, moved to another locale where a fight started that spilled out into the street, and ended up under a statue of Benjamin Franklin. "All in one shot," Scorsese marveled. "I used to watch that on TV when I was eleven or twelve." Scorsese valorizes Fuller's original by a tracking shot which follows Travis down a long corridor to the young prostitute's room.[22]

Not all the intertextual quotes were Scorsese's doing. Paul Schrader had many other written and filmic sources for his script. As he told Richard Thompson,

> Before I sat down to write *Taxi Driver*, I reread Sarte's *Nausea*, because I saw the script as an attempt to take the European existential hero, that is, the man from *The Stranger*, *Notes from the Underground*, *Nausea*, *Pickpocket*, *Le Feu Follet*, and *A Man Escaped*, and put him in an American context. There's a line in *Yakuza* which says, "When a Japanese cracks up, he'll close the window and kill himself; when an American cracks up, he'll open the window and kill somebody else." That's essentially how the existential hero changes when he becomes American.... Travis is just not smart enough to understand his problem. He should be killing himself instead of these other people.[23]

Schrader admits to a number of Bressonian elements in *Taxi Driver*: "The attention to detail, the *quotidienne*, the daily little things of one's life. The diary format [from *Diary of a Country Priest*, 1950], showing the writing." Schrader revealed that the "dress up" scene, in which Travis tries on all his new weapons, is from Bresson's *Pickpocket* (1959). Travis' breakfast of milk, bread, and apricot brandy is also from *Diary*, as is "I think I've got stomach cancer."[24] There were other, more mundane influences on Schrader. While he was in the hospital, he heard a Harry Chapin song called "Taxi," and Arthur Bremer shot George Wallace at a political rally.

The single, overriding intertextual element in *Taxi Driver*, however, is Scorsese and Schrader's reliance on the structure, theme, and a specific scene from John Ford's 1956 classic Western *The Searchers*. Stuart Byron insists (overemphatically, I believe) that "all recent American cinema derives from John Ford's *The Searchers*." Why does Byron think this? Because of *The Searchers*' impact on the young lions: Paul Schrader, Martin Scorsese, John Milius, Steven Spielberg, Michael Cimino, George Lucas, and others.[25]

Schrader admitted to Richard Thompson that *The Searchers* was one of a handful of films he tried to go back to regularly, including *Vertigo, An Autumn Afternoon, Tokyo Story, Pickpocket,* and *Diary of a Country Priest,* "to keep in mind what I'm striving for, and what can be done."[26] Scorsese, as noted in Chapter 1, also tried "to see it once a year."

Schrader, according to Stuart Byron, was initially reluctant to acknowledge that *The Searchers* was a prime influence on *Taxi Driver,* coming clean only after an Australian film scholar noted in *Film Heritage* that "the basic narrative and thematic structure of the two movies are virtually identical. . . ." In a letter to the magazine, Schrader confessed, "Although some of Mr. Boyd's points seem a little contrived, his [basic] point is valid. Scorsese and I agree that *The Searchers* is the best American film, a fact that must have influenced *Taxi Driver.*"[27]

According to Byron, neither Scorsese nor Schrader guessed that some viewers would see the *Taxi Driver's* overall resemblance to *The Searchers.* Apart from the similar structure of the two films, Scorsese and Schrader copied only one scene from the original:

> As Schrader told an audience at the Museum of Modern Art: "I wrote two scenes for the film . . . which I protested . . . [including] one for Harvey Keitel, when he dances with Jodie Foster. That one I protested because every other scene in the film is from the taxi driver's point of view. But Harvey was chafing and wanted more room to work, and Marty Scorsese wanted to give him another scene. So we made the rationalization that would be the 'Scar' scene. That's a reference to John Ford's *The Searchers.* I feel, and other people feel, that the one thing *The Searchers* lacks — and it is a great film — is a scene between Scar, the Comanche chief, and Natalie Wood, who's lived with him since she was kidnapped as a child. If Ford had had the guts to show that their life together had some meaning, it would have made the ending — when John Wayne 'rescues' her — bitterly sweet. So, too, in *Taxi Driver.*"[28]

In that scene longtime Scorsese associate Harvey Keitel gives a marvelously considered performance as Sport, Iris' (Jodie Foster) pimp. Keitel sweet talks his young ward while he enfolds her in his arms and slow-dances with her. He tells her how much he loves her and needs her love — how much he needs *her.* For a confused runaway from Pittsburgh, this tender attention is a magic elixir.

As for Travis, he "becomes a parody of John Wayne's Ethan Edwards in Ford's 1956 film *The Searchers,*" says Robert Kolker.

> Ethan is himself a figure of neurotic obsession, who wants to rescue his niece from the Indians because of his hatred of miscegenation and his desire to purify her and bring her back to white civilization. The equation — Travis Bickle as Wayne's Ethan; Iris as Natalie Wood's Debbie; and Sport as the Chief — is perfect. Travis believes in the rightness of his plan, as does his filmic forebear. What he does not see is that his whole notion of saving people is based on a movie cliché of heroic activity.[29]

Leo Braudy quotes Scorsese on Travis' mad obsession: He's "somewhere between Charles Manson and Saint Paul. . . . He's going to help people so much he's going to kill them." As Braudy observes, "Characters like Travis Bickle . . . dictate their own actions and responses by a world of film melodrama."[30]

At one point in the film, Travis picks up an obsessed man who pays for the taxi to sit outside an apartment building while he watches the silhouette of a woman inside who the man says is his wife. He tells Travis that "a nigger lives there" and that he's going to kill her with a .44 Magnum pistol. He asks Travis, "Did you ever see what it can do to a woman's pussy, cabbie?" The intense obsessive was played by Martin Scorsese himself. "The idea of that scene was that the man in the back seat would never kill anybody, but that the man in the front seat would," explained Paul Schrader. "John Milius tried to get Marty to have me play that role. I wouldn't have done it; Marty didn't ask, either."[31]

Schrader, however, saw the wisdom of collaborating with Scorsese. "I saw in Marty's work what I didn't have in the script: that sense of vibrancy, a sense of the city. What I think happened was that I wrote an essentially Protestant script, cold and isolated, and Marty directed a very Catholic film."[32]

Bernard Herrmann's score, as Charles Michener points out, operates on two levels. First, as a traditional movie score, it dramatically underscores and draws attention to the film's dramatic and emotional twists and turns, "clueing in" the listener through the established conventions of movie music. But "it heightens, by its very qualities as an old-fashioned movie score, the dreamlike nature of *Taxi Driver*, proclaiming it not a slice of life, but an exercise essentially in surrealism, a *movie*."[33]

Michener touches upon perhaps the most important structure in Scorsese's films: a dichotomous split between realism and artifice. Scorsese chooses gritty, realistic narratives and then constantly plays against those elements by subtly, and not so subtly, underscoring their essentially fantastic features. Scorsese films play with filmic conventions and normal narrative construction in ways that elevate his work to levels beyond the reach of many other young lions. A Lucas or Spielberg film will revel in its *movieness*, often making little attempt to disguise the gears and wheels. Coppola may make a film which works on several levels at once, but they are all conventional or generic levels, their self-reflexivity or intertextuality serving to link them to established norms. Scorsese's self-reflexivity, on the other hand, calls attention to itself, especially while situated in an otherwise "realistic" film (e.g., *Alice's* stylized, meant-to-be-seen-as-Hollywood-phony opening).

In this vein, Robert B. Ray sees *Taxi Driver* as a "corrected" Right film, the type of film generally aimed at a naive audience. (See the discussion of

In Taxi Driver, *director Scorsese (left) plays an obsessed man who pays to have Travis' (Robert DeNiro) taxi sit outside an apartment so he can spy on his wife.*

Coppola's *The Godfather*, in chapter two, for an explanation of Ray's theory.) The danger of correcting the Right stance was that any "corrections" stood a very good chance of appearing "arty" to the normal audience who patronized such films. Ray notes that Scorsese, Schrader, and DeNiro "together produced the most popular 'corrected' movie in the American Cinema since *Citizen Kane*."[34]

Scorsese, an ardent admirer of the New Wave and its filmmakers like Godard, copied Godardian ruptures in the narrative (the better to point out how cinema perpetuates certain ideological structures), yet he did so by so completely integrating them into his story that they lost the visibility Godard's interruptions possessed.

Ray notes that Scorsese's slow zoom-in on a glass of Alka-Seltzer until it filled the screen is a direct lift from Godard's *2 or 3 Things I Know About Her*. In Godard's film, however, the zoom took more than three minutes and reflected not the POV of the protagonist but a character lacking a role in the main narrative. Rather than prompting thoughts about the nature of subjectivity-objectivity, as Godard's shot did, Scorsese's shot underscores Travis' increasing solipsism. "By making his stylistic departures functional, therefore," writes Ray, "Scorsese kept the naive audience from seeing them as purposelessly 'arty.' In fact, narrative motivations rendered such departures largely invisible."[35]

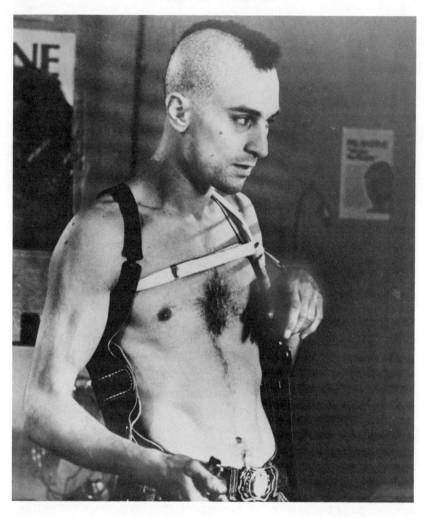

With his Mohawk haircut and his arsenal of handguns, Travis Bickle – "God's lonely man" – prepares for a bloodbath.

The "corrections" Ray speaks of come near the film's conclusion. All through the film Travis is seen as the typical individual hero, contrasted with various evildoers or impotent citizens. The audience is, through genre conventions of identification, clued to see Travis as a hero worth emulating. Then, says Ray, "*Taxi Driver* abruptly withdrew its sympathy for Travis with a single shot." Slowly panning up Travis' body, the camera arrives at his head – shaved in a Mohawk haircut. With that, Scorsese, Schrader, and DeNiro revealed that the hero the audience was manipulated into identifying with was insane. Scorsese made the audience pay for that mislaid trust in the character by being linked to Travis' final outburst of extreme violence.[36]

Those critics who missed the film's "corrections" believed it to be in the same class as the Michael Winner–Charles Bronson vigilante fantasy *Death Wish* (1974). These critics (according to Ray) did not understand that the violence, because it "punished" the audience for desiring it, was itself the primary correction.[37]

New York, New York

Before beginning production on *New York, New York*, Martin Scorsese did what he does so often — he went back to the films of the forties and fifties for inspiration: structure, pace, composition, cutting, color, and spatial manipulation.

> The pictures I ran were not artistic . . . [Scorsese said]. They . . . weren't very good. I was looking for how they made the hall look so big or . . . where do they cut people off in two shots. It's usually below the knee. . . . They never came in really tight, except for love scenes or their equivalent. So throughout *New York, New York* Jimmy Doyle and Francine Evans are always in the same frame together whether they like it or not.[38]

Scorsese said that *Lady in the Dark* (1944) "has influenced a lot of my movies. . . . The dream sequences are marvelous kitsch. I love the fantasy element. I love the Kurt Weill–Ira Gershwin songs. I screened it before shooting *New York, New York*, to look at the color and the use of lipstick, etc. Liza Minnelli was named after the Ginger Rogers character; her godfather was Ira Gershwin."[39]

According to Pye and Myles, Liza Minnelli's Francine was also based on the long-suffering June Allyson in *The Glenn Miller Story* (1954). George Cukor's 1954 *A Star Is Born*, with its story of a relationship rocked by the seesaw gyrations of the husband and wife's show-business careers and its vibrant use of color, strongly influenced Scorsese. Similarly, *Pal Joey*'s (1957) nightclub sequences contributed to Scorsese's handling of corresponding sequences in *New York*. As much as he liked some of the "stuff" in *Pal Joey*, Scorsese did not want to duplicate that film's happy-ever-after ending.

Scorsese also admits to being influenced by *My Dream Is Yours* (1949) and *The Man I Love* (1946). Both, he says, "are musical *films noirs* about night-club singers; they had a lot to do with *New York, New York*. When we asked Doris Day about *My Dream Is Yours*, she said, 'That's my life story.' The style, the color, the decor, I took it all for *New York, New York*. For the opening titles I wanted a New York skyline — the one from *The Man I Love*. We wound up painting the film."[40]

The strange studio-bound artificiality of the exteriors, which Scorsese foreshadowed with the rosy-lit nostalgic opening of *Alice*, is certainly in keeping with the happy-go-lucky, don't-take-this-too-seriously-folks attitude of the more traditional musicals of the forties, the non-*noir* ones, but it is in stark contrast to the supposedly "realistic" musical melodramas he consciously evokes.

Robert Kolker comments on Scorsese's sets:

> The forties interiors and the strange, almost abstract suggestiveness of the exteriors develop their own attraction; the control of the *mise-en-scene* seems to become more important than why that control is being exercised, so that the form threatens to refer only to itself. The viewer becomes aware not of *why* the studio sets are there (to evoke the atmosphere of the studio musical), only that they *are* there. And they are inconsistent. Most of the interiors . . . are conventionally "real." They look like interiors evocative of the forties, whereas the exteriors evoke not a time but the idea of studio sets.[41]

That Scorsese was after a stylized, unreal look seems beyond question, but it is still strange to hear him explain why he hired the man who designed *The Silver Chalice* (1954) and *Giant* (1956): "Any man who could design those two films . . . that's it, I had to have him. *The Silver Chalice*, which is a bad picture, has no authenticity. It's purely theatrical, and this is mainly due to the sets."[42]

By calling attention to the artifice, Scorsese, it seems, wants us to reexamine not only the relationship of such things to our understanding and appreciation of the film we're viewing but also to question the assumptions we bring to a forties-style movie musical. The sets, the Hollywood make-believe, are all conventional signposts pointing to a romantic happy ending; the reality of the relationship between Scorsese's two protagonists, however, suggests that no such happy ending is possible — or even desirable.

As Lawrence S. Friedman writes,

> A relentless anti-hero from the future, DeNiro's Jimmy Doyle is an alien in the tinsel and moonlight world of the 1940s. Scorsese has subverted the mythology of the big band musical by denying its basic assumption — the efficacy of romantic love. His New York conditioned by *Mean Streets* and *Taxi Driver*, as well as by Vincente Minnelli musicals, is finally, of the 1970s, a time when romantic reconciliations are barely possible.[43]

While Scorsese is a card-carrying member of the young lions, a postmodernist filmmaker, he is less concerned with commerce than his cohorts. Although Lucas, Coppola, De Palma, and Spielberg work variations on the directors, styles, and genres that influenced them as kids or student filmmakers, they rarely lose sight of their audiences. If they break new ground, they do so in a way which allows them to take the audience with them. This is not the case with Scorsese. He not only makes films primarily to please himself; he flaunts genre conventions with impunity. If we briefly examine the concept of genre, we can see why what Scorsese does in a film like *New York, New York* is not only bold and daring but dangerous and self-destructive — in a purely commercial sense.

Leland Poague cites Andrew Tudor's argument that genre is best served when it is used to describe audience expectations. Poague notes that genre, for Tudor, has very little to do "with characteristics of films but rather it serves to describe 'conceptions held by certain films.'"[44] Poague then posits that the genre of the work "is determined by reader expectation.... It is possible to understand almost any verbal or cinematic text as a 'literary construct.'"[45] Poague is saying that unless filmmakers and audiences share a horizon of expectations concerning the ways "intratextural or structural relationships" are assigned meaning and relevance, no meaningful communication between the parties can be expected. This is at the heart of what *genre* really refers to: audience expectations.

Although a genre audience's horizon of expectations demands that certain conditions be met, the audience may allow the writer and director the freedom to expand and test the boundaries of the genre. Stephen Schiff asserts that rather than being confined by genre restrictions, a good director, like Howard Hawks, for instance, could freely improvise like a "blues musician who could wring sublimity out of three chords and a standard 4/4 grove."[46]

After quoting Douglas Newton's assertion that "the musical film performs the important function of creating a modern myth," Mark Roth adds, "The importance of this cannot be overstated. The musical form is essentially ritualistic. It is meant to reaffirm faith — not to illuminate conditions or states of being."[47] Roth further posits that the "essence" of the musical is its similarity to a religious service or ritual. If the ritual is correctly followed and the proper conventions adhered to, then a happy, integrating ending must follow as surely as night follows day.

Similarly, Martin Sutton writes, "The musical is essentially a genre that concerns itself with the romantic/rogue imagination and its daily battle with a restraining, 'realistic,' social order. The battle grows out of a tension between realistic plot and spectacle/fantasy number.... The musical shows the brighter, more positive side [of the human soul] prevailing."[48]

In a sense, then, because it lacks the classic musicals' ritual function, *New York, New York* is a wedding without a bride or groom, a funeral without a body, or more importantly a church service without God. Given its willful flaunting of genre conventions, it's easy to see why *New York, New York* failed with audiences. Similarly, given its technical brilliance and its glossy professional sheen, it's also easy to see why many critics and dispassionate observers admire the film and its audacity.

When Jimmy Doyle (Robert DeNiro) and Francine Evans (Liza Minnelli) stand in studio snow in front of flat cutout trees, Scorsese is making
a powerful statement about the contrast between real life and our dreams,
but the mass audience (with the box office as proof)[49] rejected this dose of
cold-eyed reality. Robert DeNiro's Jimmy Doyle is in many ways a
superbly drawn character; he is also basically unlikable and a bit of a creep.
New York, New York did not deliver the genre goods the audience expected
and demanded.

"It is significant to [Scorsese]," says Chris Hodenfield, "that his dark,
schizo *New York, New York* opened a mere three weeks before *Star Wars*,
which, he says, 'brought about a whole new period of filmmaking.'"
Scorsese explains: "With the advent of *Rocky* and *Star Wars* and the
Spielberg pictures, on the best side they're morally uplifting. . . . And on the
worse side, they're sentimental lies. Lies. That's the problem. And where
I fit in there, I don't know."[50]

Raging Bull

Robert DeNiro had read Jake LaMotta's book *Raging Bull*, and he took
it to Scorsese and told him he wanted to play the role of the former champ.
Although Scorsese agreed, after the debacle of *New York, New York*, he
was dubious at best about the project's chances:

> And *Raging Bull*, I figured, was the end of my career. It was like a punch
> in the face. It was a violent movie that would shake them and make them
> feel something. Luckily enough, we got the money to make it because
> DeNiro was a star. I thought it was a swan song for Hollywood. By the
> time it was released in '80, I thought it was the end; that I was going to
> be living in New York and Rome, and I was going to make documentaries
> and educational films on the saints. I was going to make films for televi-
> sion, that sort of thing.[51]

One of the factors in helping Scorsese reach that sincere if over-
wrought conclusion was the release of *Rocky* in 1976. The effect of that
film's triumphal ending on audiences sent a shock wave through
Hollywood executives. Overnight, it seemed, the sort of daring and
dangerous films that directors like Scorsese often made were in danger. In
early 1989 Scorsese reflected to Chris Hodenfield what the change in atmosphere meant to him:

> Wiped out. Oddly enough, I like the ending of *Rocky*, myself. I don't like
> the picture that much, but I like the ending. I felt good. . . . But this is what
> scares me. You have films with happy endings . . . like *Rocky*. And then
> you have pictures that are a little more realistic and deal with certain emo-
> tions and psychological character studies, and they don't necessarily have

that uplifting effect. In the '50s through the '70s, they seemed to exist together. Now, it seems that some films don't even have a right to exist.[52]

When DeNiro began working out with fighters to get in shape for the role, Scorsese filmed the training sessions in 8mm, showing the footage to his good friend British director Michael Powell (*The Red Shoes*, *Peeping Tom*). After viewing the footage, Powell frowned and said to Scorsese, "But the gloves are *red*."[53] Scorsese was bothered by his friend's observation. Even at that time he was involved with the problems of preserving color films in the face of their gradual fading. In a 1980 letter to *Film Comment*, Scorsese wrote, "My own work has been severely affected, in that *New York, New York* was made to look like a Technicolor imbibition film. Within five years, its color will have faded beyond any recognition of the original concept, and the film will suffer for that loss. My present film, *Raging Bull*, was shot in black-and-white in order to avoid the color problem entirely."[54]

Scorsese's decision to film *Raging Bull* in black and white was both correct and commercially sound. The film *feels* right to anyone whose primary memories of the LaMotta era come from black-and-white newsreels and the technically primitive Friday night fights that began on NBC in 1946. The black-and-white also distinguished the film from several other boxing films released around the same time — *Rocky II*, *The Champ*, and *The Main Event*. "We just wanted to be different, to have a different look," Scorsese said.[55]

The film's second unusual departure was Robert DeNiro's decision to gain over 50 pounds to play the retired champ. "It was Bobby's idea," Scorsese told Thomas Wiener. "And when he told me about it, I thought it was great." Shooting wrapped in August and did not resume until November — when the transformed DeNiro was ready. "We did have to be careful; Bobby would get tired pretty easy from carrying that weight," Scorsese said.[56]

There is one shot of LaMotta in a jail cell restlessly tossing and turning on a cot that Scorsese may have filmed specifically to show off DeNiro's bulging beer belly as he lies shirtless on the covers. After all, it would be pointless for DeNiro to have gone through the ordeal if the effect could have been gotten by padding. Only by showing us his swollen flesh could the actor validate his stunt. And *stunt* is the right word. There's nothing about the later scenes that demanded DeNiro's unusual preparation for the role. But as a stunt, it was perfect: when people remember the film, they say, "Yeah, that's the black-and-white movie about the fighter — the one Robert DeNiro gained all that weight for."

Coming on the heels of *Rocky* and *Rocky II*, which between them earned rentals of $100 million, Scorsese faced his old nemesis once again —

Raging Bull *(voted the best film of the 1980s by a poll of film critics) was one of director Scorsese's (left) and actor DeNiro's most fruitful teamings. DeNiro played Jake LaMotta in Scorsese's black-and-white filming of the boxer's story.*

the limitations and constraints of the genre film. Luckily for Scorsese, the vehicle he'd chosen allowed him to have it both ways. Since the film was biographical, Paul Schrader and Mardik Martin's script could incorporate certain stock elements (like the mob and their demand that LaMotta throw a fight to get a chance at the title) because they were part of the boxer's history. Having paid lip service to the generic conventions, Scorsese was again able to present us with an alienated loner, self-destructive to the point of obsession.

The winning of the title, an event which happens in the middle third of *Raging Bull*, is usually seen as the Holy Grail in the average boxing film, achieved at great personal cost and sacrifice in a bitterly contested prizefight our hero wins against all odds. In Scorsese's antiheroic narrative, the title is won, lost, and all but forgotten as LaMotta's life spirals down a black hole of pointlessness.

"*Raging Bull* particularly seems to be a direct response to *Rocky*," observes Leo Braudy, "similarly contemplating the boxer in working-class and lower-middle-class Italian-American culture. In contrast to the sweet color melodrama of *Rocky*, it is shot in a lusciously harsh black-and-white neo-realist documentary style."[57]

"I don't think Scorsese knows very much about boxing," writes David Thomson. "The fight scenes are as fanciful as they are brutal. Scorsese settles for closeups cross-cut, turning every fight into a confrontation of movie manner — whereas real fights are relationships that demand the two-shot style Scorsese understood in *New York, New York*."[58]

Raging Bull's sound track is one of Scorsese's most thoughtful. In the ring, especially, the punches land like mortar shells, and the sounds of the flashbulbs and the bell are also exaggerated. Scorsese uses period music like "Big Noise from Winneka," and "Bye Bye Baby" carefully. The score's theme music, by Pietro Mascagni, is surprisingly close to "Over the Rainbow" in its melody and orchestration.[59]

Unlike many of Scorsese's protagonists, LaMotta by film's end is neither defeated nor transformed; he has survived. He goes forth to meet an audience in his second career as a stand-up comedian. After his title defense, which he lost to Sugar Ray Robinson, he has been brutally beaten — but he has not been knocked down. "Hey, Ray — I never went down. You never got me down," he taunts the new champ.

The King of Comedy

"In 1970 I saw a *David Susskind Show* on autograph hunters, and thought, My God, they're just like assassins," recalled Paul D. Zimmerman, who wrote the script for *The King of Comedy*. "I also read a piece in *Esquire* about a guy who kept a diary of talk-show hosts as though they were his friends. I began to imagine the possibility of one of these fringe people developing in his head a personal relationship with a television personality, and then their getting together somehow."[60]

Scorsese was making *Alice Doesn't Live Here Anymore* when he first read Zimmerman's script. "I didn't go for it. Didn't understand it," he told Carrie Rickey. After sending the script to Robert DeNiro as a matter of course, Scorsese began to see connections between Rupert Pupkin and himself. "I realized Rupert's an extension of me inasmuch as he'd do *anything* to get what he wanted. When I realized he was to comics as I was to movies, I understood. Rupert reminds me of the hunger I had in the sixties."[61]

Since Zimmerman's script for *King* precedes 1976's *Taxi Driver* by two years, it is a remarkable coincidence how much the two films and their two obsessed protagonists, Rupert Pupkin and Travis Bickle, resemble each other. Both men are influenced by media images so compelling and real to them that the images induce the two socially estranged loners to act out a violent (less so in Rupert's case) fantasy—which leads ultimately to a lionization by the media itself.

Leo Braudy notes that "Rupert Pupkin emerges from prison for kidnapping the talk-show host to discover that he has become a celebrity.... In *The King of Comedy* [Rupert] is a stand-in for all those in the audience who want to be celebrated merely for being themselves."[62] While *The King of Comedy*'s ironic developments do not "punish" the audience as they do in Scorsese and Schrader's *Taxi Driver* by implicating them in horrific vigilante violence, they may compel the audience to question its complicity in accepting mass-media images and ideas as reality. Scorsese does this in many ways. One of the first was to cast Jerry Lewis as Jerry Langford, the talk-show host whom Rupert eventually kidnaps. Had Scorsese been successful in convincing Johnny Carson to play the role (which he refused for obvious reasons—the danger of life imitating art), he would have given the story an effective but almost too self-reflexive spin. With Jerry Lewis, a celebrated film comedian and telethon host, Scorsese is able to pit the contrasting images not only against each other but against themselves.

Scorsese uses three sequences in particular to subvert our ideas about reality and fantasy. First, the film begins with the opening of a typical edition of *The Jerry Langford Show*. The mimesis of *The Tonight Show* is uncannily complete. The titles are superimposed over a curtain. The announcer, Ed (Herlihy), is shot standing in exactly the same position Ed McMahon stands, and the camera angle is precisely the same. Jerry walks out after the curtain rises to reveal him, accepts the cheers of the audience, and banters with the bandleader—again, located in the same position of the band and bandleader on the Carson show (later, the role of Jerry's producer is played by Frederick de Cordova, Carson's producer). As Jerry begins his monologue, Scorsese cuts to Rupert and a horde of autograph seekers waiting outside the studio on the streets of New York. The opening of *The Tonight Show (Starring Johnny Carson)* is so much a part of American popular culture that while the movie audience must get to know Rupert Pupkin, they already know Jerry-Johnny by virtue of his coming into our living rooms and bedrooms for over 20 years.[63]

The second sequence, in which Jerry and Rupert have lunch, begins with absolutely no visual or other "qualifiers" or clues to its fantasy nature. The scene simply shows the two men eating lunch in a restaurant and being interrupted by autograph seekers and fans while Jerry begs Rupert to take over the show for six weeks. Scorsese emphasizes the standard Hollywood shot–reverse shot pattern, developed as part of the classical paradigm of "invisible" construction. Jerry, on the left, is seen from Rupert's general perspective and over Rupert's left shoulder; Rupert, on the right, is seen from Jerry's general perspective and over his right shoulder. This naturalization of the narrative is meant, in classical Hollywood cinema, to

Scorsese's The King of Comedy *starred Jerry Lewis (left) as Jerry Langford, a talk-show host, and Robert DeNiro as Rupert Pupkin, an obsessive fan and would-be star. This lunch sequence turns out to be a fantasy of Pupkin's.*

hide the presence of the filmmaker and to ensure that the audience accepts the fictional events as real. Suddenly Scorsese cuts to Rupert in his basement, still talking to Jerry, still upholding his end of the conversation. Scorsese cuts back to Jerry, still in the fantasy setting, and back to Rupert again. Rupert is then shown occupying Jerry's previous position, in the basement, replying to himself. Just as filmmakers (like Martin Scorsese) do, Rupert has constructed an elaborate scene which is unreal, a fantasy. Rupert is simultaneously creating the fantasy, acting in it, and consuming it as a spectator since the standard shot–reverse shot visuals posit the viewpoint of an audience or a camera, not someone within the shot.

The third sequence is similar to the second in that it is another fantasy of Rupert's. Standing in front of a huge black-and-white photograph of an audience applauding and laughing, Rupert delivers the monologue he's written for Jerry's staff. Since most of Rupert's delivery is inaudible to us, we concentrate on the increasingly loud laughter of the noncorporeal audience. As the level of hilarity increases to near hysteria and the laughter becomes distorted, the camera slowly tracks backward. Finally Rupert is observed from the rear of a long tunnellike corridor, dwarfed by this image of people laughing at some unseen moment of comedy, their distorted faces and imagined voices subsumed by his solipsistic fantasy.

In another scene Scorsese reveals that Pupkin has arranged his base-ment to resemble the set of *The Jerry Langford Show*, going so far as to populate it with life-size cardboard cutouts of Liza Minnelli and Jerry Lewis. Then he acts out a phony show-biz conversation with them, right down to responding to one of the cutout's jokes with loud, forced, talk-show laughter.

Scorsese's choice of Liza Minnelli and Jerry Lewis (playing Jerry Langford in the digesis) is interesting and intertextual. Minnelli had played the role of Francine Evans in *New York, New York*, which also starred Robert DeNiro. As for Jerry Lewis, in addition to the associations he brings to his casting, his 1963 film *The Nutty Professor* was a favorite of Scorsese's, one that he showed to his NYU students. As Allan Arkush noted,

> "Don't ya see, don't ya see?" [said Scorsese]. "Buddy Love is Dean Martin. Professor Kelp is Jerry Lewis. The movie is a result of Jerry's years in psychoanalysis. He wants to be Dean Martin and Jerry Lewis at the same time. This is the greatest multiple personality movie ever made." Most of the class thought Marty had gone too far; I thought he was right. I . . . have spent more than a few hours defending Jerry Lewis from his detrac-tors. I've incurred the wrath of Jerry haters everywhere, but I've also seen *The King of Comedy* three times.[64]

To blur the distinction between film and video further, Scorsese shot most of *The King of Comedy* as if he were shooting *The Jerry Langford Show*. The sets are lit evenly and brightly, giving the film the flat, low-contrast look of most television shows. Whether shooting interiors or ex-teriors, Scorsese keeps the camera at eye level, the TV paradigm, and his editing is classical shot–reverse shot takes.

Although Harvey Keitel is absent from *The King of Comedy*, almost all of Scorsese's stock company make appearances. Diahnne Abbott plays Rita, and members of Scorsese's family have small roles. Catherine Scorsese, Scorsese's mother, plays the off-screen voice of Rupert's mom; Charles Scorsese, his father, plays a man in Rita's bar; Cathy Scorsese, his daughter, plays Dolores, an autograph seeker in Rupert's fantasy; and Scorsese plays Jerry's TV director. Longtime Scorsese coscripter Mardik Martin plays the "second man" at Rita's bar.

The idea of celebrity-confusing reality and fantasy is compounded by the fact that various celebrities play "themselves," thereby validating at least one thesis of the film. Ed Herlihy plays himself, as the Ed McMahon–like announcer of *The Jerry Langford Show*. Tony Randall, as "Tony Randall," guest-hosts Jerry's show, which has as its guests Dr. Joyce Brothers and Victor Borge.

The King of Comedy's final link to *Taxi Driver* is provided by the two films' endings. In each, a media-deranged man acts on his delusions. Then, after paying for his acts (Travis is wounded and hospitalized; Rupert is convicted of kidnapping and serves nearly three years in prison), each man is misunderstood by the media forces he misunderstood.

Much more satisfyingly than in *New York, New York*, Scorsese reveals the filmmaker's strings and forces the audience to confront the dichotomy between fantasy and reality in the images they watch so willingly.

The Last Temptation of Christ

> This film is not based on the Gospels but upon [Nikos Kazant-zakis'] fictional exploration of the eternal spiritual conflict.
> — Opening of *Last Testament*

> I thought for one second I wasn't gonna make it. But Ididit Ididit Ididit!
> — Martin Scorsese[65]

Scorsese has spoken about his parents, their feelings for the Catholic church, and his deeper, more religious values:

> My parents grew up Americans, Italian-Americans. Their idea was survival; my father went to work when he was nine years old; there was hardly room to sleep; you had to fight . . . with your brothers and sisters for food and attention. . . . It was survival. And I don't think the church figured into their life that much. Italian-Italian Catholics . . . say "We're really pagans . . . in the good sense. We enjoy life, we put the church into a certain perspective." My parents were able to do that. When the church wanted to delve into personal lives, how many children they should have, my parents shied away from that. They figured that wasn't any of the priest's business. *I* was the one who took the church seriously.[66]

When asked about Nikos Kazantzakis' 1955 novel on which the film is based, a book Barbara Hershey gave him to read in 1972 when they were making *Boxcar Bertha*, Scorsese said, "It took me six years to finish it! I'd pick it up, put it down, reread it, be enveloped by the beautiful language of it, then realize I couldn't shoot the language. I read most of it . . . in October 1978. And that's when I realized this was for me."[67]

Scorsese and Schrader's Christ, as taken from the novel, derives from Kazantzakis' representation of Christ as a man yearning to attain God and the author's fascination with the "merciless battle between the spirit and the flesh." Says Scorsese of Kazantzakis' philosophical examination of this idea: "I don't say the concept . . . is *the* truth, but it is a fascinating idea. In Kazantzakis' depiction, Jesus wrestles with the human side of His nature as he comes to terms with the God within Him. Because of His dual nature, human and divine, every moment in His life is a conflict and a victory."[68]

"I was taught in Catholic schools, where the emphasis is on the divine," said Scorsese. "I was always curious about Jesus' human side. I remember reading a lot about it in the Gospels—his anger at Peter, and in Matthew where he curses the fig tree. The priests and nuns would say, 'That's the human side' and quickly go on to the divine. And I'd want to stop and say, 'But wait! What about the human side? That's what interests me!'"[69]

Richard Corliss, among others, noted *Last Temptation's* structural similarity to Scorsese's earlier works, "buddy" films like *The Color of Money* and *Mean Streets*. In the latter, Robert DeNiro's Johnny Boy and Harvey Keitel's Charlie have a strange symbiotic relationship based on friendship, a sense of neighborhood, and friendly rivalry. For years Scorsese had projected that DeNiro would play Jesus to Keitel's Judas when he was finally able to make *Last Temptation*, and it would have been a nostalgic pairing for the two *Mean Streets* actors. Jesus (Willem Dafoe) and Judas, two men from the "neighborhood," plot their intertwined destinies, each needing the other to fulfill the role he has chosen to play.[70]

If the relationship between Jesus and Judas is evocative of *Mean Streets*, Schrader and Scorsese's Jesus is not unlike Rupert Pupkin in *The King of Comedy*. Just as Pupkin connives with Masha to perform a spectacular and attention-getting media stunt, so does Schrader and Scorsese's Christ connive with Judas to perform a no less attention-getting act to get the celebrity he believes he is fated for.

As he is dying on the cross, Jesus allows himself to be rescued by a guardian angel in the guise of a young girl. No longer required to die for humanity as their "messiah," Jesus marries, and fathers several children. Dying after a long and conventional family life, Jesus is confronted by an angry Judas, who shouts "Traitor! Your place was on the cross!" Realizing that the angelic little girl was really Satan in disguise, Jesus is allowed to take up his place on the cross and die for humanity's sins.

"To a filmwise viewer, the cumulative effect of all this resembles nothing so much as an inverted variation on Frank Capra's *It's a Wonderful Life*," says *Variety's* reviewer "Cart." in a startling but perceptive analysis. "Jesus is made to see that it is only by dying that his life will make a difference, that he cannot forsake his Father and future supporters because of his own acknowledged selfishness and unfaithfulness."[71]

Kazantzakis used the "demotic" speech of everyday Greeks rather than the "puristic" speech of Athenian intellectuals. Schrader and Scorsese also relied on less exalted forms of speech, allowing their characters to speak in rough, unsophisticated American accents. "Schrader said this to me," Scorsese reported. "'Unless you have them speaking in ancient Aramaic with subtitles, whoever stands behind the camera is going to be doing his 'wrong' idea of the time. You'll do your wrong idea. I'd do my wrong idea. Twenty years ago George Stevens did his wrong idea.'"[72]

Scorsese (left) directing the controversial The Last Temptation of Christ. *The film starred, left to right from the center: Barbara Hershey as Mary Magdalene, Willem Defoe as Jesus, and longtime Scorsese collaborator Harvey Keitel as Judas.*

Schrader's script was extensively tinkered with by Scorsese and former *Time* movie critic Jay Cocks. Scorsese and Cocks' reworking of Schrader's already deliberately low-key dialogue either gives Jesus and his speech back to the common people or results in prosaic renderings of vivid King James version speeches: "Uh, I'm sorry, I'm going to tell you a story," Jesus apologetically and fumblingly begins his Sermon on the Mount. Later, when Jesus tells the strong and activist Judas that he must betray him, he tells him, "You have the harder job."

Scorsese was more conventional in choosing to have the Romans — and Satan, via the little guardian angel — played by British actors, like David Bowie's dryly cynical Pontius Pilate. "Anyone from outside is going to sound different," Scorsese said. "And anyone in authority should have a British accent. It sounds authoritative to American ears."[73]

When asked about the scene in Mary Magdalene's brothel, Scorsese said it had two purposes: to show Jesus' proximity to the real world, including sex, and to show what Mary goes through, what she suffers. "The scene isn't done for titillation; it's to show the pain on her face, the compassion Jesus has for her as he fights his sexual desire for her. He's always wanted her."[74]

Finally, given all the controversy, Scorsese was asked if his Jesus really is divine, if he personally believed that to be true:

> He's God. He's not deluded. I think . . . the movie says that, and I know I believe that. The beauty of Kazantzakis' concept is that Jesus has to put up with everything we go through, all the doubts and fears and anger. He made me *feel* like he's sinning — but he's not sinning, he's just human. As well as divine. And he has to deal with all this double, triple guilt on the cross. That's the way I directed it . . . because my own religious feelings are the same. I do a lot of thinking about it, a lot of questioning, a lot of doubting, and then some good feeling. A lot of good feeling. And then a lot more questioning, doubting![75]

Made by a True Believer, a film artist whose movies may not always succeed as much as he would prefer, *The Last Temptation of Christ* is a deeply honorable film that raises questions of faith and doubt in ways few other such films have. Like all Martin Scorsese films, it exhibits the strengths and flaws of his personal vision, a vision influenced by films, television, and novels but also by religion and philosophy.

Scorsese ponders his future and the future of the sort of films he wants to continue making:

> It's very hard for me to do the uplifting, transcendental sentimentalism of most films because it's not true. And it's not because I'm this great prophet of truth — it's just like embarrassing to do it on the set. There's no doubt we've got the problem that movies are considered mainly to be escapism. You want to have fun. I even shirked, let's say, from seeing every Bergman picture after a while. It was like doing homework. I prefer the escapism of fantasy, rather than the escapism of incredible sentimentality. What I'm afraid of is pandering to tastes that are superficial. There's no depth anymore. What appears to be depth is facile character study. But they're making a product, and a product's gotta sell. And what sells is fantasy and sentimentality. You've gotta make money. And you make money [by] giving the audience what the hell they want![76]

Still, it's hard to imagine that Martin Scorsese won't continue to make films that go against the popular grain, that often frustrate audience expectations. But perhaps not. When an audience sees "a Martin Scorsese film," they probably know by now to expect the unexpected, to be prepared to confront ideas and emotions they would rather not confront. The would-be priest or gangster will continue to make his "small," quirky, angst-filled films.

Chapter 7
The Not-So-Young Lions

America after World War II was a vastly different country from the one the old guard in Hollywood grew up in and made films for. The rise of television and rock and roll, combined with a baby boom and a period of unprecedented prosperity, sowed the seeds for the youth culture that would blossom in the sixties and seventies. The old producers and directors, once young lions, had made wonderful films, but they were not the films the young postmodern generation wanted to see. Like their audiences, the five young lions grew up in a postmodern culture which immersed them in radio, comic books, movie serials, B movies, rock-and-roll music, television, and cartoons. Hollywood needed new directors badly — but where to find them?

One way of intensifying the effects of postmodern popular culture is to consume great hunks of it. As we have seen, most of the five young lions were not social lions in high school. Coppola was "funny-looking, not good in school, nearsighted," and unable to meet girls. Lucas had hot-rodder friends, but he started out in high school being not all that different from *American Graffiti*'s Terry the Toad. De Palma was the neglected third son of a self-absorbed and hysterical mother, a "science type" always up in his room with computers and other electronic gear. Spielberg, full of fears and phobias, was a nerd and so physically inept that the other boys in his gym class called him "the retard." Scorsese's asthma and pleurisy kept him off New York's mean streets; while his peers played stickball, he made movies from comic strips and pieces of paper. The lions had to develop inner resources like imagination and active fantasy lives to enliven their otherwise deprived childhoods. When they became adult filmmakers, rather than growing out of their youthful obsessions, they valorized these childhood themes and the genres that had presented them.

The lions' postmodern sensibilities are clearly shown in the music videos and other short films they've made in addition to their feature films. De Palma has done several videos, including the Frankie-goes-to-Hollywood video "Relax" featured in *Body Double* and Bruce Springsteen's "Dancing in the Dark." Scorsese directed Michael Jackson's "Bad" video, first shown on CBS in 1987 with great fanfare. Lucas and Coppola also teamed up with Michael Jackson and Disney to produce and direct *Captain Eo*, a short 3-D film seen at Disneyland.

Following the lead of Francis Ford Coppola, the young lions, wrote J. Hoberman, "elevated drive-in monster movies, Abbott and Costello–style slapstick, rock 'n' roll musicals, Saturday-morning science fiction—the most vital and disreputable genres of their youth—to cosmic heights."[1]

The young lions invested these genres, long considered to be moribund or beneath contempt, with the nostalgic glow of their childhood obsessions. Observes Hoberman:

> Following Godard, the movie brats brought an unprecedented degree of celluloid erudition to their creations. Films swarmed with allusions to *Psycho* and *The Searchers*, not to mention *Rebel Without a Cause, Forbidden Planet*, and *The Wizard of Oz*. Unlike Godard, however, the young American directors did not see this sort of intertextuality as part of a larger cultural critique. Rather than deconstruct the Hollywood system, their most successful movies strove to resurrect its greatest triumphs. As Marx did to Hegel, they stood Godard on his head.[2]

As filmmakers, the young lions blended—as did musicians, artists, architects, designers, and writers—high and popular art to create their postmodern filmic visions. Composed of repetition, pastiche, parody, and homage, their postmodern films borrowed from high and low, from directors like Lean, Kurosawa, Hitchcock, Ford, and Godard. Spielberg filmed a high-budget monster movie called *Jaws*, changing forever the idea of the "summer movie," and drew praise for his Lean-like epic *Empire of the Sun*. Both Coppola and Lucas, in *The Godfather* and *Star Wars*, borrowed liberally from Kurosawa but also from the gangster and SF genres. De Palma films such as *Sisters, Dressed to Kill*, and *Obsession* are virtual compendiums of Hitchcock techniques and shots. Spielberg and Lucas echo Fordian themes and obsessions (even to the point of shooting in Monument Valley) but lack Ford's sense of community. And Martin Scorsese owes much to Ford and Godard as well as all the lesser-known noir craftsmen he emulates.

If we return to my interpretation and expansion of Stanley Fish's idea of interpretive communities, we might posit that Coppola belongs to the Roger Corman (horror, B films, exploitation cheapies) "family" and foreign (Kurosawa, Antonioni) interpretive communities. Lucas could be said to belong to the popular-culture, foreign (Kurosawa), comics, nostalgia, and style-design interpretive communities. De Palma seems closest to the Alfred Hitchcock, horror-film, and popular-culture interpretive communities. Spielberg could belong to the TV, popular-culture, TV-film, family, suburban (middle-class values and aspirations), and David Lean interpretive communities. Finally, Scorsese, very much a New Yorker, might be said to belong to the New York City–urban, family, close-knit group, and Italian-American interpretive communities.

While the young lions raid genre films and classics alike for their narrative structures and visual styles, they often overlook other elements in the films of the older directors, shortchanging things like humanity and warmth. David Denby compares several of the young lions to Kurosawa and observes their shortcomings in comparison:

> What Spielberg and Lucas and their followers seem to have gotten from the great Kurosawa (whom they sincerely adore) is his incredibly active frame, his way of taking the spectator right into the middle of whatever he's dramatizing. What they haven't picked up — how could they? — is Kurosawa's understanding of tradition as a tragic burden as well as a standard; the astounding heartbreaking iron pride of his heroic style; his love of Shakespeare, Dostoevsky, Gorky, as well as his own culture. In other words, they haven't absorbed any of those elements that make a charge frame and physical excitement the fulfillment of a genuine dramatic conception.[3]

The young lions would not have had the chance to flaunt their postmodern borrowings, their film-school and late-night-TV knowledge of films and filmmaking, had they not come along at just the right moment. They shouldered their way through a briefly opened door of opportunity to enter the previously closed Hollywood film industry in the late sixties and early seventies, seizing the opportunity presented them by Hollywood executives seeking to satisfy an increasingly elusive — and younger — audience. In 1977, only 13 percent of movie tickets were purchased by people over 40; 57 percent were bought by young people under 25.

Knowing the tastes and cinematic sophistication of the young audience through their own adolescent and film-school-directed experiences, the young lions were well placed to fulfill the needs and desires of the new interpretive communities that longed for movies about teenagers and teenage heroes, that wanted escapism and thrills and spectacle writ large (Lucas, for one, learned to make commercially safe films like *American Graffiti* and *Star Wars*, not "downers" like *THX 1138*). It is therefore not surprising that the decline of genres like Westerns and melodramas was accompanied by a corresponding rise in the popularity of genres like SF, horror, fantasy, and brainless comedy — all favorites of the under-25 set. The young lions, well versed in these genres and aware of the sea change in Hollywood, prospered. *American Graffiti, Jaws, Rocky, Close Encounters of the Third Kind, Animal House, The Godfather, Star Wars,* and *Star Trek: The Movie* were among the highest-grossing films of the seventies.

Because they were exposed to a steady diet of classic Hollywood films in addition to the requisite number of "Art films," the postmodern auteurs were ready when Hollywood, still reeling from the excesses of the ill-considered youth movement of the sixties, beckoned in the early seventies. As Richard Corliss observed,

> If young people were to be entrusted with the millions to make a movie, they'd better be people with a strong conservative streak. And who better than kids from a university? They've learned their craft, they've delivered on time, they've worked under supervision — and they've grown up watching old movies. If we're lucky (the moguls thought), they'll do just what we want: make *new* old movies. Sure enough, when the scholars seized the asylum from the lunatics, they specialized in slick homages to traditional Hollywood genres.[4]

As Corliss says, the young lions' styles are clearly conservative and in line with the classical Hollywood cinema's paradigms. Francis Ford Coppola has admitted the limitations, limitations he ascribes to the need to hedge one's bets financially and to the audience's desire for certain types of films:

> Understand one thing. Essentially, all movies coming out — whether it be *The Exorcist*, Bergman, *The Godfather*, or *Pound* or *Putney Swope* — all movies are basically done in the same way. If you were to take the most stylistically divergent films — an Elvis Presley film and *Cries and Whispers* — they represent a teenie, teenie bit of what can happen with movies. Movies are all made the same way and the reason they're made the same way is because the audiences want them that way. The films cost so much that to really veer from that way of telling a story, you have to be independently wealthy and subsidize it.[5]

In Stanley Fish's view, "If a community believes in the existence of only one text, then the single strategy its members employ will be forever writing it." Having joined the postmodern pastiche and classical Hollywood communities via television, comic books, popular culture, and film school, the young lions are forever rewriting those texts.[6]

Unfortunately, the very conservatism that made the film-school graduates, those from USC in particular, so appealing to the Hollywood executives, all but guaranteed that their films would reflect their cautious and unimaginative approach to moviemaking. With numbing regularity, the USC graduates have produced a body of work that tends toward the derivative and the lightweight — genre movies appealing primarily to adolescents or to those with undemanding tastes: *Grease, Alien, Romancing the Stone, Conan the Barbarian, Star Wars,* and *Jaws.*[7]

Even the lightweight movies some of them make are pale imitations of their unassuming predecessors. Technically proficient and more comfortable with special effects than the older directors, some of the film-school generation have looked back at the classic science-fiction and horror films they grew up with and said, "If someone like me, with enough money and special-effects talent and technology behind him, remade those creaky old movies we love so much, they'd *really* be something." Well, the postmodern auteurs' remakes of *The Thing*, *Invasion of the Body Snatchers*, *King Kong*, and others, while having all the gee-whiz SFX one could ask for, lacked several essential ingredients: imagination, meaningful stories, and characters worth caring about. Similarly, when several of the brats produced their homage to the old *Twilight Zone* television series, the result, *Twilight Zone: The Movie*, was a mess.

Perhaps more than anything else what *some* of the young lions learned in film school was a facile lesson: the triumph of style over substance.

In the seventies, with the star system in disarray and pundits pontificating over the dearth of real movie stars, the lions and their cohorts became the stars of their films. They became "brand name" directors. Now instead of going to see the new "John Wayne" or the new "Jimmy Stewart," audiences went to see the new "Brian De Palma," "George Lucas," or "Steven Spielberg" at the corner Roxy. (This is not to suggest that directors like Ford, DeMille, or Hitchcock were not star directors.)

Nothing lasts forever, however, and the baby boomers are aging. Those in the first wave are in their forties, and those bringing up the rear are in their twenties; as all the help-wanted signs on the fast-food restaurants attest, the number of teenagers is at a low level compared to the boom times of the seventies. This means the "youth market" is not the monolithic mass it once was. As their primary audiences age, along with the not-so-young lions themselves, the former movie brats must go with the demographics or face slowly falling box-office receipts for their once massively popular youth films.

The maturing of the lions is clearly under-way. De Palma may still make escapist fare like *The Untouchables*, but it is higher-class escapism, escapism with a human face. *Casualties of War* displays a new awareness of adult themes and concerns. De Palma has apparently learned that his camera can still swoop, pan, glide, and circle his actors, but now his vaunted visual sophistication serves a meaty adult story. Of all the lions, given his past record, De Palma has the most potential for growth. He is a director whose abilities with a motion-picture camera are without equal — unless one mentions Steven Spielberg.

Spielberg seems to have forgotten all about Peter Pan. He realizes finally that all is not nice in the world; he realizes that everything is not part of one huge middle-class suburb. With *The Color Purple*, Spielberg began his process of growing up. His version of Alice Walker's novel presented us with noble black victims living in a pastel-colored Disneyized version of the Deep South. But it was a beginning. Spielberg followed this first step with a much more mature, self-assured attempt to show the darker side of life, *Empire of the Sun*. When he returned in 1989 to his popcorn days with the third Indiana Jones film, his new maturity showed in even this melodrama. Like De Palma, Spielberg has the tools if only he'll use them.

Coppola, whose early career suggested he might be the one to invest stale genre formulas with larger issues and darker undertones, seems moribund — almost dead in the water. In *Tucker* one could see flashes of the old Coppola, the Coppola of *The Godfather*. But Coppola, having stumbled a number of times with glossy, high-tech teen melodramas, seems to have lost his way. Prodigiously talented, Coppola also seems to be prodigiously spendthrift in his career choices. Indeed, when the second edition of Robert Phillip Kolker's influential *Cinema of Loneliness* was published in 1988, he had replaced his chapter on Coppola with one on Spielberg, arguing that Coppola's early prominence was no longer justified. His contribution to *New York Stories* was bloated and embarrassing, glossy but emotionally empty. One hopes that with the release of *Godfather III*, a return to the subject matter of his earliest and greatest success, Coppola will find his way again.

Scorsese, once content to tease his audiences by skewering genre-film expectations, now explores questions like the relationships between faith, duty, and self. With *The Last Temptation of Christ*, he continues to make personal films but films which challenge and goad us to think about things we'd rather not think about.

George Lucas, now exclusively a producer, seems to have few choices in front of him. If he returns to directing, it may be at the helm of a new *Star Wars* film. If he does not return to directing, it seems that his eventual fate (and wish) is to become the next Walt Disney. With *Star Wars* attractions already drawing crowds at Disneyland, Lucas could conceivably continue to spin off toys, games, video games, books, and amusement park rides for the next 10 or 20 years. If he gets behind a camera to direct or simply returns to more active filmmaking, it is questionable whether he has either the will or the ability to create more mature works.

The young lions are all the same . . . and different. As Brian De Palma said in an interview,

> Marty Scorsese and I are basically very urban kids. You know, brought up in the city. Marty went to NYU; I went to Columbia. We actually went around the city on subways and saw all kinds of weird and strange things when we were very young. Steven, you know, is sort of a product of Hollywood. George is sort of a product of northern California, as Francis is. So we all come from really different worlds and our movies are very much a part of us. And even although we all like each other and respect each other's movies, they're all very different.[8]

Francis Ford Coppola, Brian De Palma, George Lucas, Steven Spielberg, and Martin Scorsese are the result of growing up in postmodern America, the products of a film-school and/or a late-night-TV-revival exposure to the whole history of the classical Hollywood film. Responsive to their audience because they and their audience are as one and gifted with strong commercial instincts, the young lions have done much to shape modern Hollywood.

If we continue to exist in a postmodern period, as I believe we do, it may nonetheless be argued that the social and political structure that nourished the lions is undergoing changes, some minor and some radical. The aging baby boomers are, despite the almost anomalous success of a comic-book hero fantasy like 1989's *Batman*, turning away from the genre films of their youth and toward films which reflect their increasingly family-oriented perspectives.

Sensing the change, the lions are beginning to respond to the new circumstances. Having changed Hollywood films in the seventies, the lions have a chance to do the same in the nineties, to be a part of the new maturity. For the same things still apply. The lions are part of one of the largest population cohorts in American history. The baby boomers are moving through American culture like a pig through a python. If the "gray lions" understand this and can adapt their moviemaking to accommodate the changes in society, we'll be going to their films for a long, long time.

Notes

Chapter 1

1. Susan R. Suleiman, "Introduction: Varieties of Audience-Oriented Criticism," in *The Reader in the Text*, ed. Susan R. Suleiman and Inge Crosman (Princeton: Princeton University Press, 1980), p. 33.

2. Todd Gitlin, "Hip-Deep in Post-modernism," *New York Times Book Review*, 6 November 1988, p. 1.

3. Gitlin, p. 35.

4. Gitlin, p. 36.

5. Frederic Jameson, "Postmodernism and Consumer Society," in *The Anti-Aesthetic: Essays on Postmodern Culture*, ed. Hal Foster (Seattle: Bay Press, 1983), p. 112.

6. Jameson, p. 114.

7. Jameson, pp. 115–116.

8. Jameson, pp. 116–117.

9. Arthur Kroker and David Cook, *The Postmodern Scene*, 2nd ed. (New York: St. Martin's Press, 1988), p. 268.

10. Kroker and Cook, p. 270.

11. Marlaine Glicksman, "Bravo Longo," *Film Comment*, 25, no. 2 (March-April 1989), p. 43.

12. Rick Woodward, "Film Stills," *Film Comment*, 25, no. 2 (March-April 1989), p. 51.

13. White, p. 39.

14. Mike Steele, quoted in *Twenty All-Time Great Science Fiction Films*, Kenneth Von Gunden and Stuart H. Stock (New York: Arlington House, 1982), p. 185.

15. Richmond Crinkley, "The Ark of the Cinemate," *Film Comment*, 21, no. 4 (July-August 1985), pp. 76–77.

16. Richard Koszarski, "The Youth of F. F. Coppola," *Films in Review*, 19, No. 9 (November 1968), 529.

17. Francis Coppola and Gay Talese, "The Conversation," *Esquire Film Quarterly*, July 1981, p. 84.

18. Maureen Orth, "Godfather of the Movies," *Newsweek*, 25 November 1974, p. 76.

19. Dale Pollock, *Skywalking, The Life and Films of George Lucas* (New York: Harmony, 1983), p. 23.

20. Pollock, p. 17.

21. Steven Spielberg, "The Autobiography of Peter Pan," *Time*, 15 July 1985, p. 62.

22. Spielberg, p. 63.

23. Michiko Kakutani, "The Two Faces of Spielberg – Horror vs. Hope," *New York Times*, 30 May 1982, p. 30.

24. Michael Pye and Lynda Myles, *The Movie Brats, How the Film Generation Took Over Hollywood* (New York: Holt, Rinehart and Winston, 1979), p. 145.

25. Laurent Bouzereau, *The DePalma Cut* (New York: Dembner Books, 1988), pp. 16–17.

26. Diane Jacobs, *Hollywood Renaissance* (Cranbury, NJ: A. S. Barnes, 1977), p. 123.

27. Pye and Myles, pp. 189–190.

28. Pollock, pp. 47–48.

29. Pierre Maranda, "The Dialectic of Metaphor," *The Reader in the Text*, ed. Susan R. Suleiman and Inge Crosman (Princeton: Princeton University Press, 1980), p. 188.

30. Maranda, p. 193.

31. Richard Corliss, "The Seventies: The New Conservatism," *Film Comment*, 16, no. 1 (January-February 1980), p. 35.

32. Corliss, p. 35.

33. Pye and Myles, pp. 86–87.

34. Pollock, pp. 46–47.

35. Michael Pye and Lynda Myles, "The Man Who Made *Star Wars*," *The Atlantic*, March 1979, p. 47.

36. Audie Bock, "Kurosawa," *Take One*, March 1979, p. 34.

37. Stuart Byron, "The Searchers: Cult Movie of the New Hollywood," *New York*, 5 March 1979, p. 45.

38. Byron, p. 46.

39. Byron, p. 46.

40. Susan Braudy, "Francis Ford Coppola: A Profile," *Atlantic* 238, no. 2 (August 1976), p. 69.

41. Stephen Farber, "Coppola and *The Godfather*," *Sight and Sound*, 41, no. 4 (Autumn 1972), p. 219.

42. Audie Bock, "George Lucas: An Interview," *Take One*, May 1979, p. 4.

43. Pollock, p. 45.

44. Pollock, p. 52.

45. Stephen Farber, "The USC Connection," *Film Comment*, May-June 1984, p. 34.

46. Bock, "Lucas," p. 4.

47. Joel S. Zuker, *Francis Ford Coppola, A Guide to References and Resources* (Boston: G. K. Hall, 1984), p. 6.

48. Corliss, p. 35.

49. Farber, "USC," pp. 34–35.

50. Farber, "USC," p. 38.

51. Farber, "USC," p. 35.

52. Jamie Diamond, "Film School Confidential," *American Film*, 14, no. 9 (July-August 1989), p. 39.

53. John Caughie, ed. *Theories of Authorship* (London: Routledge & Kegan Paul, 1986), p. 9.

54. Stephen Crofts, "Authorship and Hollywood," *Wide Angle*, 5, no. 3 (1983), p. 20.

55. Roland Barthes, "The Death of the Author," *Theories of Authorship*, ed. John Caughie (New York: Routledge & Kegan Paul, 1986) pp. 212–213.

56. Wolfgang Iser, "The Reading Process: A Phenomenological Process," *The Implied Reader* (Baltimore: Johns Hopkins University Press, 1974), p. 274.

57. Iser, p. 275.

58. Iser, p. 278.

59. Iser, p. 280.

60. Iser, p. 282.

61. Robert Crosman, "Do Readers Make Meaning?" in *The Reader in the Text*, ed. Susan R. Suleiman and Inge Crosman (Princeton: Princeton University Press, 1980), p. 154.

62. Stanley Fish, "Interpreting the *Variorum*," *Critical Inquiry*, 2, no. 3 (Spring 1976), pp. 485–486.

63. Hans Robert Jauss, "Literary Theory as a Challenge to Literary Theory," *New Literary History*, 2, no. 1 (Autumn 1970), pp. 18–19.

64. Jauss, p. 19.

65. Suleiman, p. 36.

66. Suleiman, pp. 44–45.

67. David Bordwell, Janet Staiger, and Kristin Thompson, *The Classical Hollywood Cinema, Film Style & Mode of Production to 1960* (New York: Columbia University Press, 1985), p. 367.

68. Bordwell, Staiger, and Thompson, p. 5.

69. Bordwell, Staiger, and Thompson, p. 59.

70. Helen Starr, "Putting It Together," *Photoplay*, 14 no. 2 (July 1918), p. 54; quoted in Bordwell, Staiger, and Thompson.

71. Kristin Thompson, *Breaking the Glass Armor* (Princeton: Princeton University Press, 1988), p. 21.

72. Bordwell, Staiger, and Thompson, p. 372.

73. Bordwell, Staiger, and Thompson, pp. 373–375.

Chapter 2

1. Joel S. Zuker, *Francis Ford Coppola, A Guide to References and Resources* (Boston: G. K. Hall, 1984), p. 1.

2. Diane Jacobs, *Hollywood Renaissance* (Cranbury, NJ: A. S. Barnes, 1977), pp. 97–98.

3. Maureen Orth, "Godfather of the Movies," *Newsweek*, (25 November 1974), p. 76.

4. Brian De Palma, "The Making of *The Conversation*," *Filmmakers Newsletter*, 7, no. 7 (May 1974), p. 34.

5. James Monaco, *American Film Now* (New York: Oxford University Press, 1979), pp. 332–333.

6. Joseph Gelmis, *The Film Director as Superstar* (Garden City, NY: Doubleday, 1970), p. 179.

7. Gelmis, *Superstar*, p. 179.

8. De Palma, p. 34.

9. Zuker, p. 2.

10. Robert K. Johnson, *Francis Ford Coppola* (Boston: Twayne, 1977), pp. 24–25.

11. Richard Koszarski, "The Youth of F. F. Coppola," *Films in Review*, 19, No. 9 (November 1968), p. 530.

12. Johnson, p. 27.

13. Johnson, p. 37.

14. Stephen Farber, "Coppola and *The Godfather*," *Sight and Sound*, 41, no. 4 (Autumn 1972), 219.

15. Farber, 219.

16. Koszarski, 531.

17. Gelmist, *Superstar*, p. 180.

18. Johnson, p. 32.

19. Farber, 220.

20. Johnson, pp. 43–44.

21. Jeffrey Chown, *Hollywood Auteur: Francis Ford Coppola* (New York: Praeger, 1988), p. 4.

22. Chown, pp. 9–10.

23. Gelmis, "Superstar," pp. 182–183.

24. Johnson, p. 46.

25. Jacobs, p. 103.

26. Farber, 219.

27. Susan Braudy, "Francis Ford Coppola, a Profile," *The Atlantic*, 238, No. 2 (August 1976), p. 70.

28. Gelmis, *Superstar*, p. 184.

29. Farber, 220.

30. Johnson, p. 64.

31. Zukor, pp. 5–6.

32. Michael Pye and Lynda Myles, *The Movie Brats* (New York: Holt, Rinehart and Winston, 1979), p. 81.

33. Johnson, p. 71.

34. Farber, 220.

35. Zuker, p. 6.

36. Johnson, p. 73.

37. Pye and Myles, p. 85.

38. Monaco, p. 328.

39. Pye and Myles, p. 82.

40. Zuker, p. 6.

41. Bock, "Lucas," p. 5.

42. Gelmis, *Superstar*, p. 188.

43. Farber, 223.

44. Monaco, p. 339.

45. Joseph Gelmis, "Merciful Heavens, Is This the End of Don Corleone?" *New York*, 23 August 1971, p. 52.

46. Puzo, p. 58.

47. "The Making of the Godfather," *Time*, 13 March 1972, p. 59.

48. *Time*, "Making of," p. 60. When making *Star Wars*, George Lucas would fight virtually the same battles with *his* crew and cinematographer (Gilbert Taylor).

49. Gelmis, "Merciful Heavens," p. 53.

50. *Time*, "Making of," p. 61.

51. Robert B. Ray, *A Certain Tendency of the Hollywood Cinema, 1930–1980* (Princeton: Princeton University Press, 1985), p. 327.

52. Ray, p. 328.

53. Ray, pp. 331–332.

54. Jonathan P. Latimer, "*The Godfather*: Metaphor and Microcosm," *Journal of Popular Film*, 2, no. 2 (Spring 1973), 206.

55. Arthur Schlesinger, Jr., "The Godfather Plays on Our Secret Admiration for Men who Get What They Want," *Vogue*, May 1972, p. 54.

56. Ray, p. 331.

57. Latimer, 205.

58. William S. Pechter, "Keeping Up with the Corleones," *Commentary*, 54, no. 1 (July 1972), pp. 88–90.

59. George De Stefano, "Family Lies," *Film Comment*, 23, No. 4 (July-August 1987), p. 24.

60. Ray, pp. 335–336.

61. Clarens, p. 289.

62. Ray, p. 336.

63. John Hess, "*Godfather II*: A Deal Coppola Couldn't Refuse," *Jump-Cut*, no. 7 (May-June 1975), reprinted in *Movies and Methods*, ed. Bill Nichols (Berkeley: University of California Press, 1976), p. 83.

64. Ray, pp. 346–347.

65. Francis Ford Coppola, "*Godfather, Part II* (Nothing Is a Sure Thing)," *City*, 7, no. 54 (11–24 December 1974), p. 36.

66. Zuker, p. 10.

67. *Variety*, 11–17 January 1989, p. 58.

68. Marjorie Rosen, "Francis Ford Coppola," *Film Comment*, 10, no. 4 (July-August 1974), p. 45.

69. Joan Buck, "*Godfather II* Probes Family's Roots," *Women's Wear Daily*, 18 June 1974, p. 28.

70. Hal Aigner and Michael Goodwin, "The Bearded Immigrant from Tinsel Town," *City Magazine*, 12–25 June 1974, p. 36.

71. Jon Carroll, "Coppola: Bringing in the Next Godfather," *New York*, 11 November 1974, p. 98.

72. Mario Puzo, "Dialogue on Film," *American Film*, 4, no. 7 (May 1979), pp. 43–44.

73. Carroll, p. 98.

74. It was a critical success, however, and won six academy awards: best picture, best director, best supporting actor (DeNiro), best screenplay (adapted from other material), best art direction–set decoration, best original dramatic score.

75. Ray, p. 335.

76. William Murray, "*Playboy* Interview: Francis Ford Coppola," *Playboy*, July 1975, p. 58.

77. Hess, pp. 86–87.

78. Rosen, p. 44.

79. G. Roy Levin, "Francis Coppola Discusses *Apocalypse Now*," *Millimeter*, 7, no. 7, (October 1979), pp. 137–138.

80. John Gallagher, "John Milius," *Films in Review*, 32, no. 6 (June-July 1982), 360–361.

81. Richard Thompson, "Stoked," *Film Comment*, 12, no. 4 (July-August 1976), p. 11.

82. Zuker, p. 11.

83. Thompson, p. 15.

84. David Bordwell, Janet Staiger, and Kristin Thompson, *The Classical Hollywood Cinema, Film Style & Mode of Production to 1960* (New York: Columbia University Press, 1985), p. 375.

85. Gilbert Adair, *Hollywood's Vietnam* (New York: Proteus Books, 1981), p. 148.

86. Ray, p. 57.

87. John Hellmann, "Vietnam and the Hollywood Genre Film: Inversions of

American Mythology in *The Deer Hunter* and *Apocalypse Now*," *American Quarterly*, 34, no. 4 (Fall 1982), p. 430.

88. Veronica Geng, "Mistuh Kurtz—He Dead," *New Yorker*, 3 September 1979, p. 70.

89. Hellmann, p. 430.

90. Hellmann, p. 431.

91. George Grella, "Murder and the Mean Streets: The Hard-Boiled Detective Novel," in *Detective Fiction: Crime and Compromise*, ed. Richard Stanley Allen and David Chacko (New York: Harcourt Brace Jovanovich), p. 423.

92. Frank Rich, "The Making of a Quagmire," *Time*, 27 August 1979, p. 57.

93. Richard Grenier, "Coppola's Folly," *Commentary*, 68, no. 4 (October 1979), pp. 69–70.

94. Adair, pp. 165–166.

95. Chown, p. 145.

96. Grenier, p. 73.

97. Greil Marcus, "Journey up the River," *Rolling Stone*, 1 November 1979, p. 56.

98. Gallagher, 361.

99. Mike Bygrave and Joan Goodman, "Meet Me in Las Vegas," *American Film*, October 1981, p. 41.

100. The reason *Apocalypse Now* nearly bankrupted Coppola and forced him to mortgage his property was that he presciently put his own money into it in return for the copyright, hoping to reap future profits from cable TV, broadcast TV, and foreign distribution rights—which he did in abundance when that film became a success. Chown, p. 159.

101. Zuker, p. 13.

102. Bygrave and Goodman, p. 41.

103. Aljean Harmetz, "Coppola Buys Studio for $6.7 Million," *New York Times*, 21 March 1980, sec. C, p. 9.

104. Haller, p. 23.

105. Chown, p. 158.

106. David Ansen and Martin Kasindorf, "Coppola's Apocalypse Again," *Newsweek*, 16 February 1981, p. 79.

107. Ansen and Kasindorf, p. 79.

108. Haller, p. 23.

109. Sheila Benson, *Los Angeles Times*, 22 January 1982, Calendar, p. 1.

110. Chown, pp. 160–161.

111. David Ehrenstein, "The Aesthetics of Failure," *Film Comment*, 19, no. 3 (May–June 1983), p. 47.

112. "Coppola's ulcer-free indifference to living at the financial brink is due in part to the fact that 'he has an earning capacity of maybe three to five million dollars a year,'" according to Robert Spiotta. "'If everything goes up in smoke, Francis can go out and sell his services for that much.'" Bygrave and Goodman, p. 43.

113. Carroll, p. 98.

114. Braudy, p. 73.

115. Kroll, p. 81.

116. Jill Kearney, "Francis Ford Coppola Simply Wants to Create a Whole New Art Form," *Mother Jones*, 13, no. 7 (September 1988), p. 22.

117. Kearney, "Coppola," p. 22.

118. Kearney, "The Road Warrior," *American Film*, 13, no. 8 (June 1988), p. 52.

119. *Variety*, 11–17 January 1989, p. 76.

120. Braudy, p. 20.
121. Pye and Myles, p. 111.

Chapter 3

1. Larry Sturhahn, "The Filming of *American Graffiti*," *Filmmakers Newsletter*, 7, no. 5 (March 1974), p. 22.
2. Stephen Farber, "George Lucas: The Stinky Kid Hits the Big Time," *Film Quarterly*, 27, no. 3 (Spring 1974), pp. 8-9.
3. Sturhahn, p. 22.
4. Aljean Harmetz, "Burden of Dreams, George Lucas," *American Film*, 8, no. 8 (June 1983), p. 34.
5. Harmetz, p. 34.
6. Farber, "Stinky Kid," pp. 2-3.
7. Dale Pollock, *Skywalking, The Life and Films of George Lucas* (New York: Harmony Books, 1983), p. xvi.
8. Farber, "Stinky Kid," pp. 3-4.
9. Pollock, p. 43.
10. Pollock, p. 44.
11. Pollock, p. 46.
12. Lucas and fellow Kurosawa admirer Francis Ford Coppola persuaded 20th Century-Fox to advance the director $1.5 million for the right to distribute *Kagamusha* outside Japan, thereby assuring that the film would be made, according to Tom Buckley ("At the Movies," *New York Times*, 3 October 1980, sec. C, p. 18).
13. Pollock, p. 53.
14. Audie Bock, "George Lucas: An Interview," *Take One*, May 1979, p. 4.
15. Stephen Farber, "The USC Connection," *Film Comment*, 20, no. 3 (May-June 1984), p. 38.
16. Mitch Tuchman and Anne Thompson, "I'm the Boss," *Film Comment*, 17, no. 4 (July-August 1981), p. 53.
17. Pollock, p. 42.
18. Bock, p. 4.
19. Bock, p. 4.
20. Bock, p. 4.
21. Bock, p. 5.
22. Jean Vallely, "The Empire Strikes Back," *Rolling Stone*, 12 June 1980, p. 32.
23. Pollock, p. 92.
24. Tuchman and Thompson, p. 53.
25. Pollock, p. 92.
26. Pollock, p. 95.
27. Paul D. Zimmerman, "Future Shock," *Newsweek*, 29 March 1971, p. 98.
28. Pollock, p. 91.
29. Ernest Callenbach, "Short Notices," *Film Quarterly*, Summer 1971, inside back cover.
30. Vallely, p. 32.
31. Harmetz, p. 34.
32. Farber, "Stinky Kid," p. 5.
33. Vallely, p. 32.
34. Vallely, p. 32.
35. Michael Pye and Lynda Myles, *The Movie Brats* (New York: Holt, Rinehart and Winston, 1979), p. 120.

36. Pye and Myles, p. 121.
37. Sturhahn, p. 22.
38. Vallely, p. 32.
39. Sturhahn, p. 20.
40. Farber, "Stinky Kid," p. 2.
41. Sturhahn, p. 24.
42. Morris, p. 10.
43. James Monoco, *American Film Now* (New York: Oxford University Press, 1979), p. 169.
44. Sturhahn, p. 24.
45. Pollock, p. 115.
46. Monoco, p. 169.
47. Farber, "Stinky Kid," pp. 6–7.
48. Farber, "Stinky Kid," p. 2.
49. Frederic Jameson, "Postmodernism and Consumer Society," *The Anti-Aesthetic: Essays on Postmodern Culture* (Seattle: Bay Press, 1983), pp. 115–116.
50. Sturhahn, p. 22.
51. Marc Le Sueur, "Theory Number Five: Anatomy of Nostalgia Films: Heritage and Methods," *Journal of Popular Film*, 6, no. 2 (1977), p. 193.
52. Pye and Myles, p. 122.
53. Farber, "Stinky Kid," p. 4.
54. Bock, p. 6.
55. Stephen Zito, "George Lucas Goes Far Out," *American Film*, April 1977, p. 13.
56. Harmetz, p. 36.
57. Paul Scanlon, "The Force Behind George Lucas," *Rolling Stone*, 25 August 1977, p. 43.
58. Harmetz, p. 36.
59. Zito, p. 10.
60. Scanlon, p. 43.
61. Maranda, p. 192.
62. D.J.R. Bruckner, "Joseph Campbell: 70 Years of Making Connections," *New York Times Book Review*, 18 December 1983, p. 27.
63. James Joyce, *Finnegans Wake* (New York: Viking Press, 1939), p. 581.
64. Campbell, p. 30.
65. Campbell, p. 256.
66. Zito, p. 10.
67. Scanlon, p. 45.
68. *Time*, 30 May 1977, pp. 57–58.
69. Pollock, p. 169.
70. Pollock, p. 181.
71. John Williams, "Themes," *Star Wars* album liner notes (Los Angeles: 20th Century Records, 1977).
72. Scanlon, p. 48.
73. Pye and Myles, *The Movie Brats*, p. 137.
74. Harlan Jacobson, "The Seventies: exhibition," *Film Comment*, 16, No. 1 (January-February 1980), p. 42.
75. Jane Feuer, "Reading *Dynasty:* Television and Reception Theory," *South Atlantic Quarterly*, 88, no. 2 (Spring 1989), p. 446.
76. Tony Bennett, "Texts and Social Processes: The Case of James Bond," *Screen Education* (Winter/Spring 1982), 9.

77. Zito, p. 10.

78. Monoco, p. 170.

79. Zito, p. 12.

80. Pye and Myles, *The Movie Brats*, p. 136.

81. Denis Wood, "The Stars in Our Hearts: A Critical Commentary on George Lucas' Star Wars, *Journal of Popular Film*, 6, no. 3 (1978), 278–279.

82. George Morris, "George Lucas' *Star Wars*," *Take One*, July-August 1977, p. 9.

83. Terry Curtis Fox, "Star Drek," *Film Comment*, July-August 1977, p. 9.

84. Schiff, p. 36.

85. Wood, 274–275.

86. Pollock, p. 173.

87. Harmetz, "Burden of Dreams," p. 33.

88. Tuchman and Thompson, p. 53.

89. David Ansen, "The Raider of Lost Art," *Newsweek*, 23 May 1988, p. 70.

90. Harmetz, p. 33.

91. Ironically, when *Star Wars* appeared, many critics commented upon its similarity to a Walt Disney film—the sort of Walt Disney film the studio seemed unable to make anymore in the seventies and early eighties. Now, however, while Disney has found its way back to its original formula (*Roger Rabbit* and *Honey, I Shrunk the Kids*), the studio also makes harder-edged adult fare like *Down and Out in Beverly Hills*, recognizing the changing audience in ways Lucas seems unable to.

Chapter 4

1. Michael Bliss, *Brian DePalma* (Metuchen, NJ: Scarecrow Press, 1983), p. 138.

2. David Bartholomew, "DePalma of the Paradise," *Cinefantastique*, 4, no. 2 (Summer 1975), p. 14.

3. Georgia A. Brown, "Obsession," *American Film*, 9, no. 3 (December 1983), p. 32.

4. Brown, "Obsession," p. 33.

5. Bruce Weber, "Cool Head, Hot Images," *New York Times Magazine*, 21 May 1989, p. 116.

6. Weber, p. 116.

7. Bartholomew, p. 11.

8. Joseph Gelmis, *The Film Director as Superstar* (Garden City, NY: Doubleday, 1970), pp. 23–24.

9. Frank Lovece, "Brian DePalma," *Video*, 12, no. 3 (June 1988), p. 59.

10. Gelmis, "Superstar," p. 29.

11. Reference sources are almost evenly split between two spellings: *Wotan* and *Woton*.

12. Gelmis, "Superstar," p. 24.

13. Pye and Myles, p. 143.

14. Gelmis, "Superstar," p. 29.

15. Royal S. Brown, "Considering DePalma," *American Film*, July-August 1977, p. 56.

16. Gelmis, "Superstar," p. 24.

17. Richard Rubinstein, "The Making of *Sisters*." *Filmmakers Newsletter*, 6, no. 11 (September 1973), p. 26.

18. Laurent Bouzereau, *The DePalma Cut* (New York: Dembner, 1988), p. 27.

19. Pye and Myles, p. 151.

20. Rubinstein, p. 28.

21. Bartholomew, p. 12.

22. Lovece, p. 60.

23. Rubinstein, p. 25.

24. Rubinstein, p. 25.

25. Richard Fisher, "*Sisters,* a Filmic Critique," *Filmmakers Newsletter,* 6, no. 11 (September 1973), p. 22.

26. Alfred Hitchcock, interview with Charles Higham and Joel Greenberg, in *The Celluloid Muse: Hollywood Directors Speak* (Chicago: Regnery, 1971), p. 92.

27. Rubinstein, p. 25.

28. Mike Childs and Alan Jones, "DePalma Has the Power," *Cinefantastique,* 6, no. 1 (Summer 1977), p. 9.

29. Rubinstein, pp. 25–26.

30. Rubinstein, p. 26.

31. Bartholomew, p. 14.

32. John Coates, "The Making of *Phantom of the Paradise*," *Filmmakers Newsletter,* 8, no. 4 (February 1975), p. 24.

33. Bartholomew, pp. 8–10.

34. Bartholomew, p. 10.

35. Coates, p. 24.

36. Bartholomew, p. 10.

37. Coates, p. 26.

38. Matt Wolf, "DePalma Hopes for International Success," *Centre Daily Times,* 26 October 1987, sec. D, p. 6.

39. Bliss, p. 49.

40. Childs and Jones, p. 9.

41. Gerald Peary, "Working His Way Through College," *Take One,* January 1979, p. 14.

42. Peary, "Working," p. 14.

43. Peary, "Working," p. 17.

44. Peary, "Working," p. 18.

45. Peary, "Working," p. 18.

46. Weber, p. 116.

47. Bliss, p. 125.

48. Brown, "Obsession," p. 33.

49. Brown, "Obsession," p. 34.

50. Bliss, p. 132.

51. Bliss, p. 135.

52. Kenneth MacKinnon, "*Dressed to Kill*," *Film Quarterly,* 35, no. 1 (Fall 1981), p. 42.

53. Brown, "Obsession," p. 32.

54. Bruce Weber, "Cool Head, Hot Images," *New York Times Magazine,* 21 May 1989, p. 105.

55. Tom Mathews, "The Mob at the Movies," *Newsweek,* 22 June 1987, p. 64.

56. Richard Corliss, "Shooting Up the Box Office," *Time,* 22 June 1987, p. 79.

57. Wolf, p. 6.

58. Bouzerau, p. 76.

59. Tom Mathews, "The Mob at the Movies," *Newsweek,* 22 June 1987, p. 64.

60. Corliss, p. 79.

61. Jesse Kornbluth, "Shot by Shot," *Premiere*, 1, no. 1 (July-August 1987), p. 38.

62. Mathews, "Mob," p. 66.

63. Weber, pp. 105, 116.

64. Weber, p. 116.

65. Kornbluth, p. 39.

66. Al Harrell, *The Untouchables:* A Search for Period Flavor," *American Cinematographer*, July 1987, p. 90.

67. Jack Kroll, "DeNiro as Capone: The Magnificent Obsessive," *Newsweek*, 22 June 1987, p. 65.

68. Weber, p. 117.

69. Brian DePalma, *Variety*, 30 August 1989, p. 7.

70. Norman, p. 13.

71. Weber, p. 126.

72. Norman, p. 13.

73. Weber, p. 117.

74. Pauline Kael, "A Wounded Apparition," *New Yorker*, 21 August 1989, p. 78.

75. DePalma, p. 6.

76. Weber, p. 105.

Chapter 5

1. Michael Sragow, "A Conversation with Steven Spielberg," *Rolling Stone*, no. 374 (22 July 1982), p. 26.

2. Donald R. Mott and Cheryl McAllister Saunders, *Steven Spielberg* (Boston: Twayne Publishers, 1986), p. 9.

3. Richard Corliss, "Steve's Summer Magic," *Time*, May 31, 1982, p. 57.

4. Susan Royal, "Steven Spielberg, In His Adventures on Earth," *American Premiere*, 3, no. 5 (1982), p. 24.

5. Mitch Tuchman, "Close Encounter with Steven Spielberg," *Film Comment*, 14, no. 1 (January-February 1978), p. 50.

6. Mott and Saunders, p. 12.

7. Charles Michener, "A Summer Double Punch," *Newsweek*, May 31, 1982, p. 64.

8. Corliss, "Steve's Summer Magic," p. 57.

9. Corliss, "Steve's Summer Magic," p. 57.

10. Tuchman, p. 49.

11. Steven Spielberg, "The Autobiography of Peter Pan," *Time*, July 15, 1985, p. 63.

12. Spielberg, "Autobiography," p. 63.

13. Royal, p. 24.

14. Judith Crist, *Take 22* (New York: Viking Press, 1984), p. 372.

15. Richard Corliss, "I Dream for a Living," *Time*, July 15, 1985, p. 57.

16. Myra Forsberg, "Spielberg at 40: The Man and the Child," *New York Times*, January 10, 1988, p. 30.

17. Crist, p. 364.

18. Michael Pye and Lynda Myles, *The Movie Brats* (New York: Holt, Rinehart, and Winston, 1979), p. 222.

19. Michiko Kakutani, "The Two Faces of Spielberg — Horror vs. Hope," *New York Times*, May 30, 1982, p. 30.

20. Nancy Griffin, "Manchild in the Promised Land," *Premiere*, 2, no. 10 (June 1989), p. 93.

21. Tuchman, p. 51

22. Kakutani, p. 30.

23. Corliss, "Steve's Summer Magic," p. 55.

24. Spielberg, "Autobiography," p. 63.

25. Kakutani, p. 30.

26. Pye and Myles, pp. 223–224.

27. Tom Allen, "The Semi-Precious Age of TV Movies," *Film Comment*, 15, no. 4 (July-August 1979), p. 23.

28. Crist, p. 358.

29. Mott and Saunders, p. 20.

30. Tuchman, p. 53.

31. Steven Spielberg, "Dialogue on Film," *American Film* 3, no. 10 (September 1978), p. 51.

32. Crist, p. 371.

33. Crist, p. 367.

34. Tuchman, p. 55.

35. Royal, p. 22.

36. Pye and Myles, p. 237.

37. Stephen Farber, "L.A. Journal," *Film Comment*, 11, no. 5 (September-October 1975), p. 2.

38. Frank Rich, "The Aliens Are Coming," *Time*, November 7, 1977, p. 102.

39. Andrew Gordon, "Close Encounters: The Gospel According to Steven Spielberg, *Literature/Film Quarterly*, 8, no. 3 (1980), p. 160.

40. Tony Crawley, *The Steven Spielberg Story: The Man Behind the Movies* (New York: Quill Press, 1983), pp. 59–60.

41. Spielberg, "Dialogue," p. 49.

42. Pye and Myles, p. 242.

43. Jack Kroll, "*Close Encounters of the Third Kind:* The UFOs Are Coming," *Newsweek*, November 21, 1977, p. 92.

44. Rich, p. 102.

45. Tuchman, p. 54.

46. Stanley Kauffman, *Before My Eyes* (New York: Harper and Row, 1980), p. 159.

47. Royal, p. 22.

48. Steve Fox, Interview with Steven Spielberg, *20/20*, ABC-TV, June 24, 1982.

49. Royal, p. 18.

50. Sragow, p. 26.

51. Sragow, p. 26.

52. Kakutani, p. 30.

53. Crist, p. 385.

54. Royal, p. 19.

55. Spielberg, "Autobiography," p. 62.

56. Robert Phillip Kolker, *A Cinema of Loneliness: Penn, Kubrick, Scorsese, Spielberg, Altman*, 2nd ed. (New York: Oxford University Press, 1988), pp. 271–272.

57. Richard T. Jameson, "*E.T.*," *Film Comment*, 19, no. 1 (January-February 1983), p. 13.

58. Jameson, p. 12.

59. Charles Michener, "A Summer Double Punch," *Newsweek*, May 31, 1982, p. 63.

60. David Breskin, "Steven Spielberg," *Rolling Stone*, no. 459 (October 1985) p. 76.

61. Sragow, p. 28.

62. Crist, p. 379.

63. Steven Spielberg, Introduction, *Raiders of the Lost Ark: The Illustrated Screenplay* (New York: Ballantine Books, 1981), no page number.

64. Steven Spielberg, "Of Narrow Misses and Close Calls," *American Cinematographer*, November 1981, p. 1101.

65. Todd McCarthy, "Sand Castles," *Film Comment*, 18, no. 3 (May-June 1983), p. 59.

66. David Ansen, "Cliffhanger Classic," *Newsweek*, 15 June 1981, p. 60.

67. Veronica Geng, "Spielberg's Express," *Film Comment*, 17, no. 4 (July-August 1981).

68. Spielberg, "Narrow Misses," p. 1160.

69. Crist, p. 382.

70. Ansen, p. 62.

71. Spielberg, "Narrow Misses," p. 1138.

72. Mott and Saunders, p. 101.

73. Harlan Jacobson, "Two For the Rude," *Film Comment*, 20, no. 4 (July-August 1984), p. 51.

74. Breskin, p. 74.

75. Breskin, p. 74.

76. Richard Corliss, "The Three Faces of Steve," *Time*, 23 December 1985, p. 78.

77. Kolker, p. 294.

78. "Jagr.," "*The Color Purple*," *Variety*, December 1985, p. 16.

79. Spielberg, "Dialogue on Film," p. 14.

80. Forsberg, p. 21.

81. Forsberg, p. 21.

82. David Ansen, "A Childhood Lost to War," *Newsweek*, 14 December 1987.

83. Vincent Canby, "Evoking Childhood Isn't Kid Stuff," *New York Times*, 7 February 1988, p. 21.

84. Molly Haskell, "*Empire of the Sun*," *Video Review*, September 1988, p. 54.

85. Richard Corliss, "The Man-Child Who Fell to Earth," *Time*, 7 December 1987, p. 79.

86. Robert B. Woodward, "Meanwhile, Back at the Ranch," *New York Times*, 21 May 1989, sec. 2, p. 16.

87. Griffin, p. 89.

88. Woodward, p. 16.

89. Woodward, p. 16.

90. Corliss, "*Indy 3*," p. 84.

91. Pauline Kael, "Hiccup," *New Yorker*, 12 June 1989, p. 103.

92. David Heuring, "*Indiana Jones and the Last Crusade*," *American Cinematographer*, 70, no. 6 (June 1989), p. 59.

93. Corliss, "*Indy 3*," p. 83.

94. Griffin, p. 89.

95. Kauffmann, p. 159.

96. Corliss, "I Dream for a Living," p. 55.

97. Spielberg, "Dialogue," p. 52.

98. Griffin, p. 93.
99. Vincent Canby, "Spielberg's Elixir Shows Signs of Mature Magic," *New York Times*, 18 June 1989, p. 15.
100. Kael, p. 105.
101. Kenneth L. Zimmerman, *Premiere*, 3, no. 1 (September 1989), p. 12.
102. Spielberg, "Dialogue," p. 52.
103. Griffin, p. 89.

Chapter 6

1. Mary Pat Kelly, *Martin Scorsese, The First Decade* (Pleasantville, NY: Redgrave, 1980), p. 22.
2. Martin Scorsese, "Martin Scorsese's Guilty Pleasures," *Film Comment*, 14, no. 5 (September-October 1978), p. 66.
3. Marjorie Rosen, "Martin Scorsese Interview," *Film Comment*, 11, no. 2 (March-April 1975), p. 45.
4. Rosen, "Interview," p. 45.
5. Rosen, "Interview," p. 45.
6. Pye and Myles, p. 191.
7. Allan Arkush, "I Remember Film School," *Film Comment*, 19, no. 6 (November-December 1983), pp. 58–59.
8. Pye and Myles, p. 192.
9. Kelly, p. 14.
10. Andrew C. Bobrow, "The Filming of *Mean Streets*, *Filmmakers Newsletter*, 7, no. 3 (January 1974), p. 29.
11. Rosen, "Interview," p. 46.
12. Robert Kolker, *A Cinema of Loneliness: Penn, Kubrick, Scorsese, Spielberg, Altman*, 2nd ed. (New York: Oxford University Press, 1988) p. 171.
13. Stuart Byron, "*The Searchers*: Cult Movie of the New Hollywood," *New York*, 5 March 1979, p. 46.
14. Scorsese, "Guilty Pleasures," p. 66.
15. Arkush, p. 59.
16. Kelly, p. 31.
17. Rosen, "Interview," p. 42.
18. Rosen, "Interview," p. 42.
19. Rosen, "Interview," p. 43.
20. Scorsese, "Guilty Pleasures," p. 66.
21. Kolker, p. 188.
22. Pye and Myles, p. 211.
23. Richard Thompson, "Screen Writer," *Film Comment*, 12, no. 2 (March-April 1976), pp. 10–11.
24. Thompson, p. 11.
25. Byron, p. 45.
26. Thompson, p. 18.
27. Byron, p. 46.
28. Byron, "The Searchers," pp. 46–47.
29. Kolker, pp. 197–198.
30. Leo Braudy, "The Sacraments of Genre: Coppola, DePalma, Scorsese," *Film Quarterly*, 39, no. 3 (Spring 1986), pp. 25, 27.
31. Thompson, p. 13.
32. Thompson, p. 13.

33. Charles Michener, *"Taxi Driver," Film Comment*, 12, no. 2 (March-April 1976), p. 5.

34. Robert B. Ray, *A Certain Tendency of the Hollywood Cinema, 1930–1980* (Princeton: Princeton University Press, 1985), p. 349.

35. Ray, pp. 350–351.

36. Ray, p. 357.

37. Ray, p. 358.

38. Pye and Myles, p. 216.

39. Scorsese, "Guilty Pleasures," p. 64.

40. Scorsese, "Guilty Pleasures," p. 64.

41. Kolker, p. 222.

42. Scorsese, "Guilty Pleasures," p. 63.

43. Lawrence S. Friedman, "Vision and Revision in Scorsese' *New York, New York* and Sorrentino's 'The Moon in its Flight,'" *Literature/Film Quarterly*, 9, no. 2 (1981) p. 109.

44. Leland A. Poague, "The Problem of Film Genre: A Mentalistic Approach," *Literature/Film Quarterly*, 1, no. 2 (Spring 1978), p. 147.

45. Poague, p. 153.

46. Stephen Schiff, "The Repeatable Experience," *Film Comment*, 18, no. 2 (March-April 1982), p. 34.

47. Mark Roth, "Some Warners Musicals and the Spirit of the New Deal," *The Velvet Light Trap*, no. 17 (Winter 1977), reprinted in *Genre: The Musical*, ed. Rick Altman, (London: Routledge & Kegan Paul, 1981), p. 45.

48. Martin Sutton, "Patterns of Meaning in the Musical," in Altman, p. 191.

49. According to *Variety* (11 January 1989), *New York, New York* earned rentals of only $6.5 million.

50. Chris Hodenfield, "You've Got to Love Something Enough to Kill It," *American Film*, 14, no. 5 (March 1989), p. 51.

51. Hodenfield, p. 49.

52. Hodenfield, p. 51.

53. Thomas Wiener, "Martin Scorsese Fights Back," *American Film*, 6, no. 2 (November 1980), p. 34.

54. Martin Scorsese, "Letters," *Film Comment*, 16, no. 1 (January-February 1980), p. 79.

55. Wiener, p. 34.

56. Wiener, p. 34.

57. Leo Braudy, "The Sacraments of Genre: Coppola, DePalma, Scorsese," *Film Quarterly*, 39, no. 3 (Spring 1986), p. 26.

58. Thompson, p. 12.

59. Jay Scott, *Midnight Matinees, Movies and Their Makers, 1975–1985* (New York: Ungar, 1987), pp. 225–226.

60. Carrie Rickey, "Marty," *American Film*, 8, no. 2 (November 1982), p. 72.

61. Rickey, p. 68.

62. Braudy, p. 27.

63. One wonders what if anything this opening sequence meant to even English-speaking foreign audiences—Johnny Carson, since he is an American television star, is virtually unknown in the rest of the world. A few attempts at syndicating *The Tonight Show* in Australia and Great Britain have failed.

64. Arkush, p. 59.

65. Richard Corliss, "...And Blood," *Film Comment*, 24, no. 5 (September-October 1988), p. 42.

66. Corliss, "Blood," p. 36.

67. Corliss, "Blood," p. 38.

68. Jonathan Rosenbaum, "Raging Messiah," *Sight and Sound*, 57, no. 4 (Autumn 1988), 281.

69. David Ansen, "Wrestling with *Temptation*," *Newsweek*, 15 August 1988, p. 57.

70. Corliss, "Body," p. 43. Corliss also argues that the unusual overheard shots in Scorsese's films can now be read as God's POV.

71. "Cart.," "*The Last Temptation of Christ*," *Variety*, 10 August 1988, p. 12.

72. Corliss, "Blood," p. 38.

73. Corliss, "Blood," p. 38.

74. Corliss, "Blood," p. 42.

75. Corliss, "Blood," p. 36.

76. Hodenfield, p. 51.

Chapter 7

1. J. Hoberman, "Ten Years That Shook the World," *American Film*, 10, no. 8 (June 1985), p. 37.

2. Hoberman, pp. 37–38.

3. David Denby, "Can the Movies Be Saved?", *New York*, 21 July 1986, p. 28.

4. Richard Corliss, "The Seventies: The New Conservatism," *Film Comment*, 16, no. 1 (January-February, 1980), p. 35.

5. Majorie Rosen, "Francis Ford Coppola," *Film Comment*, 10, no. 4 (July-August 1974), p. 48.

6. Stanley Fish, "Interpreting the *Variorum*," *Critical Inquiry*, 2, no. 3 (Spring 1976), pp. 485–486.

7. Stephen Farber, "The USC Connection," *Film Comment*, 20, no. 3 (May-June 1984), p. 35.

8. Brian DePalma, interview on USA cable network's *Nightflight*, 1988.

Bibliography

Books

Adair, Gilbert. *Hollywood's Vietnam*. New York: Proteus Books, 1981.
Allen, Richard Stanley and Chacko, David, eds. *Detective Fiction: Crime and Compromise*. New York: Harcourt Brace Jovanovich, 1974.
Altman, Rick, ed. *Genre: The Musical*. London: Routledge and Kegan Paul, 1981.
Bliss, Michael. *Brian De Palma*. Metuchen, NJ: Scarecrow Press, 1983.
Bordwell, David, Staiger, Janet, and Thompson, Kristin. *The Classical Hollywood Cinema, Film Style Mode of Production to 1960*. New York: Columbia University Press, 1985.
Bouzereau, Laurent. *The De Palma Cut*. New York: Dembner Books, 1988.
Caughie, John, ed. *Theories of Authorship*. London: Routledge and Kegan Paul, 1986; reprint.
Chown, Jeffrey. *Hollywood Auteur: Francis Ford Coppola*. New York: Praeger, 1988.
Crawley, Tony. *The Steven Spielberg Story: The Man Behind the Movies*. New York: Quill Press, 1983.
Crist, Judith. *Take 22*. New York: Viking Press, 1984.
Foster, Hal, ed. *The Anti-Aesthetic: Essays on Postmodern Culture*. Seattle: Bay Press, 1983.
Gelmis, Joseph. *The Film Director as Superstar*. Garden City, NY: Doubleday, 1970.
Higham, Charles, and Greenberg, Joel. *The Celluloid Muse: Hollywood Directors Speak*. Chicago: Regnery, 1971.
Iser, Wolfgang. *The Implied Reader*. Baltimore: Johns Hopkins University Press, 1974.
Jacobs, Diane. *Hollywood Renaissance*. Cranbury, NJ: A. S. Barnes, 1977.
Johnson, Robert K. *Francis Ford Coppola*. Boston: Twayne, 1977.
Joyce, James. *Finnegans Wake*. New York: Viking Press, 1939.
Kasdan, Lawrence. *Raiders of the Lost Ark: The Illustrated Screenplay*. New York: 1981.
Kauffmann, Stanley. *Before My Eyes*. New York: Harper and Row, 1980.
Kelly, Mary Pat. *Martin Scorsese, the First Decade*. Pleasantville, NY: Redgrave, 1980.
Kolker, Robert Phillip. *A Cinema of Loneliness: Penn, Kubrick, Scorsese, Spielberg, Altman*. 2nd ed. New York: Oxford University Press, 1988.
Kroker, Arthur, and Cook, David. *The Postmodern Scene*. 2nd ed. New York: St. Martin's Press, 1988.

Medhurst, Martin J., and Benson, Thomas W., eds. *Rhetorical Dimensions in Media, A Critical Casebook*. Revised printing. Dubuque, Iowa: Kendall/Hunt, 1984.

Monaco, James. *American Film Now*. New York: Oxford University Press, 1979.

Mott, Donald R., and Saunders, Cheryl McAllister. *Steven Spielberg*. Boston: Twayne Publishers, 1986.

Pollock, Dale. *Skywalking, the Life and Films of George Lucas*. New York: Harmony, 1983.

Pye, Michael, and Myles, Lynda. *The Movie Brats, How the Film Generation Took Over Hollywood*. New York: Holt, Rinehart and Winston, 1979.

Ray, Robert B. *A Certain Tendency of the Hollywood Cinema, 1930-1980*. Princeton: Princeton University Press, 1985.

Scott, Jay. *Midnight Matinees, Movies and Their Makers, 1975-1985*. New York: Ungar, 1987.

Suleiman, Susan R., and Crosman, Inge, eds. *The Reader in the Text*. Princeton: Princeton University Press, 1980.

Thompson, Kristin. *Breaking the Glass Armor*. Princeton: Princeton University Press, 1988.

Von Gunden, Kenneth, and Stock, Stuart H. *Twenty All-Time Great Science Fiction Films*. New York: Arlington House, 1982.

Zuker, Joel S. *Francis Ford Coppola, a Guide to References and Resources*. Boston: G. K. Hall, 1984.

Articles

Aigner, Hal, and Goodwin, Michael. "The Bearded Immigrant from Tinsel Town." *City Magazine*, 12-25 June 1974.

Allen, Tom. "The Semi-Precious Age of TV Movies." *Film Comment*, 15, no. 4 (July-August 1979).

Ansen, David. "A Childhood Lost to War." *Newsweek*, 14 December 1987.
_____. "Cliffhanger Classic." *Newsweek*, 15 June 1981.
_____. "The Raider of Lost Art." *Newsweek*, 23 May 1988.
_____. "Wrestling with Temptation." *Newsweek*, 15 August 1988.

Ansen, David, and Kasindorf, Martin. "Coppola's Apocalypse Again." *Newsweek*, 16 February 1981.

Arkush, Allan. "I Remember Film School." *Film Comment*, 19, no. 6 (November-December 1983).

Bartholomew, David. "De Palma of the Paradise." *Cinefantastique*, 4, no. 2 (Summer 1975).

Bennett, Tony. "Texts and Social Processes: The Cast of James Bond." *Screen Education* (Winter-Spring 1982).

Benson, Sheila. "Calendar." *Los Angeles Times*, 22 January 1982.

Bobrow, Andrew C. "The Filming of *Mean Streets*." *Filmmakers Newsletter*, 7, no. 3 (January 1974).

Bock, Audie. "George Lucas: An Interview." *Take One*, May 1979.
_____. "Kurosawa." *Take One*, March 1979.

Braudy, Leo. "The Sacraments of Genre: Coppola, De Palma, Scorsese." *Film Quarterly*, 39, no. 3 (Spring 1986).

Braudy, Susan. "Francis Ford Coppola: A Profile." *Atlantic*, 238, no. 2 (August 1976).

Breskin, David. "Steven Spielberg." *Rolling Stone*, no. 459 (24 October 1985).

Brown, Georgia A. "Obsession." *American Film*, 9, no. 3 (December 1983).

Brown, Royal S. "Considering De Palma." *American Film*, July–August 1977.

Bruckner, D. J. R. "Joseph Campbell: 70 Years of Making Connections." *New York Times Book Review*, 18 December 1983.

Buck, Joan. "*Godfather II* Probes Family's Roots." *Women's Wear Daily*, 18 June 1974.

Bygrave, Mike, and Goodman, Joan. "Meet Me in Las Vegas." *American Film*, October 1981.

Byron, Stuart. "*The Searchers*: Cult Movie of the New Hollywood." *New York*, 5 March 1979.

Callenbach, Ernest. "Short Notices." *Film Quarterly*, Summer 1971.

Canby, Vincent. "Evoking Childhood Isn't Kid Stuff." *New York Times*, 7 February 1988.

_____. "Spielberg's Elixir Shows Signs of Mature Magic." *New York Times*, 18 June 1989.

Carroll, Jon. "Coppola: Bringing in the Next Godfather." *New York*, 11 November 1974.

"Cart." "*The Last Temptation of Christ*." *Variety*, 10 August 1988.

Childs, Mike, and Jones, Alan. "De Palma Has the Power." *Cinefantastique*, 6, no. 1 (Summer 1977).

Coates, John. "The Making of *Phantom of the Paradise*." *Filmmakers Newsletter*, 8, no. 4 (February 1975).

Coppola, Francis Ford. "*Godfather, Part II* (Nothing Is a Sure Thing)." *City*, 7, no. 54 (11–24 December 1974).

Coppola, Francis, and Talese, Gay. "The Conversation." *Esquire Film Quarterly*, July 1981.

Corliss, Richard. ". . . And Blood." *Film Comment*, 24, no. 5 (September–October 1988).

_____. "Body . . ." *Film Comment*, 24, no. 5 (September–October 1988).

_____. "I Dream for a Living." *Time*, 15 July 1985.

_____. "The Man-Child Who Fell to Earth." *Time*, 7 December 1987.

_____. "Steve's Summer Magic." *Time*, 31 May 1982.

_____. "The Seventies: The New Conservatism." *Film Comment*, 16, no. 1 (January–February 1980.

_____. "Shooting Up the Box Office." *Time*, 22 June 1987.

_____. "The Three Faces of Steve." *Time*, 23 December 1985.

Crinkley, Richmond. "The Ark of the Cinemate." *Film Comment*, 21, no. 4 (July–August 1985).

Crofts, Stephen. "Authorship and Hollywood." *Wide Angle*, 5, no. 3 (1983).

Denby, David. "Can the Movies Be Saved?" *New York*, 21 July 1986.

De Palma, Brian. "The Making of *The Conversation*." *Filmmakers Newsletter*, 7, no. 7 (May 1974).

_____. *Variety*, 30 August 1989.

De Stefano, George. "Family Lies." *Film Comment*, 23, no. 4 (July–August 1987).

Diamond, Jamie. "Film School Confidential." *American Film*, 14, no. 9 (July–August 1989).

Ehrenstein, David. "The Aesthetics of Failure." *Film Comment*, 19, no. 3 (May–June 1983).

Farber, Stephen. "Coppola and *The Godfather*." *Sight and Sound*, 41, no. 4 (Autumn 1972).

_____. "George Lucas: The Stinky Kid Hits the Big Time." *Film Quarterly*, 27, no. 3 (Spring 1974).

————. "L.A. Journal." *Film Comment*, 11, no. 5 (September–October 1975).

————. "The USC Connection." *Film Comment*, 20, no. 3 (May–June 1984).

Feuer, Jane. "Reading *Dynasty*: Television and Reception Theory." *South Atlantic Quarterly*, 88, no 2 (Spring 1989).

Fish, Stanley. "Interpreting the *Variorum*." *Critical Inquiry*, 2, no. 3 (Spring 1976).

Fisher, Richard. "*Sisters*, a Filmic Critique." *Filmmakers Newsletter*, 6, no. 11 (September 1973).

Forsberg, Myra. "Spielberg at 40: The Man and the Child." *New York Times*, 10 January 1988.

Fox, Terry Curtis. "Star Drek." *Film Comment*, July–August 1977.

Gallagher, John. "John Milius." *Films in Review*, 71, no. 6 (June–July 1982).

Gelmis, Joseph. "Mericiful Heavens, Is This the End of Don Corleone?" *New York*, 23 August 1971.

Geng, Victoria. "Mistuh Kurtz — He Dead." *New Yorker*, 3 September 1979.

————. "Spielberg's Express." *Film Comment*, 17, no. 4 (July–August 1981).

Gitlin, Todd. "Hip Deep in Post-modernism." *New York Times Book Review*. 6 November 1988.

Glicksman, Marlaine. "Bravo Longo." *Film Comment*, 25, no. 2 (March–April 1989).

Gordon, Andrew. "*Close Encounters*: The Gospel According to Steven Spielberg." *Literature/Film Quarterly*, 8, no. 3 (1980).

Grenier, Richard. "Coppola's Folly." *Commentary*, 68, no. 4 (October 1979).

Griffin, Nancy. "Manchild in the Promised Land." *Premiere*, 2, no. 10 (June 1989).

Harmetz, Aljean. "Burden of Dreams, George Lucas." *American Film*, 8, no. 8 (June 1983).

————."Coppola Buys Studio for $6.7 Million." *New York Times*, 21 March 1980.

Harrell, Al. "*The Untouchables*: A Search for Period Flavor." *American Cinematographer*, July 1987.

Haskell, Molly. "*Empire of the Sun*." *Video Review*, September 1988.

Hellmann, John. "Vietnam and the Hollywood Genre Film: Inversions of American Mythology in *The Deer Hunter* and *Apocalypse Now*." *American Quarterly*, 34, no. 4 (Fall 1982).

Hess, John. "*Godfather II*: A Deal Coppola Couldn't Refuse." *Jump-Cut*, no. 7 (May–June 1975).

Heuring, David. "*Indiana Jones and the Last Crusade*." *American Cinematographer*, 70, no. 6 (June 1989).

Hoberman, J. "Ten Years That Shook the World." *American Film*, 10, no. 8 (June 1985).

Hodenfield, Chris. "You've Got to Love Something Enough to Kill It." *American Film*, 14, no. 5 (March 1989).

Jacobson, Harlan. "The Seventies: Exhibition." *Film Comment*, 16, no. 1 (January–February 1980).

————. "Two for the Rude." *Film Comment*, 20, no. 4 (July–August 1984).

"Jagr." "*The Color Purple*." *Variety*, December 1985.

Jameson, Richard T. "*E.T.*" *Film Comment*, 19, no. 1 (January–February 1983).

Jauss, Hans Robert. "Literary Theory as a Challenge to Literary Theory." *New Literary History*, 2, no. 1 (Autumn 1970).

Kael, Pauline. "Hiccup." *New Yorker*, 12 June 1989.

————. "A Wounded Apparition." *New Yorker*, 21 August 1989.

Kakutani, Michiko. "The Two Faces of Spielberg — Horror vs. Hope." *New York Times*, 30 May 1982.

Kearney, Jill. "Francis Ford Coppola Simply Wants to Create a Whole New Art Form." *Mother Jones*, 13, no. 7 (September 1988).

————. "The Road Warrior." *American Film*, 13, no. 8 (June 1988).

Kornbluth, Jesse. "Shot by Shot." *Premiere*, 1, no. 1 (July–August 1987).

Koszarski, Richard. "The Youth of F. F. Coppola." *Films in Review*, 19, no. 9 (November 1968).

Kroll, Jack. "*Close Encounters of the Third Kind*: The UFOs Are Coming." *Newsweek*, 21 November 1977.

————. "DeNiro as Capone: The Magnificent Obssessive." *Newsweek*, 22 June 1987.

Latimer, Jonathan P. "*The Godfather*: Metaphor and Microcosm." *Journal of Popular Film*, 2, no. 2 (Spring 1973).

Le Sueur, Marc. "Theory Number Five: Anatomy of Nostalgia Films: Heritage and Methods." *Journal of Popular Film*, 6, no. 2 (1977).

Levin, G. Roy. "Francis Coppola Discusses *Apocalypse Now*." *Millimeter*, 7, no. 7 (October 1979).

Lovece, Frank. "Brian De Palma." *Video*, 12, no. 3 (June 1988).

McCarthy, Todd. "Sand Castles." *Film Comment*, 18, no. 3 (May–June 1982).

MacKinnon, Kenneth. "*Dressed to Kill*." *Film Quarterly*, 35, no 1 (Fall 1981).

Marcus, Greil. "Journey Up the River." *Rolling Stone*, 1 November 1979.

Mathews, Tom. "The Mob at the Movies." *Newsweek*, 22 June 1987.

Michener, Charles. "A Summer Double Punch." *Newsweek*, 31 May 1982.

————. "*Taxi Driver*." *Film Comment*, 12, no. 2 (March–April 1976).

Morris, George. "George Lucas' *Star Wars*." *Take One*, July–August 1977.

Murray, William. "*Playboy* Interview: Francis Ford Coppola." *Playboy*, July 1975.

Orth, Maureen. "The Godfather of the Movies." *Newsweek*, 25 November 1974.

Peary, Gerald. "Working His Way Through College." *Take One*, January 1979.

Pechter, William S. "Keeping Up with the Corleones." *Commentary*, 54, no. 1 (July 1972).

Poague, Leland A. "The Problem of Film Genre: A Mentalistic Approach." *Literature/Film Quarterly*, 1, no. 2 (Spring 1978).

Puzo, Mario. "Dialogue on Film." *American Film*, 4, no. 7 (May 1979).

Pye, Michael, and Myles, Lynda. "The Man Who Made *Star Wars*." *The Atlantic*, March 1979.

Rich, Frank. "The Aliens Are Coming." *Time*, 7 November 1977.

————. "The Making of a Quagmire." *Time*, 27 August 1979.

Ricky, Carrie. "Marty." *American Film*, 8, no. 2 (November 1982).

Rosen, Marjorie. "Francis Ford Coppola." *Film Comment*, 10, no. 4 (July–August 1974).

————. "Martin Scorsese Interview." *Film Comment*, 11, no. 2 (March–April 1975).

Rosenbaum, Jonathan. "Raging Messiah." *Sight and Sound*, 57, no. 4 (Autumn 1988).

Roth, Mark. "Some Warners Musicals and the Spirit of the New Deal." *The Velvet Light Trap*, no. 17 (Winter 1977).

Royal, Susan. "Steven Spielberg, in His Adventures on Earth." *American Premiere*, 3, no. 5 (1982).

Rubinstein, Richard. "The Making of *Sisters*." *Filmmakers Newsletter*, 6, no. 11 (September 1973).

Scanlon, Paul. "The Force Behind George Lucas." *Rolling Stone*, 25 August 1977.

Schiff, Stephen. "The Repeatable Experience." *Film Comment*, 18, no. 2 (March–April 1982).

Schlesinger, Arthur, Jr. "The Godfather Plays on Our Secret Admiration for Men Who Get What They Want." *Vogue*, May 1972.

Scorsese, Martin. "Martin Scorsese's Guilty Pleasures." *Film Comment*, 14, no. 5 (September–October 1978).
Spielberg, Steven. "The Autobiography of Peter Pan." *Time*, 15 July 1985.
————. "Dialogue on Film." *American Film*, 3, no. 10 (September 1978).
————. "Of Narrow Misses and Close Calls." *American Cinematographer*, November 1981.
Sragow, Michael. "A Conversation with Steven Spielberg." *Rolling Stone*, no. 374 (22 July 1982).
Starr, Helen. "Putting It Together." *Photoplay*, 14, no. 2 (July 1918).
Sturhahn, Larry. "The Filming of *American Graffiti*." *Filmmakers Newsletter*, 7, no. 5 (March 1974).
Sutton, Martin. "Patterns of Meaning in the Musical." In Altman.
Thompson, Richard. "Screen Writer." *Film Comment*, 12, no. 2 (March–April 1976).
————. "Stoked." *Film Comment*, 12, no. 4 (July–August 1976).
Time. "The Making of *The Godfather*." 13 March 1972.
Time. 30 May 1977
Tuchman, Mitch. "Close Encounter with Steven Spielberg." *Film Comment*, 14, no. 1 (January–February 1978).
Tuchman, Mitch, and Thompson, Anne. "I'm the Boss." *Film Comment*, 17, no. 4 (July–August 1981).
Vallely, Jean. "The Empire Strikes Back." *Rolling Stone*, 12 June 1980.
Weber, Bruce. "Cool Head, Hot Images." *New York Times Magazine*, 21 May 1989.
Weiner, Thomas. "Martin Scorsese Fights Back." *American Film*, 6, no. 2 (November 1980).
White, Armond. "Celluloid Songs." *Film Comment*, 25, no. 2 (March–April 1989).
Wolf, Matt. "De Palma Hopes for International Success." *Centre Daily Times*, 26 October 1987.
Wood, Denis. "The Stars in Our Hearts: A Critical Commentary on George Lucas' *Star Wars*." *Journal of Popular Film*, 6, no. 3 (1978).
Woodward, Rick. "Film Stills." *Film Comment*, 25, no. 2 (March–April 1989).
Woodward, Robert B. "Meanwhile, Back at the Ranch." *New York Times*, 21 May 1989, Sec. 2.
Zimmerman, Paul D. "Future Shock." *Newsweek*, 29 March 1971.
Zito, Stephen. "George Lucas Goes Far Out." *American Film*, April 1977.

Other Sources

De Palma, Brian. Interview on *Nightflight*. USA cable network, 1988.
Fox, Steve. Interview with Steven Spielberg. *20/20*, ABC-TV, 24 June 1982.
Scorsese, Martin. "Letters." *Film Comment*, 16, no. 1 (January–February 1980).
Williams, John. "Themes." *Star Wars* album liner notes. Los Angeles: 20th Century Records, 1977.
Zimmerman, Kenneth L. "Letters." *Premiere*, 3, no. 1 (September 1989).

Index

Numbers in **boldface** refer to pages with photographs.